The Complete Guide to

EDITING YOUR FICTION

MICHAEL SEIDMAN

WRITER'S DIGEST BOOKS
CINCINNATI, OH
www.writersdigest.com

The Complete Guide to Editing Your Fiction. Copyright © 2000 by Michael Seidman. Manufactured in the United States of America. All rights reserved. No part of this book may be reproduced in any form or by any electronic or mechanical means including information storage and retrieval systems without permission in writing from the publisher, except by a reviewer, who may quote brief passages in a review. Published by Writer's Digest Books, an imprint of F&W Publications, Inc., 1507 Dana Avenue, Cincinnati, Ohio 45207. (800) 289-0963. First edition.

Visit our Web site at www.writersdigest.com for information on more resources for writers.

To receive a free weekly E-mail newsletter delivering tips and updates about writing and about Writer's Digest products, send an E-mail with "Subscribe Newsletter" in the body of the message to newsletter-request@writersdigest.com, or register directly at our Web site at www.writersdigest.com.

04   03   02   01   00   5   4   3   2   1

Library of Congress Cataloging-in-Publication Data

Seidman, Michael.
   The complete guide to editing your fiction / by Michael Seidman.—1st ed.
     p.   cm.
  Includes index.
  ISBN 0-898179-938-4 (hardcover: alk. paper)
    1. Editing. 2. Fiction—Technique. I. Title.

  PN162.S43   2000
  808.3—dc21   99-088526
                                                            CIP

Designer: Angela Lennert Wilcox
Cover designer: Cindy Beckmeyer/Beckmeyer Design
Cover illustration: Brian Steege/Guildhaus Photographics
Production coordinator: Emily Gross

DEDICATION

With respect and affection this book is dedicated to David Bradley who, with patience and goodwill, has taught and continues to teach me the things I have to know about what I'm doing as a writer. Everything good here comes from him; the bad is my own.

ABOUT THE AUTHOR

Michael Seidman is the author of *From Printout to Published* and *Living the Dream*, both published by Carroll & Graf, and *Fiction: The Art and Craft of Getting Published*, Pomegranate Press. He has been an editor since 1970, working at Fawcett Crest, NAL, Ace/Charter, Tor, Zebra/Pinnacle (as editorial director), and Mysterious Press (as editor-in-chief) before moving to Walker, where he is the senior mystery editor. He has written for a variety of publications, including *Writer's Digest, Mystery Scene, Twilight Zone* and *West Coast Review of Books*. A popular speaker, he lectures at more than a dozen writers conferences every year. He also is the moderator of a writer's discussion board for AOL and writes an online column called "Ask the Editor." He lives in New York City.

TABLE OF CONTENTS

PART THREE

Refining and Reworking

APPENDICES

INTRODUCTION

There are as many reasons not to edit and revise as there are reasons not to write. But one of the things that separates the professional writer from the amateur and hopeful is the pro's willingness to take the time to read, revise and edit her manuscript before sending it off to an agent or publisher.

There's really nothing to it, beyond giving priority to the job once you've typed "The End" when you finish your first draft. And when you think about it, you're editing and revising many things in your life constantly.

Have a favorite daydream? How many times have you changed it, tweaked it, brought new characters or items into it? That's revision.

Have you ever decided it was time to talk to your boss about a raise, to talk to a friend about a needed change in a relationship? You sat down, began with a basic script and then said, "No, that doesn't work, sounds too threatening." So, you took out that phrase, replaced it with another and then rehearsed it again. Sounds okay? Well, maybe if you beg a little here . . . that's revision.

How about this scene: You've asked for the job, the raise, the hand in marriage. Now you're home and, "If only I'd said . . ." That's editing: a change made in a scene already finished.

See, you do it all the time. You do it watching television and movies: Remember how you groaned when the ingenue went down into the cellar? If you'd written the scene, you'd have had her go into the backyard, instead, and then . . . well, and then something else would have happened, maybe something more credible, maybe something that would have increased suspense, something that would have allowed you to create a surprise, rather than offer the trite and true. How many times have you been comfortably reading a book or a story and then something happens that jars you out of the narrative and back into the room? Maybe it was a word that didn't resonate correctly, that sounded wrong; maybe it was an action that wasn't motivated, that ran counter to the character as he'd been presented to you for the last 150 pages, but that the author placed there because if it didn't happen the story couldn't continue. No matter what it was, how many times have you reacted to it by saying, "I can do it better, if I only had the chance." This is your chance.

◆——————————————————————————————◆

Why are you going to do all this work? Well, for one thing, you don't want some other hungry, young writer to look at your finished book and say, "I can do it better. . . ." If she can, you could lose your place in line.

For another, you want your manuscript to be the best one on the editor's or agent's desk; it is the best one that is going to be acquired.

Not too long ago, I received a manuscript from a gentleman who was a long way from ready. It was clear that the novel in my hands was, at best, a first draft. It had been run through spell checking and grammar checking programs, but that was the extent of the work the writer had done. When I sent the material back to him, I pointed out some of the problems, told him he had more work to do, gave him a few pointers. His response was a nasty letter making it clear that it was my job to fix the manuscript. That's right and wrong.

I know you've been hearing the nonsense about editors no longer editing. There may not be as many of us, and we may have more work to do, but we still edit. Because of the time constraints, however, we're editing less because we're looking for manuscripts that don't need quite as much work. We still want to help you write the best book of which you're capable *at this moment*, but too many of us too often are looking for manuscripts that are closer to finished. So, we do still edit and revise; some still do a little rewriting (or, generally, suggesting where the rewrites might be necessary). The manuscript will still be put through the copyediting process so that any glitches you and I missed (and we'll both miss something) might be fixed. But we won't do your work for you, and your job, right now, is to present the manuscript in the best possible form.

You do that by rereading the manuscript, in type, not on the computer's video display, after you've given it a chance to cool down a little, and making notes on the typescript of changes that have to be made. Then you go back to the keyboard and start making the fixes. If you're really interested in writing a good book, one that is going to impress an editor, you'll rekey the entire work. I know, outrageous; that's why you bought your computer, so you wouldn't have to do that. Well, the reality is this: As you retype, as you, literally, rewrite, you find other places to make changes, new word choices occur to you—the work benefits. If you only do a search and replace, you're cheating yourself and your characters.

Also important is that you do whatever work you're going to do with some distance between yourself and the creative process. This is a good time to sharpen your editing skills by practicing with a pencil what you've been doing in your head all your life. Pick a book, any book, from your shelves and *edit* it! Right. It doesn't matter that it's already been rewritten, revised and edited; do it anyway. Remember, you decided you could do a better job, so fix the book that inspired that thought.

Look for those places where a point-of-view shift was too abrupt, for the word that struck you the wrong way, for the hole in the plot or the character acting out of character. Make notes in the margins about how you would fix the problems.

Then, take your manuscript and do the same thing. Do it ruthlessly, do it painstakingly, do it thoroughly.

Then, and only then, send the manuscript into the world. We'll know if you don't care enough to send the very best. . . .

Michael Seidman
New York, New York
July 1999

The Building Blocks

CHAPTER 1

Beginning

It's said that Michelangelo, when asked about his statue of David, replied that he began with a block of stone and chipped away everything that wasn't the young king. The writing process is much the same: You begin with something, take away everything that isn't what you want in the finished work, and what's left is the novel or story or essay or poem that you want to present. It doesn't matter what you're writing—you have to do the same thing.

To extend the metaphor, if revision is the act of removing what doesn't matter, your first draft is quarrying the stone with which you'll work.

But keep this in mind: PEN/Faulkner Award–winning novelist David Bradley reminds us that a sculptor takes the chips and flakes that have come away and sweeps them out at the end of the day; as a writer, you have the opportunity to pick those pieces up and blend them into the almost-finished work later. So keep your chips. Today, with digital files instead of cabinets filled with yellowing pages, saving material is a snap. The importance of it?

Well, if you've written something and it's good (though wrong for what you're working on), you can always use it later in something else. There's another reason to keep things, and keep them safely. As I sat down to begin outlining this book, I searched out my old files, many of them stacks of paper in folders and envelopes. Because I know that revision is rewriting, I wanted to share the process of writing my first story with you.

"Sands of Expiation" was set on a military base in the South; it featured a young private, a black man named Linc who worked in the motor pool. His sergeant was named Henderson; they came from the same area in West Virginia. Henderson was married to a woman twenty years younger than he; her name was Lilah. And Henderson, it is revealed, was responsible for the death of Linc's mother in Shantytown, an event witnessed by the boy who grew into a man. Lots of Army stuff, lots of mixing things up. Linc and Lilah begin an affair; Henderson dies.

Much of my fiction deals with Fate (there are those who uncharitably call it coincidence). The end of the story hinges on one of those twists. Nice, neat; my mentor at the time, the poet Dr. Alfred Dorn, started encouraging me to submit the manuscript. But I was working for *New American Review* by then, an important literary magazine, and I knew the story wasn't publishable. I put it away.

Ten years later, I took it out and rewrote it. The themes and the nature of the characters were the same, but Linc was now called Junior and he was white; the setting had moved from Ft. Bragg to New York City; Henderson was a retired MP who worked two jobs, as a bank security guard and a cabdriver; Lilah was looking for a job as a waitress . . . and the story, as published in *Mystery Magazine* in March 1981, was called "Perchance to Dream."

The two versions are the same story, and yet completely different. And that repeated revising is not only easy, but also worthwhile. After all, if I hadn't done it, the story would never have appeared, I wouldn't have been asked to contribute another story and the rest of my ideas might very well have died aborning.

When you begin, you have an idea. Usually (and one seriously hopes) you've started by thinking about the idea, carrying it with you: You've really begun revising by considering the story you want to tell, choosing most of the characters, creating scenes that you're going to use, maybe even hearing some of the dialogue.

Then you've—gasp—done your outline. A scene you've been working on between two characters, Rose and Danny, (the scene that was, in your mind, designed to get the action going) doesn't seem to work where you have it, so you move it back and create another piece of business to get the couple together: *That's what was missing,* you realize, *a reason for them to be in the same place at the same time.*

Satisfied, you begin to write. If you're smart enough to realize that writing isn't a race, that getting done first doesn't mean getting done better, you won't spend too much time worrying as you write the first draft. Anne Lamott, in her classic *Bird by Bird,* tells us,

> All good writers write them [shitty first drafts]. This is how they end up with good second drafts and terrific third drafts. People tend to look at successful writers, writers who are getting their books published and maybe even doing well financially, and think that they sit down at their desks every morning feeling like a million dollars. . . . But this is just the fantasy of the uninitiated.
>
> For me and most of the other writers I know, writing is not rapturous. In fact, the only way I can get anything written at all is to write really, really shitty first drafts.
>
> The first draft is the child's draft, where you let it all pour out and then let it romp all over the place, knowing that no one is going to see it and that you can shape it up later. You just let this childlike part of you channel whatever voices and visions come through and onto the page.

Lamott is, of course, a best-selling writer.

Writing is rewriting. Revision is a matter of looking again, of re-visioning, taking what's been done, of looking at it and fixing it. It begins, as we've said, before you begin writing; you have to consider every aspect of what you're doing in the story, why you're writing it, what the point is, what the theme is, what the story means, what it is about.

Theme, or meaning, is a term that's in a certain state of disrepute, especially among genre writers (and many of their readers). After all, the books are an entertainment, not an education; they're read for escape and relaxation and we don't want to be fed, by spoon or force, some philosophy, some lesson, while we're kicked back and enjoying ourselves.

Beyond that, most categories have an inherent theme: Whether it is the orderly universe and justice of the mystery novel, the triumph of the Judeo-Christian ethic over the (evil) supernatural in horror fiction, or the love that conquers all of the romance book, we assume the theme before we begin writing and reading and too rarely think beyond that. And that is one of the reasons too many critics and readers find it easy to mock the categories. (An insight: Lots of poets and academics read crime fiction; they enjoy it for the same reason the more public fans do, and, if you look carefully, you'll discover that lots of so-called mainstream and/or literary novelists use the mystery form—though not the formula. Consider the work of Joyce Carol Oates, under her own name and as Rosamund Smith.)

It's easy (well, as easy as writing ever is) for a category novelist—in this instance we mean one devoted to the genre, not someone who thinks that's what she should write because it's what's selling—to simply fulfill reader expectation, to create a "good enough" story within the parameters of the form. But have you ever heard writers complaining about being considered hacks, about not getting respect, about not breaking through to mainstream and bestsellerdom? The reason they don't, given equal talent between two writers, is because they don't resee their novels and stories, don't look beyond the set pieces from which they work. Those writers who do become noteworthy are those who know that coming up with a story is only the beginning. They write their stories, first, as Lamott suggests, throwing everything in, letting imagination (and subconscious) run wild, childlike. It is in seeing the idea again, and revisiting it regularly, in revising and rewriting, that a finished piece of writing is honed, perfected and made good enough for someone else to look at, for an editor or agent to consider. And that's your goal, isn't it?

Asking Questions

Let's take a broad look at how you might approach revision of a first draft; we'll use a mystery novel as an example because I've spent most of my career editing them. But as you'll see, the principles pertain regardless of the form.

Okay, you're writing a private eye novel, and you're doing what's expected: first-person narration, boiled to the hardness with which you're comfortable, paying homage to the idea of the mean streets as expressed by Raymond Chandler. You're well read in the genre, you know what the current tastes are and you've created your story: a missing woman, several suspects (a spouse, a lover, a fortune hunter, someone spurned—and you know whodunit), two or three credible motives and a police officer who insists that there was no foul play. You have a conflict, you have actions and reactions—all the required elements are in place, including an idea or two for subsequent adventures.

Take a moment, now that you've finished your first draft, and think of your story as it might be told from the perspective of the guilty party (or one of the suspects). What insight does that give you into your hero? What more have you learned about the new point-of-view character? Does any of that change the way in which the sleuth sees things? And does it lead you to an idea of what the story might be about beyond solving the puzzle, to some meaning or point or theme?

If you're a romance novelist, consider your story as it might be told from the viewpoint of the swain, or the troublemaker. Does that change how you see your heroine? Does it give you more insight into her character? Does it lead to another kind of novel, a mainstream women's fiction possibility, or a more traditional historical novel, one that can take you from category author to an Oprah Book Club selection?

What's going to happen, do you suppose, if you change the setting of one of the scenes? A confrontation at a company dinner might be crucial, may even have been the impetus of the story. (You watched something unfold and began to play the novelist's "what if?" with the situation.) But a later scene (or an earlier one, it doesn't matter) set in an office (Why did you set it there? Was it simply easier, because of your day job? Does it make a difference?) might be very different, more meaningful, if it occurs in a restaurant or in a formal dining room, where the etiquette of a meal will cause people to react differently. How do those reactions offer new insights to you and your reader?

Will it make a difference if the victim is a man rather than a woman? If a lover is a widower rather than a bachelor, or a manufacturing magnate rather than a plantation owner?

Every possible change should be considered, if only to allow you to see all the variations on your theme (whether it's known to you or not), even if it is, in this story and all that follow, the same theme, the one called for by the genre. Does it make sense, for instance, to move your series private eye to a new locale? How will having to work in a rural setting change someone used to the inner city? One of the failings I see in series proposals is that the characters are static; they act or react in the same way every time, which means to me that they're pawns, not players, moved and not moving. That can also be a problem in *any* given manuscript: Characters don't evolve, develop and change as a result of what they've experienced. If it has no impact on them, why should it have an impact on the reader? Predictability makes for dull reading—just consider the way in which you react when you know the punch line of a joke long before it is delivered.

Your characters have to be accepted as real—within the context of the tale. Readers will grant you a certain latitude in that: After all, high fantasy wouldn't work if the reader didn't accept wizards; the amateur sleuth novel doesn't hold together if the reader is someone who knows that the police actually *do* know what they're doing and are far better equipped to solve the case. And being real means they should reveal all the aspects of the people we know in our daily lives. (There are those who believe that our fictional heroes should be without warts; I'm not one of them because I can't relate, identify with or recognize people like that. But I'm only one reader.)

To a certain extent, some of the revision we're talking about can be (and often is) done before you sit down to write. You tweak characters and situations as you think about them during the creation stages and as you outline. That experience gives you insights into the situations you'll be writing about and will offer discoveries about your characters.

That doesn't mean that you don't have to revise later, after the draft is finished; it means that revision is an ongoing process and that if an idea occurs to you early on, don't wait until later to put it down.

The most important thing is to do the revising. The reader isn't going to know what you went through to get the finished product, but the discoveries you make will be discoveries that he makes; he will be touched by it and remember it. And talk about it with his friends. He doesn't have to understand what you've done (and won't), but *you* do. To the reader, the novel should seem to flow easily. He shouldn't be aware of your effort, but if you make that effort he *will* be impressed. Impressed, he will look for your next work. And so the overnight success is created: by spending days and nights revising what seemed like a good idea until it becomes a great one.

CHAPTER 2

Quarrying

Since revision begins even before we begin writing, let's start digging out the raw material for a story. We'll make it a love story, because they're universal, timeless, and because we're going to use various drafts of my Spur Award–nominated story, "The Dream That Follows Darkness," as an example, watching things as they evolve.

The story is about two people, probably in their thirties or forties. (I often tend toward some ambiguity in matters like that, feeling that if you specify certain details, the reader might not identify as easily. It's something that works for me, especially in short stories.) They're going to meet accidentally, and something is going to begin between them; it is something that shouldn't begin because she is married.

Who is she? Middle American, the girl next door, no matter where we live. Because one of my themes is universality of people, she's going to have to be a Christian; the hero will be Jewish. (Assimilation is also going to play a role.) She has to have a name . . . we'll call her Peg Wright: Peg—something upon which something else might depend.

He's Jewish. We'll call him David and give him a last name, Malek. Why that? Because the Hebrew word for king is "melech," and I want that pun there because . . . because part of the inspiration for the story is the biblical tale of David and Bathsheba. We won't, at this point (or ever, really), worry about whether or not the reader "gets" it and makes that particular connection. It will be clear in the story for those who are aware; for those who aren't, it isn't going to matter.

Both characters are searching for something: identity, peace, happiness, love—basic human needs. She will be an artist: a painter, someone who wanted to be a dancer, once. He is a photographer, with something in his past. Maybe we'll discover it as we go along. And he is, as we see him now, uncertain, questioning.

The setting is America, contemporary. The story will start somewhere in the West—a rugged place, still untamed in spots. But the characters will travel.

Oh, yes, they'll travel. After all, as a writer, I'm fascinated by magic realism, by events that can't always be explained, that seem, well, strange to everyone but those who've experienced them. So, our story will begin "today." I may discover those elements later. Right now, we're just going to write. And like so many writers, I like to have a title when I begin. The title may (and in this case, does) change throughout the process of revision, but it's a place from which to start. There's a line I remember from every good Native American memoir of the years of the Plains Wars: "It's a good day to die." A good day? No. A perfect day.

"The Dream That Follows Darkness"—first draft [under the title "A Perfect Day"]

A Perfect Day

And later that night, after the rain stopped, the wind began, cold and scouring the sky of clouds. It was a strong wind that blew in circles and people curled into tight balls in their sleeping bags and under blankets, in tents and campers and lean-tos. The wind would stop, of course, and then the dawn would begin, a mad palette followed by a sky so clear and blue and high that it would hurt to look at it. It would be a beautiful day. A perfect day.

For an accident. That's how David Malek always thought of it, anyway. An accidental meeting, just one of those things. Just one of those things. They happen, they're forgotten.

He had gone to his blind next to the lake between the moments when the wind died and the dawn began; a grey time. He put his camera onto the tripod, focussed on the spot where he knew the deer would come to drink. He wondered, but just for a moment, about smoking a

continued on next page

cigarette and for another moment about what he was doing there. His fame, such as it was, came from photographs of the bizarre, Helmut Newton out of Diane Arbus: tortured people, wrecks mechanical and human. Pictures framed to reflect pain. Now he was next to a mountain lake, cold and wet—his own pain personified—waiting to take photographs of a herd of deer drinking water. An assignment designed by a magazine to "stretch" him out, to test him. A silly effort, doomed to failure. He wondered about it for a minute; then slept and missed the dawn.

And how had she come there? Was it accident that brought Peg Vogel Wright from Billings in the north to Beaumont in the south, and finally to the night of rain and wind on the edge of a mountain lake? She didn't think about it at all; if she had she wouldn't have considered it anything more than right. But she didn't think about it then, and later it didn't matter. What mattered is that she rose from her husband's side, saw the play of color in the sky, and walked past David's blind (it was a good one), removed her clothes and, taking a deep breath, dove from a rock into the icy embrace of the water.

Malek woke to the sound, a splash. Automatically, eyes still closed, he released the shutter, trusting to the camera's automatic features to take care of exposure. Then, he looked out. Tendrils of mist whispered up out of the lake, fading into the air. Small ripples played on the surface of the water, then disappeared. There were no deer. A fish, Malek thought, jumping for a fly. A rock loosened and rolling into the lake.

But he was awake now, and he crawled to the front of the blind and looked at the day. He turned the camera's motor drive on, and watched what was in front of him as if he were peering through the camera, framing each shot. His thumb played idly against the shutter release button on the cable release. The lake's now still again surface began to pulse, the surface tension preparing to break.

She rose from the water in a straight line, up gleaming, droplets of water prisming her skin. She was facing him as she came up and than

continued on next page

swam toward him. Even strokes, strong, as if she had been born to water. Vaguely, he heard the sound of the camera as frame after frame was exposed.

Her towel was thirty feet from where he hid and he watched as she dried herself, as she wrapped the towel about her and ran her fingers through her hair, short light brown shading to blonde locks that began to curl. She stood at the edge of the lake then, and stretched; the lean lines of a dancer silhouetted against the blue of sky and water's gleam.

Dry and warmed, she dropped the towel and moved at the lake's edge. To her right, a buck peered out from the trees, watching, waiting to see if it would be safe to come to the water. She saw the deer and smiled, knowing perhaps that this place was his territory. Then, nodding, she wrapped the towel around herself again, and walked away, passing the blind, passing David Malek, and humming to herself.

The photographer sat silently, unmoving, and watched the deer moving. This is what he was here for, not naked sprites; this was money, this was the freedom to do what he wanted to do again. He kept his camera going, the thunk of the moving mirror loud in his ears. The buck noticed the sound, sniffed the air, and went back to his drinking.

Now Malek's thoughts went to the woman, to the grace with which she moved, to the play of light on her body. And he wondered. Behind him, somewhere, he heard sounds of laughter and talk, warm sounds carried on the still air. The deer turned and walked with dignity back into the woods. This part of the day was done.

Malek packed his cameras and began to walk toward the sounds he had heard. He smelled smoke and sausages cooking. He saw the woman, dressed and lounging against a tree while a tall man with lank hair crouched by the fire and tended to the food. The woman was looking directly at him, at David, as he walked into the clearing, and she smiled in greeting.

Malek knew that smile. Calm and self-possessed, it said, willing to say hello if the occasion demanded it, or ignore you. Now her voice fol-

continued on next page

lowed the smile and she said, "Hello."

Her husband looked up, setting weak grey eyes on the intruder. They were questioning, jealous, fearful. Malek looked into them, through him, and said, "Hi. Sorry to disturb you. I was on my way back," he pointed into a vague distance, "to my car." He held up his camera bag. "Just down at the lake, taking some pictures of the deer."

"They were beautiful, weren't they?" Her voice danced into his ears. She turned to the man, to her husband. "I saw them, too, when I went down to wash." She looked at Malek. "My name is Peg Wright. And this is my husband, Thomas."

"David Malek." He paused, uncertain. Something was very wrong. Or very right. He watched Peg watching him. She knew that he had seen her. Must know. He looked at her and found her within herself. He remembered the sound and feel of the wind in the night. "Well," he said, and started walking.

"No, wait. Why don't you join us. We have enough." Her voice was an entreaty to Malek, a command to her husband. Thomas Wright grunted.

The sat and talked and ate. Tom Wright was quiet, watchful. A psychiatrist with a thriving practice in Beaumont, Texas and a collector's mentality: Books, art, black powder weapons—whatever there was to acquire and eventually make a profit on was fair game. His dream was to breed horses. When he learned that David Malek was an "artist," he asked about collecting his work.

"I don't know," David said. "I have gallery showings here and there, but nothing in Texas. Yet." He dug into his pocket, found his wallet, and gave Wright the card of the Soho gallery that handled most of his work. "They should have a catalogue, I guess."

"Thanks."

"No big thing. I don't think there's any special value to me yet, but I'm good. It'll be there."

continued on next page

Tom nodded and shook a cigarette out of a crumpled pack. "Mind?"

David shrugged, and pulled out one of his own. "Guess not."

Tom looked at Peg. "I don't give a tinker's damn. It's your body." She got up and walked away from the group, sitting again a few feet away from the men.

"She doesn't like cigarette smoke, but what the hell, right? There's a lot of space here. Women."

"Yeah, women." David watched Peg watching the sky. How did she put up with this jerk, he wondered; why didn't she take off? Even after an hour, he knew they were wrong for each other, that he . . . He pushed himself up. "Thanks for everything, people. I think I'd better get going. Tom. Peg. So long."

He started walking along the path, passing Peg. she smiled up at him. "I hope you got some nice pictures, David."

She knew. "Thanks. Listen," he turned so that we facing both of them, "why don't you give me your address, and I'll send you a print. Start your collection."

"How mu—" Wright started to say, but Peg interrupted him. "Thank you, David. That's very kind." She gave him their address, and then, as he let another cigarette, she added, "If you cared about yourself, you wouldn't do that."

"I guess you're right." He ground the unsmoked cigarette underfoot. "See ya round, guys. and, oh, Tom, the prints on me. This time."

Wright smiled uncertainly, then waved.

He didn't wave three months later, though, when David Malek met them for the second time. And Malek knew this time was not an accident.

But before that he went to New Orleans, renting a small room in the Quarter, and lived a life as desperate as that of the people walking the night-streets. He found bars and bistros, drank and ate, and drank again, ending each night with the sticky sweet kiss of sazeracs at the Old

continued on next page

Absinthe House. He listened to stories and took his photographs and felt time go out of sequence. soon, he knew. Soon. but what? The search continued and he danced through streets that sleep forgot.

And then it was time to go, the time of the beginning, beginning to end. In a magazine shop on Bourbon Street, he read of a meeting of black-powder enthusiasts, an attempt to recreate the rendezvous of old. It seemed reasonable to Malek that the Wrights would be there, that a collector like Wright would not miss the event. He packed some prints and his cameras and left New Orleans, stopping only for the sticky-sweet kiss of a sazerac on a humid night. On the Mississippi, the whistle of the steamboat *Natchez* screamed and echoed and sheet lightning played against the sky. The sky was not blue as Malek flew into it. In a bar on a corner, a stripper sighed. It was not a perfect day. there are no accidents.

"David, how nice to see you again." Peg's voice was filled with joy, the words danced from her lips. "Tom, you remember David Malek, don't you?"

"Of course. He was supposed to send us a copy of one of the pictures he took when were camping at the lake. I guess you weren't satisfied with them."

David felt something curl up and die inside himself, someplace deep and dark, something once warm. "As a matter of fact, I brought them with me. Hi, Peg."

"What made you think we'd be here?" Wright's voice didn't dance, it attacked, cracked. He looked at his wife, appraising her infidelities, seeing what was behind his eyes and not in front of them. she brought her hand to her neck, fondled the pink ribbon there; a small gold cross sparked in the hollow of her throat.

"I didn't know. My agent told me you'd been in touch, though, that you'd bought a couple of my portraits. And when I heard about this convention I figured I'd take a chance. If you weren't here, I'd have

continued on next page

mailed them on to you.

"How do you like the ones you got?"

Wright smiled for the first time. "Well, I'll tell you, they're certainly different. I don't know that I'd want to display them, but as a psychiatrist, they certainly intrigue me. They look like some of the nightmares my patients describe.

"I've read some of your reviews, though, and asked around about you. I guess you're worth collecting." He reached out and took the envelope from his wife's hand. "Let's see what these look like."

There were three prints. Two showed the herd of deer at the edge of the lake, a spot of mist around their hooves, as if they were walking on clouds. The third was just the lake and the sky of blue clarity. The surface of the lake rippled, as if a rock had tumbled into it. Peg looked at David and back at the last photograph, knowing just where her form was hidden by the water, willing herself to see the play of light against herself. David touched the spot delicately, casually. "Like them?"

"David, they're beautiful. And so different. Do these look like your patients' nightmares, Tom?"

"No. No, not at all. Why the change in style, Dave?"

"That was the purpose of the shoot, just to try something new. My work hasn't changed, though."

And then the uncomfortable small talk began and ended, the where have you been, what've you been doing, where are you going next kind of talk. Wright made certain to always be between his wife and David, to hover. On the last night of the end of the beginning, there was a dance and prizes awarded to the best marksmen at the meeting. Tom Wright won in the pistol category. And on the dance floor, with Peg in David's arms, lightly and gracefully, Tom Wright started to lose.

"David," she asked during one dance, "Did you happen to . . . ?"

"To what?"

"Get any pictures of me at the lake." Her grace fell in front of her discomfort.

continued on next page

***"Yes." And that's all he said.

And she asked no more about them.

A year later, in Houston, she saw them when David had is first gallery showing there. They weren't on display, but on the afternoon of the opening, she came there and he showed them to her, and shook his head when her eyes asked the question.

"They are mine, alone," and he packed them away and Peg went home to dress for the opening because the Wrights had been invited because Tom Wright had one of the major collections of Malek prints in the world. And a new collection was beginning, the collection of horses for breeding.

Wright was distant at the party, royal, as if he owned Malek as well as the majority of the pieces in the show. He walked the floor, challenging anyone to challenge him. There were two more gatherings for the Wrights and Malek: One the night after the opening, a party at the ranch in David's honor. And one later, in the future. But they didn't know about that one, yet.

For the next two years, David and Peg danced around the edges of what was happening to them, touching when they could, but not touching most of the time. She kept assuring him that time was on their side, that all they had, finally, was time. There were light moments of flirtation and delicate kisses, and the darker hours of separation. There were phone calls and parties, meetings by chance and by design. And there was Tom.

He, Tom, laughed at Peg the night she asked for a divorce. "Never," he said and left the house to go out the ranch where the horses bred successfully and he collected women.

So David killed him—at the ranch, calling out to Tom, yelling "Fire," and watching the glow build behind the barn and move toward the stables and finally pushing Tom under the thrashing legs of the packing horses hearing the thuds and whinnies and the rushing sound of the hands coming to fight the fire, save the horses, and the shrill sirens

continued on next page

of emergency vehicles, concerto of fear—David killed Tom Wright and claimed Peg as his prize.

The sky was so clear and blue and high that it hurt to look at it. It was a beautiful day. A perfect day for a wedding.

Yisgadal v'yskadash shemay rabo . . . David Malek mouthed the ancient Aramaic words of the mourner's prayer and shivered in the chill of the early autumn West Virginia morning.

They had had two and a half years of near perfect happiness, marred only by the lack of a child. Two and a half years of***◆

And that was the first attempt to get the stone from the quarry. Somewhere in those 2,700 words is a story, but it's going to need a lot of chipping and carving. Just to offer an idea of how the process will work, what follows is part of the second draft, replacing the section on pages 20-21 that's been marked by three asterisks at the beginning and end.

"Yes." And that's all he said.

And she asked no more about them.

Until a year later, when Malek had his first showing in Houston. They weren't on display, but on the afternoon of the opening, Peg came to the gallery and he showed them to her, and shook his head when her eyes asked the question.

"They're mine. Alone. Maybe yours. Someday." He put a cigarette in his mouth, but before he could light it, she took it from his lips.

continued on next page

"I told you," she said, "that if you—"

"—cared, I wouldn't do that. And if you cared. . . ."

She broke the cigarette, dropping the pieces on the floor. "One of us has to." Then she left, to go home and change her clothes. The Wrights were hosting a party in Malek's honor and celebrating Logan's latest acquisition—a stud farm.

That evening, with the stars as witness and the wind for company, David kissed Peg.

Logan refused to give Peg the divorce she asked for two years later; he was getting involved in politics, it just wouldn't do. In that time, David and Peg danced around the edges of what was happening to them, touching when they could; not touching most of the time. She kept assuring him that time was on their side, that all they had, finally, was time. There were light moments of flirtation and delicate kisses; darker hours of separation. There were phone calls and parties, meetings by chance and design. But there were no accidents, just the beginning, beginning to end.

Until the night Logan was found trampled near the door to his stables. Or what had been his stables before the fire. The horses had all been saved. Malek's last pack of cigarettes had not been. He killed Logan Wright and claimed the widow as his prize.

The sky was so clear and blue and high that it hurt to look at it. It was a beautiful day. A perfect day for a wedding.

Yisgadal v'yiskadash shemay rabo . . . David Malek mouthed the ancient Aramaic words and shivered in the chill of the early autumn West Virginia morning. *Two and a half years* he thought with that part of himself that had split away and was watching the group at the gravesite. He had never felt more alone. Or less lonely.

They traveled to the places that had been special to them separately: Moose Creek, Idaho and Santa Fe, a deserted cay between Florida and the south Pole; and San Francisco, and a corner of Oklahoma and the

continued on next page

edge of Maine, made them something to share. Their laughter filled the days and nights. But no place was home.

On a steamy Bourbon Street night, David told Peg of a place he knew, of trees and stone and running water, of a mountain and a cave. "I was there, for a while, when I got out of the army. Sort of running away from home. It's in West Virginia. I knew we'd be able to get the land, build a cabin. It'll be marvelous."

She took his hand in hers and traced the lines on his palm with a fingernail. "It sounds wonderful, perfect. Or it will be, at least for a while. Look at us; neither of us has stayed in one place for any time. we're nomads, David, looking for the next oasis. But we're traveling together now, and looking for the same thing. Let's try it, let's go."

But they didn't go together, at first.

The town they arrived at used to have a name, but after the dam broke and the creek swept through in a rage, it was considered dead. But it wasn't deserted. Like Lazarus, the spirit moved within it. Some of those who had left before and through the racing waters traced back through the mud as the water receded, reclaiming what was theirs. the mining company didn't care. the company store was no more, of course, but that was a minor inconvenience. The beer hall remained, that was enough. time would tell. They had time. And now they had David and Peg.

They arrived at the beginning of summer, pitched a tent on the mountainside, across the creek from the town, on a level piece of land near the mouth of a cave. By the middle of September, as the chill began to grasp the clapboard homes, the sounds of David's axe resounded in the hollow as he chopped at trees, clearing space, building the cabin. There were homes they could have moved into, but that isn't what they wanted. They built, using the living rock of the mountain as a wall, encroaching on the mouth of the cave.

When they were done, their home had four rooms; three they had built, the last was the cave which David used as a darkroom. There had

continued on next page

> been some argument with local authorities about running
> power lines up, but by now both David and Peg were respected
> artists: His photographs and her watercolors brought top dollar in gal-
> leries around the country. Their presence was a boom to the county.
> Things were done.◆

Among other things, you'll notice that Tom has become Logan. Why? I liked the name better. Later, we'll look at the complete third draft and the story as it was finally published in *The Twilight Zone Magazine* in June 1987. The story began for me in 1981; I spent almost two years thinking about it before I typed the first word.

As I looked at what I had written, at the stone I'd quarried, I realized that most of what I wanted to see was still hidden: the David and Bathsheba metaphor hadn't appeared; the magic was missing; the story I was carving was not the one I wanted to see. There was a lot more to do.

And we'll also look at the changes I still want to make; polishing can become an obsession. It's also true that we're always learning— or should be. That can't be used as an excuse not to submit a piece of work—"I'll know more next year, so I can revise it then"—but is offered as a gentle reminder that the more you work, the more you'll learn, and that the learning crosses genre and form. When we discuss point of view, you'll see how what is learned in fiction can be applied to the essay.

There's something else you should have noticed: There are typos, misspellings and errors of form throughout the draft you just read. Which is as it should be, because as you're writing the first pass you shouldn't be worrying about that. The corrections can be (and will be) made during the subsequent rewrites. Keep reading to see how this piece evolves.

Before we can do any more work, we have to consider the elements of story.

The Elements of Story

CHAPTER 3

Character

Okay, you've let yourself go, written from the heart and imagination, taken your idea and transcribed it, put it on paper. Give yourself a week, then sit down again with your manuscript and begin reading. What you're looking at are not spelling and grammar and punctuation and usage errors (all of which are important to varying degrees, but not yet), but the larger matters—the elements of your story, those things that are going to keep the reader interested and caring.

What are the building blocks of a good narrative? Story line, certainly: the action, the "What happened and what happens because of it?" Scenes are made up of action and dialogue; action is created, and dialogue spoken, by characters. That's where you have to begin.

The easy thing to say about characters is that they're your story people. So, having said it, let's consider what constitutes character. There's the physical reality: size, coloring, scars, physique, disabilities if any. Each of these aspects of a person may have a very real impact on how that character acts, and how people react to her. The reactions may be due to cultural considerations (which change from area to area as dramatically as they may change from nation to nation), or they may result from a character's (or your own) biases and prejudices.

There's a social reality, which can be seen as an aspect of culture: Someone raised in a particular milieu is going to act in a certain way in a given situation. This can be seen as a class issue, upbringing or peer pressure. Whatever background you choose, you have to be aware of not only how that person acts, but how others react to her.

Have you considered education? That's certainly going to make a difference in how your character is going to see and understand the world around her . . . and, again, how people react to her. Just think about the so-called town-and-gown clichés: The way city folk look down on those from rural areas, or the people who can't stand those intellectuals who cloud the issue with discussion rather than simply going to the heart of the matter.

There's also this: It is not only how *you* see a character that matters but how the characters in your work see each other.

Finally, your novel is about your characters, not about the events. Events don't happen in a vacuum; they happen to people, affect them, and the story is, ultimately, about a character resolving a conflict of some kind. Without the characters, you don't have anything.

That's why you want to look at your characters before you create them. Build biographies for them; use photos from your albums or magazines to help you visualize them. But if you haven't done that, you're going to have to do it now, with your draft in front of you and your pencil in hand.

Here's the opening scene from Bill Pronzini's masterful *A Wasteland of Strangers* (Walker and Company, 1997).

John Faith has just arrived in the town of Pomo. The speaker is Harry Richmond, manager of a motel.

> I didn't like him the minute I laid eyes on him.
>
> He made me nervous as hell, and I don't mind saying so. Big, mean-looking. Cords in his neck thick as ax blades, eyes like steel balls, pockmarks under his cheekbones, and a T-shaped scar on his chin. The way he talked and acted, too. Cold. Hard. Snotty. Like you were dirt and he was a new broom. . . .
>
> He wrote as hard as he looked, but I could read his scrawl plain enough. No street address, and you're supposed to list one, but I wasn't about to make an issue of it. Not with him.

The next speaker is a woman.

> He scared me half to death. And not just because he startled me, sneaking up as quiet as an Indian or a thief. My flesh went cold

when I saw him looming there. He was a sight to give any decent soul the shudders even in broad daylight. . . . I turned around and there *he* was, the sneaky stranger. . . .

I wished Howard wasn't away traveling for his job until tomorrow night. With a man like that one in town, a woman and her little girl weren't safe alone in their own home.

Many other characters in the novel describe their first meeting with Faith, but I'm going to quote only one other here, Richard Novak, Pomo's police chief.

I swung the cruiser around onto Fifth and got out. The Porsche's driver was coming up onto the sidewalk when he saw me approaching; he stopped and stood waiting. I'm not small at six feet and two hundred pounds, but I felt dwarfed in this one's massive shadow. Rough-looking, too, with a hammered-down face and hard, bunched features. But there was nothing furtive or suspicious about him, nothing to put me on guard.

Pronzini's taken on a complicated task: The novel is told from nineteen different first-person points of view; John Faith, however, clearly the protagonist, never comments directly—though he is quoted by the others. During his reading of the first draft, then, the author had to be certain that each speaker had an individual voice, that each saw Faith consistently from his or her own perspective, and that any interactions between characters (singly or in combination) with him also remained consistent. The proof of Pronzini's success is made clear in the reading.

Generally, your job is not as complicated. That doesn't mean that it's any easier. Reread your work, concentrating only on one character at a time. It's not only the physical details you're considering (size, eye color, mannerisms), but the way the character presents herself and the way others see her. Again, are they consistent?

In the examples from *A Wasteland of Strangers*, people are seeing Faith as a threat. But the police chief, the man we count on to recognize danger in someone, says that there was nothing suspicious about him. Those reactions are telling and have to hold through the story.

Unless there's a reason for the change. Just as your opinion of people you know alters subject to events and experience, the characters in your novel can change their minds—as long as the proper motivations have been put in place. Remember Danny and Rose, that couple I threw at you on page 6? Well, if Rose decides that Danny is a good guy, there has to be a reason for it; if the acceptance happens only because the story demands it, you have to add a scene or two, some action, some dialogue to warrant it.

You'll ask yourself these questions:

• Are the characters true to themselves (in terms of personalities, opinions, behaviors) and if they change, is there a reason for it?

• Are their actions motivated, a result of preceding (and proceeding, ongoing) events, or do they act more as a result of your needs?

• Are the characters' goals and drives, their needs, appropriate to them and to the story, and are they clear to the reader?

• Do their physical characteristics and mannerisms remain constant?

• Are the things they say in keeping with the characters as you've presented them? If you remove all the identifiers in dialogue, would the reader still know who is speaking?

• And while this isn't a character issue specifically, it's worth paying attention to point-of-view issues at the same time: If you've written in first person, does your character have knowledge of events that haven't been shared with the reader. Have you inadvertently gotten out of the skin of the character and presented information to the reader from another perspective?

If there are any problems, anachronisms, dichotomies or questions about any of those aspects of your characters, you have to correct them. We'll talk more about how to do that in the next chapter.

CHAPTER 4

Dialogue

Dialogue is one of the parts of the craft of writing that is the most difficult to master, not only in the choice of language but in the presentation of the conversation. It is also, in most stories, a keystone in the structure.

What purposes is your dialogue going to serve?

1. **Dialogue aids character definition, development and evolution.** Readers "listen" to what your characters are saying and interpret the statements in the same way that we, in our daily lives, hear people and form opinions.

2. **Dialogue brings information to the reader.** We receive clues in a mystery novel from what is said to the sleuth, either in the course of general conversation or as a result of questions; we learn about lovers through the things they say (and don't say) to each other. Don't forget, the two characters aren't always on stage together; events occur out of sight or hearing. The reader is aware of these happenings and will interpret what a participant says about them. If we know that Toni lied about where she was last night—either directly or by omission—it will shade our opinion of her. That's what you want to do, but the question is, Are you shading us in the right direction in terms of the story's needs?

Dialogue does not stand alone, entire unto itself. It's part of a scene, of an ongoing action: It takes place in a setting that will, when done correctly, have an influence on what's being said and how the characters say it. Do they lean forward, to be heard over the noise of a party? Are they whispering? Is their manner furtive? What's their body language? Are you using those elements to further the story? Why not?

Because dialogue is not only the words and what they mean but also movement, you'll want to be sure you don't give your readers a stretch of unrelieved talking heads (or, what's worse, long speeches and/or orations).

Dialogue is also intrinsic to character: You and I speak differently because of our backgrounds and interests; that's a given. But there are times when, as individuals, we vary our own speech patterns. It may have to do with the place we find ourselves in. It may also have more than a little to do with our intentions. In her 1987 essay, "From Outside, In," Barbara Mellix describes this scene with her ten-year-old daughter. Mellix is working on an essay; Allie is bored and pesky:

> Finally, she pulled up a chair to my desk and watched me, now and then heaving long, loud sighs. After two or three minutes (nine or ten sighs), I lost my patience. "Looka here, Allie," I said, "you too old for this kinda carryin' on. I done told you this is important. You wronger than dirt to be in here haggin' me like this and you know it. Now git on outta here and leave me off before I put my foot all the way down."
>
> I was at home, alone with my family, and my daughter understood that this way of speaking was appropriate in that context. She knew, as a matter of fact, that it was almost inevitable; when I get angry at home, I speak some of my finest, most cherished black English. Had I been speaking to my daughter in this manner in certain other environments, she would have been shocked and probably worried that I had taken leave of my sense of propriety.
>
> Like my children, I grew up speaking what I considered two distinctly different languages—black English and standard English (or as I thought of them then, the ordinary everyday speech of "country" coloreds and "proper" English)—and in the process of acquiring these languages, I developed an understanding of when, where, and how to use them.

Characters in our stories face situations like this daily, so they must vary consistently—consistent with their backgrounds and with the background against which you've placed them at that moment.

A scene from life: A friend of mine was raised—and still lives—in

Brooklyn. The nature of her job requires that she speak "properly," and she does. Usually. Every now and again, though, something will slip by, generally when she's comfortable, sitting in the office casually. Then she'll refer to "youse guys." Another friend, a writer raised in the same neighborhood, will say, "I'm comin' by you." He doesn't mean that he's passing me on his way to somewhere else; he's letting me know he's coming to visit. It doesn't happen in his writing. His editor will often add it.

Idioms and slang are, clearly, part of what you have to consider. Every culture, region, every neighborhood has a manner of speech; recognition and use of this is what adds flavor, a reality that allows for continued suspension of disbelief on the part of your reader. It is what makes Southern writing immediately identifiable and makes all writing vivid. In her collection *Close Range: Wyoming Stories*, Annie Proulx, author of *The Shipping News*, tells the story of Diamond Felts, a rodeo performer. A character says, "Well, you rodeo, you're a rooster on Tuesday, a feather duster on Wednesday." What the line reveals about the human condition is beside the point for us here; what matters is that Proulx captured the cadence of a place.

Other expressions are a root cause of debates about the use of language in novels, and touch on questions of so-called political correctness. Is it necessary to use the infamous four-letter words, the seven words George Carlin based a comic routine around because he couldn't say them on television? What about "the 'N' word" that is no longer used, but only referred to in that way? My answer is an unqualified *yes*! With the exclamation point.

While it's true that people can and do speak without resorting to vulgarities, it's also true that most people do use them. Sometimes it's a matter of emphasis, sometimes of anger, sometimes peer pressure, sometimes a lack of education. And sometimes, especially when considering racial epithets, it is a simple bias or prejudice. Denying those realities—because they are painful, because they might be deemed hurtful or because of the same peer pressures that are so often the reason they're used in the first place—results in a story that isn't honest, that doesn't reflect a true world.

Your characters have to speak in the way that we all speak, and that "all" includes everyone. As I read a novel, if I sense that a writer has compromised the dialogue, I begin to distrust everything, expect other compromises, even while acknowledging that there are places and people for whom that isn't a compromise.

What can dialogue accomplish? Here's a line from a scene in Keith Snyder's *Coffin's Got the Dead Guy on the Inside.* The novel, the second in a series, features Jason Keltner, a musician and composer who functions as a reluctant sleuth, along with his two buddies, Martin and Robert. In this adventure, Jason is called upon to "babysit" someone who appears to be involved in some kind of computer scam. The simple job becomes complex when one man dies and a group of men show up at Jason's home, looking for "the dongle." From that point, the novel becomes a high adventure. The speaker is Robert, one of three ongoing characters in the series the author has created. First, here's the line as it was written originally:

> Robert glanced down. "Three-quarters of a tank and we haven't touched the five-gallon can. I'm being careful not to do any sudden surges of speed so we don't waste gas."

We get some information (a reminder that they've got extra gas in a can) and learn that Robert is paying attention to what he has to do. But in the following revised version, as the author tells us, "I've made Robert's line more Robertish, which both shows his way of talking and thinking and allows the reader to infer his disinterest in things automotive":

> Robert glanced down. "Three-quarters of a tank. I'm being very smooth with the thing, the what is it, the pedal thingy."

We've lost the fact that they're carrying a gas can (but that information shouldn't need repeating—if the reader is paying attention to the story, he will remember it; if he isn't paying attention, the author has more serious problems). We've also lost nine words of text, none of which were particularly important to the story. But we've gained an insight into Robert and kept his dialogue "honest": This is the way he speaks and thinks; we've been hearing it throughout the story. The first version would have furrowed the brow of the reader—that just isn't the way Robert speaks.

Another point: sound. One of the best tests of dialogue is to read it aloud or, even better, have someone unfamiliar with it do the reading. Does it sound like someone speaking, or does it sound like an author trying to create "realism"?

Our normal way of speaking is filled with stops—"umm," "huh," "ya know," "like"—and our conversations are social events, talk about nothing, filled with minutiae. Some of the trivial detail may be important to one or another of the speakers, but is it important to a reader? Remember: Fiction is a *reflection* of life; it isn't life itself. Life goes on, often in spite of us; if you want someone to get to the end of your story, though, you have to make it necessary. Pacing is part of that, and the pacing of dialogue is as important as what's being said.

Also remember that even as the reader is listening to you, as the storyteller, she is also listening to the characters. If the voices aren't right, if what's said is trivial, she'll eavesdrop elsewhere. And if it doesn't sound like people talking, your characters won't be talking to your readers for very long—or very often.

So far we've been talking about dialogue in a broad perspective. Let's focus a bit more closely now, looking at some of the aspects discussed, as well as the mechanics of dialogue—the way it is presented as well as the way it is said.

"I think it is time to go," Rose pouted.

"If you say so," Danny shrugged.

"I do say so," Rose repeated.

"Okay, okay. Where did you put your coat? I will go and get it," Danny explained.

"You hung it in the closet," Rose observed.

"Oh, yes, that is right," Danny conceded.

"If you would only pay more attention, we would not have these arguments all the time," Rose said angrily.

"You are the one who is arguing. I am ready to go," Danny snorted, hotly.

We'll begin with the sound of the conversation. Read it aloud. Can you hear two people having this talk? Do you care about what's being said? (If you answered yes to either of those questions, go directly to jail. Do not pass Go. Do not collect $200.) So, how can it be corrected, made at least a little more engaging, more realistic even within the context of the contrivances of fiction?

Look first at the language: There isn't one contraction used. There may be people who speak that way, but how many of them do you know? Uh-huh. As exaggerated as the example is, the awful truth is that too many of the manuscripts I receive are filled with dialogue that stiff. (I think the authors think it is formal, reflective of how a certain class of people speak.) We'd begin correcting this by changing some of the words: "it is" would become "it's"; "that is" becomes "that's." Do we change them all? Not necessarily. "Where did you put your coat?" contains a beat that could be important to the scene. "Where'd you put your coat?" might be acceptable; it's a simple question. But by leaving "did" in the phrase, you give that word particular weight. Speak the two sentences and notice how you emphasize it. The texture and rhythm are both different, and make a slightly different point.

It doesn't hurt, at times like that, to think as a director might. The words the playwright puts into the mouths of the characters are there in black and white on the page; it is in the delivery that they come to life. By choosing your words, and trusting the reader to hear them (as good readers do), you do what the director does.

That part's simple: Pick words your characters would use, make full use of your vocabulary and pay attention to the cadences of speech. Listen to people, not only for what they say but how they say it.

What are Rose and Danny doing? All we see, if we see anything, are two people placed on their marks, speaking to each other. There's no action at all, no movement. Here's a better version, with some contractions added (and an assumption that we've met these folks earlier, so we know what they look like):

> Rose brushed her bangs out of her eyes. "I think it's time to go," she pouted.
>
> "If you say so," Danny shrugged.
>
> "I do say so," Rose said. She stood up and crossed her arms under her breasts.
>
> "Okay, okay. Where did you put your coat? I'll go and get it," Danny explained. He stood, too, careful not to touch Rose.
>
> "You hung it in the closet," Rose observed.
>
> "Oh, yes, that's right," Danny conceded, nodding.
>
> "If you'd only pay more attention, we wouldn't have these arguments all the time," Rose said angrily.
>
> "You're the one who's arguing. I'm ready to go," Danny snorted, hotly.

Still weak, but at least something's happening—there's some activity beyond speech. The next problem we have to fix are the attributions. There are only two people in the scene; once we've established who they are (which should be clear in context, especially in a case like this), it isn't necessary to tell the reader who's saying what.

At the same time, the author has used dialogue tags indiscriminately: "pouted," "observed," "conceded." Those words, used to avoid using the word "said," are, contrary to popular belief, the sign of an unimaginative writer: someone who recognizes that the dialogue is weak, that it isn't carrying its message, and so resorts to the tag device as a way of explaining (nine times out of ten, ineffectively) what's being said.

> Rose brushed her bangs out of her eyes. "I think it's time to go."
>
> Danny shrugged. "If you say so."

"I do say so." Rose stood and crossed her arms under her breasts.

"Okay, okay. Where did you put your coat? I'll go get it." He stood, too, careful not to touch Rose.

"You hung it in the closet."

"Yeah, that's right." Danny nodded.

"If you'd only pay more attention, we wouldn't have these arguments all the time," Rose said angrily.

"You're the one who's arguing. I'm ready to go," Danny snorted, hotly.

Are you, as the reader, missing anything important as a result of these changes? (If you read carefully, you'll note that I also edited some of the words.) Rose is no longer pouting; her attitude, though, is clear by the end of the conversation. Danny's concession is implicit in his agreement, so we got rid of that. Notice, too, that there's a period after the word "right." A comma would indicate that he nodded the words, rather than spoke them; it's a physical impossibility.

Still a couple of problems, though: "angrily" and "hotly." Adverbs are like a good spice: They have to be used delicately. Whenever I see them in dialogue, I know the author has missed an opportunity to show, not tell. What would Rose do, physically, that gives the reader a real sense of what the emotions are? She might knock an object over, she might stiffen, her face could redden . . . or pale. She could raise her voice. Any one of those actions (or the one you will choose, based on how you've developed the character) will serve.

As for Danny snorting hotly, visualize that. Not a pretty picture, nor one that serves your purposes as a storyteller. Hotly also implies anger; tempers are rising, the argument that is developing is getting out of hand—as arguments do. What are the physical manifestations of Danny's emotional state? Remember, too, that every word you use has weight and meaning and should be creating an image in the reader's mind. The words call attention to themselves.

Another consideration: Even now the dialogue is spoken without pauses. Because this example is short, that isn't a serious problem. However, in a scene that goes on for several paragraphs (or even pages), you'll want to use some kind of beat: You can break the dialogue with an attribution or action:

> "You're the one who's arguing." Danny spun and stomped toward the closet. "I'm ready to go," he said, not looking back at Rose.

This is an alternate version:

> "You're the one who's arguing . . . I'm ready to go." Danny stomped toward the closet, fists clenched.

The ellipsis indicates a pause, a break, in this case maybe a consideration of what he might want to say next. The techniques can be mixed:

> "You're the one who's arguing . . ." Danny took a deep breath. "I'm ready to go."

He's stopped speaking; the ellipsis tells the reader that the words trail off into silence. He takes a breath—another pause—and then action. Is he trying to calm himself? Is he choosing his words more carefully now that this silly argument is about to get out of hand? The rest of the scene will offer the answers.

◆ Take these few lines and begin to rewrite them so that the scene you create makes a difference to you. And to the reader.

◆ Look at the dialogue in your novel: Are you explaining what's being said, or is it clear? Are you using adverbs to indicate emotion? Are you beginning or ending every line of dialogue?

◆ Write a scene that is only dialogue; there's nothing that doesn't appear between quotation marks. Make all the emotions clear through language. Once you've done that, you'll be able to look at any dialogue you write and pinpoint what's working and what's not.

Once you have your characters really speaking, they'll be speaking to your readers, helping you tell your story effectively.

CHAPTER 5

Scenes

The story line is the linear action of your piece: It's made up of scenes, of the things that happen, all chosen to bring your characters from the beginning—their conflict or crisis—to a resolution. It's a timeline, a record of events caused by and causing other events. Jack Bickham and Dwight Swain wrote about and taught the principle of scene and sequel; your job in revision is to make certain that cause and effect are solidly in place.

The scenes that you write are the description of the action, and in addition to defining the action, they serve additional purposes: They continue the evolution of character and add ambiance and tone (important aspects of involving the reader, placing her *there*, in the story). They also create tension, worry on the part of the reader, a need to turn the page.

If you've taken Lamott's advice and not worried about your first draft, just written it, when it comes time to read the printout you're going to find scenes that actually make a difference to the plot, and those that are there just because you felt like writing them at the time. You have to be able to tell the difference and, in the old phrase, be able to mercilessly kill your darlings—all those bits of writing that are just so wonderful . . . and so pointless. (Don't worry; you can always adapt them for another novel—one in which they belong.)

We've already taken a look at a brief piece of Keith Snyder's *Coffin's Got the Dead Guy on the Inside.* Here's the whole scene as first written.

Coffin's Got the Dead Guy on the Inside—First Draft

Robert glanced down. "Three-quarters of a tank and we haven't touched the five-gallon can. I'm being careful not to do any sudden surges of speed so we don't waste gas."

"Onward."

On the way through Santa Maria, still trailing behind the white Taurus, Jason said, "I got it!"

Robert glanced at him expectantly and then returned his attention to the road.

"Whatever it is," Martin said, "I hate it. A lot."

Robert gave Jason a second glance of increased expectation.

"Yeah . . . " Jason said. "Yeah . . . that'll work."

Robert held his expectant glance for a few moments, and then burst out, "What!"

"I figured out how to communicate with Platt in such a way that only Platt would know how to decode it. I think."

He turned half around on the front seat so he could see both Robert and Martin and said, "When I was at Platt's place, I noticed that he has one of the same pieces of gear that I own. A Roland U-220. So I figure—"

"What's a Roland Whatever-Twenty?" Martin interrupted.

"Oh. Sorry. Um . . . see that road case next to you?"

"Yeah."

"Open the front."

Martin unclamped the front of the road case and removed the front lid.

Jason pointed. "See it?"

All the faceplates visible in the open road case had buttons and small, dark LCD displays. One of them said ROLAND U-220 on it in thin white and blue silkscreening.

"Yeah."

continued on next page

"It's a sound module. Basically it's a box of sampled sounds—piano sounds, drum sounds, whatever—that a keyboardist can play from his keyboard by attaching it with a cable."

"Okay."

"Okay, I'll try to explain this simply." He stopped to put his thoughts straight. "All right. When you buy a sound module, you don't just have to be content with the sounds that came pre-made from the factory. For instance, I can make a really cool, eerie sound by removing the beginning of a piano note. If you truncate the sound of the piano hammer striking the piano string and then give it a little fade-in instead, it's a really neat sound. With me so far?"

Martin said, "You can do that? I didn't know you could do that."

Robert nodded.

Jason said, "Yeah, that's just the beginning of what you can do."

On the way through Pismo Beach, Martin started talking.

"I knew this guy in Turlock named Hector Jenkins," he said. "He worked at one of the peach canneries in the summer. He used to work there every year, seven days a week, just insane hours. Like a hundred and ten degrees inside the cannery. He was just on the line, you know, the what do you call them . . . the conveyor belt. He didn't have any responsibilities except just watch the peaches go by and find the bad ones or something like that.

"So every year Hector works his cannery job for four months and then every year he gets laid off at the end of the peach season and draws unemployment for the rest of the year. Not enough to live like a king or anything, but ol' Hector's doing okay, you know? He's got his health benefits all year and he can eat and pay rent and buy a little beer and see a movie sometimes.

"Hector's got no wife and kids—he's just a single guy with average luck. Nothing special. You get the picture."

He stopped talking, but not as though he had finished. Neither

continued on next page

Robert nor Jason interrupted the pause. Highway flowed by around them and the Taurus maintained speed.

"One day," Martin continued presently, "Hector comes into the bar at the bowling alley and there's something different about him. It wasn't anything you could really point at, but he's just some cannery worker with a regular check from the government and that doesn't fit with this new vibe I'm picking up from him, if you follow.

"So I give him his Coors and he's leaning against the bar, kind of surveying the action around pool tables, and I just casually end up cleaning the bar right where he is, and I say, 'Hector, you got something different about you. What's the story?'

"He says, 'Man, you're not gonna believe it even if I told you.' I say, 'Try me.' 'Okay,' he says, 'try this on for size.'

"He turns around and leans over the bar with one forearm flat on the bartop and says, 'Martin, my man, I just won the fucking lottery.'

"So I say, 'You mean that like a figure of speech, or is this like the lottery lottery, the State lottery?' 'No figure of speech,' he says. 'No figure of speech. I won the fucking lottery.'

"I say, 'Jesus Christ, that's great, Hector,' even though I'm not sure he's not bullshitting me.

"He says, 'Yeah. You want to see it?'

"I say, 'Sure.'

"He reaches into his shirt pocket and pulls out this lottery ticket. Sure enough, I match the numbers on the Lotto machine and he's got the winning ticket. Thirteen million and some dollars.

"I say, 'Hector, this is the honest-to-Petie-the-dog-from-Our-Gang winning ticket.'

"He says, 'Yeah, that's what I told you.'

"So when I'm finished saying 'Wow,' I ask him what he's going to do with it.

"He says, 'I been thinking about just that all week, and I tell you what. You know what this ticket really gives me, Martin?'

continued on next page

"I say no. He leans way over toward me like he wants to tell me a secret and says, 'Freedom, man. This gives me freedom.'

"I say, 'Hector, it's none of my business, but money has a way of not being able to give you freedom.'

"He looks at me like I missed the point and he's sure of something I don't get. Then he nods at me, puts the ticket back in his shirt pocket, and while I'm still trying to puzzle a little sense out of this, he drains his Coors, leaves me a dollar tip, and says, 'Catch you later,' and leaves.

"That's the last time I saw him in Turlock. I stayed on there for, oh, a year, year and a half, and then I moved down to L.A."

He stopped again, and again, Robert and Jason waited.

A few miles went by.

Finally, Martin said, "About four years later, I was in San Diego visiting my mom. She had this thing for Tom Cruise so I took her to see whatever movie he was in that year, I don't remember which one . . ."

Robert said, "Was it the one where he plays the good-looking cheesy guy who learns to have a heart?"

"Yeah, I guess," Martin said. "Anyway, mom's in the theatre and I'm out in the lobby waiting in line to buy some Good'n Plenties or something when the guy in front of me turns around with his root beer to go into the theatre and it's Hector Jenkins.

" 'Hector!' I say, 'Hey, what's up? It's me, Martin Altamirano.'

"He says, 'Martin, what's up?' and we take a couple of minutes and blah this and blah that, and he finally says, 'Hey, my wife's waiting for me in the movie, I gotta go,' and I say, 'Okay, but I gotta ask you one thing because I always wondered it and I gotta know: Did that thirteen mil give you your freedom like you thought?'

"He gets this look on his face and says, 'No.' And he looks like he's deciding whether he's going to say something more, so I just wait. After he sees I'm just going to keep waiting, he says, 'No, man it didn't. But this ticket did,' and takes it out of his shirt pocket and *shows it to me.*"

Robert said, "The ticket?"

continued on next page

"Yeah."

Jason said, "He never cashed it?"

"Never cashed it."

Robert angled his head as he considered the scenario. "Why not?"

"I asked him that, but Hector's not the world's most articulate human. I got the feeling he'd been trying—unsuccessfully—to answer that question for a long time. He got real uncomfortable and just ended up saying, 'I dunno, man; sorry.' Then we went into the movies and that was it. I didn't even see the movie, my mind was so whirled up trying to get what he was getting at. When my movie let out, he was long gone. That's it."

A few more miles rolled by.

"I'll tell you what I think," Martin said, and he leaned back into his seat as though to punctuate. "I think it was Plan B. I think before he won the lottery, he already wanted just a little better life than he had. Not a lot better, just a little. And once he had that lottery ticket to fall back on, he thought he could try for what he always wanted. Like, it meant he could quit the cannery and get a better job? And if it didn't work out, he could always fall back on the thirteen mil safety net." ◆

There's material here that makes a difference to the story, of course, some of the techie information plays a role, but as Snyder says in presenting the rewrite:

> In the unrevised version, I'm vamping around and trying to fig-
> ure out what to write. Here [in the excerpt below], I've lost the
> computer/audio/techie angle and Martin's Hector story. I've also
> made Robert's line [the first one on p. 46] more Robertish, which
> both shows his way of talking and thinking and allows the reader
> to infer his disinterest in things automotive.

Coffin's Got the Dead Guy
on the Inside—Revised

Robert glanced down. "Three-quarters of a tank. I'm being very smooth with the thing, the what is it, the pedal thingy."

They went through San Luis Obispo, Paso Robles, and a string of smaller towns with Spanish names. Afternoon became evening. Nobody talked for a while.

After about an hour without conversation, the Pontiac decelerated abruptly and lurched toward the center divider. Martin said, "Watch it, watchitwatch*watchit!*" Jason lunged for the steering wheel and overcorrected the course into the next lane and Robert snapped awake and insisted, "Queen to . . . oh, no!" He stomped convulsively on the brake pedal and something metallic in the front part of the car immediately responded by making a horrific grinding noise and not slowing down much.

Jason and Robert did contradictory things to the steering wheel but the car eventually came back into true behind the Taurus.

After a long stretch of scenery, Jason said, "When's the last time you slept?"

"Last night."

"How long?"

Robert looked sheepish. "About an hour."

"You were playing chess all night."

"Not all night. I slept for an hour."

"Great," Martin said. "The driver's falling asleep and we can't stop to switch."

"I'm fine," Robert said overly brightly.

"Okay," Jason said, "how do we keep Robert awake?"

"I'm fine."

"You're not fine. You just fell asleep in the fast lane. What should we do to keep you awake?"

continued on next page

"Play chess?"

There was a long pause. Hopefulness radiated from the driver's seat.

Jason said, "Robert, is that one of your better ideas?"

Robert looked offended and said, "Sure it is. Chess exists in the mind, not on the board."

"Yeah, that's what we need, you drifting off in deep thought."

"I won't drift off."

"Ixnay," Martin said, terminating the debate, "on the goddamn esschay."

"All right," Robert said. "In that case, keep me talking."

Jason said. "Okay. Tell us a story."

"About what?"

"Um . . . let's see. Since you'd drift off into deep thought if we asked you to make something up, let's go with true stories. How about . . . someone you know who did something unusual."

Robert considered the topic. "I know this guy who caught the killer of a performance artist."

"Someone not in this car."

"Okay, let me think. I get to embellish . . ." ◆

End of chapter.

The lottery story was just a story, guys talking; the earlier technical information was also important, but it could be worked in at other times (not everything has to be said at once, remember). So, for the sake of pacing, and so as to make a point, material had to be shifted.

Sometimes, however, a scene may appear that seems to advance the story (it was meant to when it was originally considered, at any rate) but later proves to be, well, simply unnecessary. Here's another example from Snyder's novel:

Coffin's Got the Dead Guy
on the Inside—First Draft

Jason's apartment had been ransacked. Dishes spilled from the wheeled dish cabinet, the bathroom medicine cabinet was on the toilet seat, the clothes from the closet were scattered on the floor, and all the books from the short hallway between the front room and the pseudo-kitchen lay in a heap below the shelves. In the front room, the sofa was away from the wall with its cushions pulled off. The music equipment on the black tube stand had been disconnected and rearranged. Several pieces were on the piano bench or on the floor.

He went out the front door onto the porch, into the door to the rest of the Manor, and up the stairs to Robert and Martin's room. The dusty boxes of paperbacks that Robert kept in the short hallway outside his door were in disarray. Jason picked his way through the books on the hallway floor and knocked on the door. There was no answer. He tried the knob. It was unlocked, and he opened the door.

The room looked only a little messier than usual. For a minute, he wasn't sure whether anything was actually wrong with it, but then he saw the garage sale turntable on its side on the floor and the walnut-veneer speaker overturned on the table. Some of the clothes in piles on the floor were still half-folded, and more of Robert's boxes of paperback books had been tipped over into little square landslides. There was no telling where Robert and Martin were, but they usually didn't stay out past about two-thirty on Friday nights. They wouldn't be happy about their room being tossed, but Jason bet himself that they wouldn't clean it up, either.

At the sound of a car in the lot, Jason threaded his way out through the clutter, went down the front stairs and onto the porch, and followed a narrow sidewalk around the side of the Manor to its corner, until he could see the parking lot in back. Paul's little hatchback was in its space, and Jason heard footsteps going up the old back stairs. He stepped

continued on next page

around the corner and walked toward his back door. Paul was on the landing above, going through his keys. He looked down at Jason.

"Hey," he said.

"My place was ransacked," Jason said. "Better check out yours."

Paul looked concerned and said, "Anything missing?"

"Not that I can tell," Jason said, "but I've only been here a few minutes." He started up the stairs.

"Shit," Paul said. "It's unlocked." He swung the door open and slid his hand around on the near inside wall until he found the light switch. Jason reached the top of the staircase as the light came on.

Paul's apartment was in the same state as the others. Paul looked at the tumbled mess of moving boxes. Jason stood in the doorway and said, "Yeah, that's what my place and Robert and Martin's looks like, too."

"Those dicks," Paul said angrily.

"What dicks?" Jason said.

Paul glared at him. "Those dicks that did this," he said. "What did you think I meant?"

"I'll go call the cops," Jason said. "Don't touch anything." He realized that he'd been touching all kinds of things and added, "More than we already have, I mean."

"It doesn't matter," Paul said. "There won't be any fingerprints anyway."

"Why not?"

"They wouldn't be dumb enough to leave fingerprints."

"Who wouldn't?"

"Are you deaf or something? The guys that did this!"

"How about I call the cops anyway?"

"How about you do whatever the fuck you want," Paul said. "Shit, look at this! I can't believe those assholes!"

Jason stood in the doorway, looking at Paul, and then went down-

continued on next page

stairs into his front room and called the police on their non-emergency telephone number. The police were busy with their non-emergencies, so they put him on hold.

Robert and Martin came home while he was still on hold, and Jason heard them enter through the front door and clomp up the interior stairs, talking about a movie in which someone turned into an ape. When they got to the top of the stairs, the ape talk stopped and Jason heard Martin say, "Hey!"

The police came on the line and Jason told them what had happened. They told him that they were very busy, and it would be at least three hours before they could send a car, and offered to mail him a form he could fill out, detailing what was stolen. He accepted the offer in case it turned out that something was missing after all, and dithered briefly about whether he wanted a car sent. Then he decided against it, thanked the dispatcher, and hung up.

Martin and Robert clomped back down the interior stairs and knocked on Jason's front door. Jason opened it, and Martin looked in with Robert behind him and said, "They got you too?"

"Yup," Jason said. "Anything missing from your place?"

Robert said, "What would they take?"

"Good point."

"Anything missing from yours?"

"No."

Robert said, "Weird."

Jason said, "They hit Paul, too. I want to go see how he's doing."

Paul was sitting on his floor, talking on the phone with his back to them. Jason rapped on the doorframe with his knuckles, and Paul turned and looked at him, said, "I've got to go. We'll talk later," to whoever was on the phone, hung up, and stood.

"What a mess, huh?" he said.

Robert said, "Anything missing?"

"No," Paul said. "What about everybody else?"

continued on next page

Excerpt #2, continued

"I don't know," Jason said. "Let's go see."

They went through Paul's other door into the Manor's second floor. No one else was home, but several doors were ajar, and all the apartment contents were strewn on floors and tables. Chuck's door was locked, as was the door to the attic apartment occupied by a woman named Patrice who worked at a bank.

"I wonder what they were after," Martin said. "It looks like they hit just about everybody."

"Looking for drugs, maybe," Robert said.

Jason said, "Then why wouldn't they have taken my music stuff and sold it?"

Martin said, "Maybe they were kids."

Jason nodded. "Could be."

Paul said, "What about your car? Was it here? Is it okay?"

Jason said, "No, I was out in it."

"That's good," Paul said. "That would suck big time."

Robert laughed. "Your car being ransacked would be worse than your apartment being ransacked?"

Paul glared at him. "All I meant," he said, "is that it would suck. You have some kind of fucking problem with that?"

After the briefest pause, something in Robert's face seemed to click to a different setting.

"That word!" he said intensely. "What was it? What *was* it?" He shut his eyes. Paul gave him a look that could decapitate rodents. Robert pressed his fingertips to his forehead and concentrated fiercely. "A jewel of meaning, a tiny, shimmering perfection of poetry . . . I almost have it . . . aha!" He half-opened his eyes in pleasure and touched the tips of his forefingers to his thumbs. " '*Suck.*' " He drew in a great breath, as though filling his lungs with sheer beauty, and then let it out, opening his hands. " '*Suck!*' Angels weep and bards forsake their souls! The simple magnificence of that mere utterance conjures images of scintillating splendor, such coruscating opalescence—"

continued on next page

"Shut up," Paul said. "You know what I meant."

"Suck," Robert said, savoring the word. "Suck. Suck. Suck. Suck. Suck. Suck."

Martin said, "You're a weird guy, Robert."

Robert sang, "Suuuuuuuuuck!" in a loud, trembling falsetto.

Paul went *humph* and said, "That's an understatement."

"Cretins!" Robert shouted, rolling the *r*. "Cretins and weenies all!"

Paul just looked at him.

"Suck," Robert concluded thoughtfully. He nodded his head wisely.

Paul opened his mouth to say something. Robert interrupted him with another, "Suck!" and then looked expectant. Paul tried again and Robert did it again.

Paul gave Robert a tough look, and when Robert didn't acknowledge it, he shook his head in disgust and said, "Later." Still shaking his head, he went back into his room and closed the door.

Robert's face clicked back into a normal expression.

"And they say vaudeville is dead," Jason said.

"Paul is my favorite person," Robert said nicely.

They went downstairs. Robert and Martin came in to help clean up and to drink decaf coffee. When the apartment was straight again, Robert and Jason got onto the subject of books, and then spent forty minutes making Martin defend his assertion that comic books existed which were equal in literary value to books by James Joyce, Ernest Hemingway, and Maya Angelou. The argument ended when Robert got Martin to admit that he'd never actually read anything by Joyce, Hemingway, or Angelou. Martin argued for another few minutes, but no one would listen to him.

"Hey," Jason said, "you're getting pretty good with that butterfly knife."

Martin snorted through his decaf. "I figure if I just get that one move down, I can intimidate people enough that they'll never find out I don't know anything else."

continued on next page

Excerpt #2, continued

"Sounds a little risky to me," Jason said. "What if it doesn't intimidate them?"

"Then Robert sings."

Robert cleared his throat and sang "Try to Remember" from *Man of La Mancha.*

When he was done, Jason said, "Try to be merciful. Just use the knife on them."

At three-thirty in the morning, Robert and Martin left and went upstairs, and Jason sat on his piano bench, put on his headphones, switched all his music equipment on, and opened UNTITLED #23.

He moved the mouse so that the onscreen cursor was positioned over a picture of a button labeled "Play," and clicked. The music began to play in his headphones. It was all wrong, and he couldn't leave town to work on it like he really needed to. He stopped playback in mid-note and began restructuring the piece, disliking the fact that he was doing so at home in Pasadena. ◆

Now, the rewrite. Note that not only is some of the language changed, but the Manor is not even ransacked.

Excerpt #2 revised

Coffin's Got the Dead Guy on the Inside—Revised

At the sound of a car in the lot, Jason moved aside the orange towel that hung over the window in his back door and looked out. Paul's little hatchback was in its space, and Paul was going up the rickety back stairs. Jason went out. Paul was on the landing above, going through his keys. He looked down at Jason.

continued on next page

"Hey," he said.

"Score some good stuff?"

Paul came down the stairs. "Nah. Not tonight. Why, you want some?"

"Nope."

"It's been a weird night. I could see you wanting to relax."

"Not for me."

"Oh, right. I forgot. You never relax."

Martin's little CVCC pulled into the lot and Robert and Martin got out and walked toward them.

"How was the party?" Martin said.

"Short," Jason said. "A guy died."

"Died like died?"

"Yeah."

"You saw it?"

"Yeah."

Paul said, "He tried to save the guy. Totally heroic. I was impressed."

"That's why I was doing it, Paul," Jason said. "To impress you."

"Hey," Paul said. "Don't take it out on me that it didn't work. Look at the bright side. At least we didn't die on the way home in that car of yours. That would have really sucked."

Robert said, "But, since it wasn't you who died, it didn't suck."

Paul looked at him without saying anything.

Robert said, "I'm just trying to understand."

Paul glared at him. "All I said, Robert, is that it would suck. You have some kind of fucking problem with that?"

After the briefest pause, something in Robert's face seemed to click to a different setting.

He leaned closer to Paul.

Martin shuffled back to give him a little space and looked as though he expected to enjoy whatever happened next.

Robert paused.

continued on next page

Excerpt #2 revised, continued

Then, "That word!" Robert emoted intensely, his gaze burning into Paul's. "What was it? What *was* it?" He shut his eyes and concentrated. Paul gave him a look that could decapitate capybaras.

Robert pressed his fingertips to his forehead and concentrated fiercely.

"That jewel of meaning," he keened. "That tiny, shimmering perfection of poetry . . ." He half-opened his eyes in pleasure and touched the tips of his forefingers to his thumbs. " '*Suck!*' " He drew in a great breath, as though filling his lungs with sheer beauty. " '*Suck!*' Angels weep. Bards forsake their souls! The simple magnificence of that mere utterance conjures images of scintillating splendor, such coruscating opalescence—"

"Shut up," Paul said. "You knew what I—"

Robert silenced him with one upheld hand. "Suck," he entreated, savoring the word deliciously.

Martin said, "You're a weird guy, Robert."

Robert sang, "Suuuuuuuuck!" in a loud, trembling falsetto.

Paul went *humph* and said, "Weird is an understatement."

"Suck," Robert insisted. "Suck. Suck. Suck. Suck. Suck."

Jason froze his face in a casual expression, clamped his jaw so he wouldn't crack up, and didn't look at Martin.

"Robert—" Paul began.

"Suck," Robert hissed murderously.

"Suck!" Robert ululated warblingly.

"Suck?" Robert implored querulously.

"Ro—" Paul began.

"Suck!" Robert interrupted. He nodded his head wisely and looked like a dog waiting for the next throw of a stick.

Paul said, "Ro—"

"Suck," Robert interrupted joyously.

Paul gave Robert a tough look. Robert twisted his lips around and snuffled like a warthog.

Paul shook his head in superiority and disgust. "Later." He turned

continued on next page

and went upstairs.

Robert's face clicked back into a normal expression. No one said anything until they went into Jason's back room and he closed the door. Then Martin lost it, spinning on one heel, slapping his thighs, and cackling.

"And they say vaudeville is dead," Jason said.

"Paul is my favorite person," Robert said nicely. "Also, I win."

Jason didn't feel like being by himself, so he got Robert onto the subject of books. Then they spent forty minutes making Martin defend his off-handed assertion that comic books existed which were equal in literary value to books by Ernest Hemingway and Maya Angelou. Despite the fact that Martin probably didn't believe his own assertion or even really care about the issue, he argued doggedly. It ended when Robert got him to admit that he'd never actually read anything by Hemingway or Angelou.

"Hey," Jason said, "you're getting pretty good with that butterfly knife."

Martin snorted through his decaf. "I figure if I just get that one move down, I can intimidate people enough so they never find out I don't know anything else."

"Sounds a little risky to me," Jason said. "What if it doesn't intimidate them?"

Robert said, "Then I sing the timeless classic "I'm Only Thinking of Him" from *Man of La Mancha.*"

He demonstrated. Martin said over the singing, "Or I could show some mercy and just slash their throats."

At three-thirty in the morning, Robert and Martin left and went upstairs, and Jason sat on his piano bench, put on just one side of his headphones so he could hear if Paul left again, switched all his music equipment on, and opened UNTITLED #23.

He moved the mouse so that the onscreen cursor was positioned over a picture of a button labeled "Play," and clicked. The music

continued on next page

began to play in his headphones. It was all wrong, and he couldn't leave town to work on it like he really needed to. He stopped playback in mid-note and began tinkering with it, disliking the fact that he was doing so at home in Pasadena, and wondering whether the death earlier that evening would affect the creative process. ◆

The ransacking, at this point in the story, was happening too soon. The point of the scene became the establishment of character (and the relating of events to other characters). It's about attitudes, laying the foundation for events and reactions later: We can expect certain things from the characters because of what we've seen here.

Now's also a good time to take a look at something else that's happening. What have you noticed about the dialogue and the way it's presented? And consider that in terms of the admonitions offered earlier about the use of adverbs and dialogue tags.

As you make your changes, keep in mind that your style and tone, the affect, effect, and impact of what you want to accomplish, are going to have to take priority positions as you consider what to do. Would Robert's litany on page 55 have been as effective if either the tags or adverbs had been cut? There's no effective way (that I can think of) to present that bit of business in a more straightforward and "acceptable" manner.

Clearly, then, no matter what aspect of the novel you're considering during revision, you have to remain open to all the things that are going on. A piece of fiction is a coherent whole, each part dependent upon all of the others; concentrating on any one part to the detriment of any other is to the detriment of the whole.

A scene is a single piece of action; it is constant in time and place. There's no break, no fast cuts forward, creating a new scene. The entire opening of "A Perfect Day," from the storm through David leaving Peg and Logan at their campsite, is one scene: It is unified and complete unto itself.

Is the dialogue part of the unity of the scene? In Snyder's first version, the car ride, the dialogue didn't sufficiently fill that role. As he said, he was trying to figure out what to write, vamping as a musician might. Cutting it completely (as in the lottery story) or shortening and/ or moving it, as was done, keeps everything that happens in the scene *part* of the scene. If David, when talking to the Wrights, had offered a short course in photography, that would not have been integral to the scene because it wouldn't have advanced events—unless the technology was part of the story. The idea of the dialogue being part of the unity of the scene, then, means that what is there has to be present for the story to continue and for the character to grow.

Is this the right place for the scene? One of the advantages writers have over the sculptor is that if we put an arm in one place and realize that it's better somewhere else, we don't have to begin again: We just move the arm. No matter how carefully you've outlined, the creative process (if you're writing and not simply filling in the pieces presented by a guideline) will lead you to do things that weren't part of your plans. Sometimes they work (and they almost always strike you as working because they were written in a fit of inspiration caused by whatever came before); sometimes they don't. And sometimes they work better elsewhere. Pulling a scene (or series of scenes) like that from the fabric of your text is not going to cause it to fall apart. If it does, it means it did belong where it was.

As you begin reading for the revision of your own work, ask yourself:

* What were you trying to accomplish? What is the purpose of every scene and every bit of a scene (description, dialogue, action)? How does the material on the page serve not only the story, but the reader?

* Are things moving too slowly, as they were as we watched Jason and his buddies in the car? Is the tension weakened because the action has nothing to do with what's going on for the characters?

* Does the dialogue lack tension because you've used too many explanations, used the dialogue to offer the reader background or

other information (Jason's explanation of the electronics) that detracts from the problem at hand?

♦ At the same time, make certain that all your scenes are part of *this* novel, of this particular piece of writing. Have you added scenes (actual scenes with characters on the stage, or sections of exposition) that don't have anything to do with the conflicts that are driving those characters? While subplots enrich a story, some may actually be the basis of another novel, not an integral part of the one you're writing now. As an example, if I had concentrated more on Peg and Logan in "A Perfect Day", giving their relationship more weight, it would have detracted from the theme or concept I had in mind: that some events may be dictated, predestined perhaps. And that if they are, "we" respond, regardless of anything else that may be at play.

While you're looking at the characters and how they're behaving, what they're saying and doing, it's an excellent time to be sure that you've picked the right point of view for the story—and stuck with it.

CHAPTER 6

Point of View

Every guide to writing discusses point of view, so we can satisfy ourselves right now with a few comments and move on from there. (John Gardner's *The Art of Fiction* offers an excellent introduction to the subject.)

Your story is seen through someone's eyes: It may be one of the characters—one of the participants in the action; or it may be an observer—removed from events but aware of them and able to share them with your readers.

There's an unwritten rule that point of view should never shift or, if you are changing from one character's perception of events to another's, that it must be done carefully, or you'll confuse the reader. While it pays to heed the rule, it doesn't make much sense to live by it: As shown earlier, Bill Pronzini has no problem shifting, and most competent writers can handle the situation as well. There are some very simple techniques in place to help you, and we'll examine them as we continue. Don't forget, however, that in certain genre traditions (e.g., the traditional private eye novel) the story is told from one point of view only. Playing with formula, however, is what keeps the formula and the category interesting, so feel free to do what seems right, as long as you know what you're doing.

Conventionally, there are two acceptable points of view: first-person and third-person singular. The former is a participant in the events, the latter a reporter. Some authors are using (with various degrees of success) a second-person approach; the storyteller very much includes the reader in the experience through the use of the pronoun "you." *Bright Lights, Big City* by Jay McInerney is a best-selling example of the approach; Italo Calvino's *If on a winter's night a traveler* is a more experimental attempt.

Within the framework of the first-, second- and third-person points of view there are endless possibilities, each with strengths and weaknesses, unless you break with the usual as Stephen Dobyns does in his book *The Church of Dead Girls*. The anonymous narrator tells the story of the search for a serial murderer in a small, upstate New York town. The following bits are taken from the end of one chapter and the beginning of the next:

> When they got back to the Blazer, they found the windshield smashed and a cinder block sitting on the front seat. The bits of glass on the dashboard looked like diamonds in the light of the streetlight.

The next paragraph includes information that might be considered conjecture:

> Ernie Corelli and Jimmy Feldman wanted to go back to Bud's Tavern. Jeb wanted to go home. His truck, as he called it, was busted up and he'd had enough. Hark saw his control over his cronies sliding away. But he also had a sense of widespread wickedness, which came in part from the time he had spent helping the Friends of Sharon Malloy. Something was dreadfully wrong and Hark didn't want to go home until he had done something about it.
>
> "Let's drive by the Arab's house," he suggested.

Neither of those passages would create a second thought but for this, the opening few paragraphs of the novel:

> This is how they looked: three dead girls propped up in three straight chairs. The fourteen-year-old sat in the middle. She was taller than the others by half a head. The two thirteen-year-olds

sat on either side of her. Across the chest of each girl was an X of rope leading over her shoulders, down around her waist, and fastened in the back . . . .

I didn't witness this. I only looked at the photographs my cousin showed me. There were many photographs. And he said the police had a videotape of the entire attic, but I never saw it.

The Church of Dead Girls is a first-person narrative; there is no way the storyteller could be aware of anything just described. We might consider the possibility that he was told about the condition of the Blazer, but Hark's emotions, his "sense of widespread wickedness," are being related by an omniscient storyteller, a style that is in even less favor than second person.

Most commonly, first person is limited: The storyteller can only relate what he knows. That's one of the reasons it's so popular as a technique in writing the classic puzzle mystery. The reader is made aware of the clues as the sleuth discovers them (though no mention is made of the fact that such-and-such is a clue). First person's limitation is also a drawback in attempting to tell a story that has any depth. The narrator may say that someone looked nervous, but cannot know, with certainty, what's going on in the character's mind. The same holds true of the third-person limited (or subjective): What is really being done in that case is a simple change of the word "I" to "he."

All of which may be why the traditional third-person omniscient is the most common point of view used in storytelling. It allows the author/narrator to add information at will while at the same time permitting her to back away and let the characters have center stage when intrusion will disrupt what's happening. A final variation on the theme is the essayist/narrator. This is usually a minor character, someone who may or may not be reliable as a witness to events but who has an identifiable voice in the story.

As you began drafting your story, you fell naturally into a point of view that was comfortable for you, either because of training or because it is what you're used to as a reader. That isn't always the right choice, and it's possible to become bogged down because of it. Sometimes what you're saying just doesn't feel right. Sometimes you realize that the character you really care about, the one whose story you're telling, has fallen by the wayside. Sometimes you realize that a shift will make things stronger, will involve the reader more closely with events. Whichever choice you're facing, now's the time to correct it.

Here's an example of how a point-of-view shift can make a story stronger, from a piece of narrative nonfiction about a trip to Amarillo. Because contemporary essay writing draws so much from the narrative techniques of fiction, and looks to accomplish many of the same things, it strikes me as a valid example for us. Originally, because this was my experience, I told it in first person:

> There isn't much to see from 38,000 feet: When the solid illusion of the clouds finally breaks, there'll be a patchwork of land broken by jagged roads and ox-bowed rivers, lakes and ponds and un-identifiable *things,* blocks of dark green and others of color as autumn travels south touching some woodlands but not others. As we start our descent, the view will change, the ground come into some kind of focus. Rooftops and parking lots, a track over there, a stadium of one kind or another over here. The crooked lines that mark the highways straighten and knife across the land-scape, and the assorted colors in which cars and trucks have been dipped scoot along. The dark amorphous forms of bodies of wa-ter take on polluted colors.
>
> At night, flashes of light spark through the darkness, marking progress or traffic jams; the idea that life exists down there be-comes credible.
>
> Lower now, and the conch swirl of communities begins to define itself; the isolated farm houses and ranches and homes of the rich give way to suburbs and bedroom communities. If I'm flying in the right direction, blue freckles make themselves clear behind the homes: everyone has a swimming pool in the back-

yard, their shapes indicating something or other; few of them are square or oblong or made up of straight lines.

And again, in the deepening dark, lights go on in windows, byways become crowded with traffic, patterns of people on their way home from work or out for an evening. There are stories down there, I know, though the drama is lost at this distance. What do I know, after all, about what's going on in that car, there, the one parked on the shoulder of I-40 or Route 3 or US 95, its emergency flashers syncopated and strobing? If I tune the television to the local news tonight in some anonymous motel room at the other end of the trip, will I hear about a carjacking, about missing children, about a businessman's suicide or a young wife's murder?

Flying out of Chicago one evening, crushed against the side of the plane by the bulk of a man too fat to sit in one seat, I saw a dark cloud forward and to port. As the plane banked, the cloud became a column, like the one that helped guide the Israelites out of Egypt and through the desert on their way to a land of promises kept and still waiting. Tracing it down as the plane rose, the pillar of fire that was the source, surrounded by the reds and blues and whites of emergency vehicles, spread: it looked like a square block at the edge of the city was involved. We banked away and lifted, leaving it all behind to be considered by those whose lives would be touched by the event.

Flying into Bozeman, Montana in 1988, we listened as the pilot told us not to worry if we smelled smoke; it wasn't our aircraft, it was only Yellowstone burning. I'd live with the smell for a week, camped in the Gallatin National Forest, I'd watch the cars and tents and people become covered with ash as the sun, fighting through, turned orange, looked like an apricot flung against a brown backdrop. Six years later, I'd finally drive through Yellowstone, and see the results of an incident barely witnessed from a distance years ago, the gray trunks of trees scratching the sky, the young trunks of new growth surrounded by a mad palette of flowers. Things are happening to the flyover people; sometimes they touch us, even at cruising altitude—or later.

Usually, I don't see those things, though, from my preferred seat on the aisle, a seat in which I can have at least one side of my body free from pressure, in which I can, if the service cart isn't in service, stretch my legs, at least a little.

You'll notice that while this opening is written in first-person singular I did, occasionally, slip into first-person plural, including everyone on the flight: "As we start our descent . . ." As I began rereading the finished portion, it occurred to me that the essay would be stronger if that became the dominant point of view, thus:

> There isn't much to see from 38,000 feet: When the solid illusion of the clouds finally breaks, there'll be a patchwork of land broken by jagged roads and ox-bowed rivers, lakes and ponds and unidentifiable *things*, blocks of color as autumn travels south touching some woodlands but not others. As we start our descent, the view will change, the ground come into some kind of focus. Rooftops and parking lots, a track over there, a stadium of one kind or another over here. The crooked lines that mark the highways straighten and knife across the landscape, and the assorted paints in which cars and trucks have been dipped scoot along. The dark amorphous forms of bodies of water take on polluted colors.
>
> At night, flashes of light spark through the darkness, marking progress or traffic jams; the idea that life exists down there becomes credible.
>
> Lower now, and the conch swirl of communities begins to define itself; the isolated farm houses and ranches and homes of the rich give way to suburbs and bedroom communities. If we're flying in the right direction, blue freckles make themselves clear behind the homes: every house has a swimming pool in the backyard, their shapes indicating something or other; a few of them are square or oblong or made up of straight lines.

And again, in the deepening dark, lights go on in windows, byways become crowded with traffic, patterns of people on their way home from work or out for an evening. There are stores down there we know, though the drama is lost at this distance. What do we know, after all, about what's going on in that car, there, the one parked on the shoulder of I-40 or Route 3 or US 95, emergency flashers syncopated and strobing? If we tune the television to the local news tonight in some anonymous motel room at the other end of the trip, will we hear about a carjacking, about missing children, about a businessman's suicide or a young wife's murder?

Flying out of Chicago one evening, crushed against the side of the plane by the bulk of a man too large to sit in one seat, I saw a dark cloud forward and to port. As the plane banked, the cloud became a column, like the one that helped guide the Israelites out of Egypt and through the desert on their way to a land of promises kept and still waiting. Tracing it down as we rose, the pillar of fire that was the source, surrounded by the reds and blues and whites of emergency vehicles, spread: it looked like a square block at the edge of the city was involved. We banked away and lifted, leaving it all behind to be considered by those whose lives would be touched by the flames.

Flying into Bozeman, Montana in 1988, we listened as the pilot told us not to worry if we smelled smoke; it wasn't our aircraft, it was only Yellowstone burning. We'd live with the smell for a week; camped in the Gallatin National Forest, we'd watch the cars and tents and us become covered with ash as the sun, fighting through, turned orange, looked like an apricot flung against a brown sky. Six years later, I'd finally drive through Yellowstone, and see the results of an incident barely witnessed from a distance years ago, the gray trunks of trees scratching the sky, the young trunks of new growth surrounded by the splashes of color spilled by summer blossoms. Things are happening to the flyover people; sometimes they touch us, even at cruising altitude—or later.

Usually, we don't see those things, though, from a seat on the aisle, a seat in which at least one side of a body is free from pressure, in which we can, if the service cart isn't in service, stretch our legs, at least a little.

In addition to changing "I" to "we," you'll be aware of other changes that were made. They are made, however, because instead of just changing the pronouns, I reread the hard copy of the essay and, as I marked the changes I knew I wanted to make, I was struck by other things that needed editing. One instance: in the original version, I wrote about a "mad palette of flowers." Obviously, as a writer, I like the "mad palette" image: I also used it in describing the sky after the storm in the story "The Dream That Follows Darkness" that we've been looking at. The first time, it's effective; the second time, well, it indicates that I'm falling into a habit, repeating myself rather than finding new ways of looking at colors. As writers, that's something we want to avoid.

I went back to first-person singular ("I") in talking about my trip through Yellowstone years after the fire; that's a memory I'm sharing with "us" on this particular journey. However, even though any given reader's memories of a flight may be different, there's enough shared experience for flyers that anyone can place himself on that plane. Once I have him there, taking him into the classroom with me later will be easy; he'll see and feel what happens along with me as it occurs, with the desired effects. While the events are "mine," the point of view is "ours."

Let's take a look back, now, at Danny and Rose. When last seen, they were getting ready to leave . . . somewhere. We don't know what's going on, beyond a disagreement. The dialogue read:

> Rose brushed her bangs out of her eyes. "I think it's time to go."
> Danny shrugged. "If you say so."

"I do say so." Rose stood and crossed her arms under her breasts.

"Okay, okay. Where did you put your coat? I'll go get it." He stood too, careful not to touch Rose.

"You hung it in the closet."

"Yeah, that's right." Danny nodded.

"If you'd only pay more attention, we wouldn't have these arguments all the time," Rose said angrily.

"You're the one who's arguing . . ." Danny took a deep breath. "I'm ready to go."

The point of view is omniscient; we're not privy to anyone's thoughts and are, essentially, simply getting a report from an observer. And, worse, we don't know if we can trust him. The tag "Rose said angrily" is that narrator's opinion. He might as easily have said "pettishly," "peevishly," "with exasperation" or "softly." That sense of remove from the action works against what we want to accomplish.

Also missing, and it's something we're discovering right now, in our rereading of what we've written, is that the characters have no dimension or depth; they're there simply to speak the words. That happens frequently, especially with minor or supporting characters, when we don't take the time to create their biographies and get to know them. Even though we're reading now for problems with point of view, by paying attention to what we're reading, we find other difficulties and, having found them, take the time to correct them. So, who are Danny and Rose?

Danny's in his early fifties, brought up in New York by conservative parents. Like so many people his age, he has the fifties experience— Elvis was more important than The Beatles, and rock and roll has a completely different meaning for him; he has the sixties experience— the threat of the draft, the assassinations, man on the moon, the evolution of feminism. That last has had an effect on how he treats women: The male chauvinism that was normal to his teen years (or of which he would be accused, right or wrong) is tempered by what he's learned about women. Once, in his mid-twenties, a woman said to him, "We've really made things difficult for you, haven't we? You spend so much time worrying about what you think we want or need that you've lost all sense of self." Now he jokes about being "an alpha male in a beta body. Beta living through politics." (In the late seventies a friend would say that everything is politics and he'd argue the point for hours. Eventually, he'll agree.)

Now it's the nineties: He's at loose ends; divorced. (Why? It might make a difference. Okay, divorced because his ex-wife found someone more successful, who could give her more of what she thought she deserved. Danny didn't fight to keep her: "Whatever you need," he said when she told him she was leaving. He never learned that what she needed was for him to take control.)

And what about Rose? She's younger than Danny (at times he thinks everyone is younger than he is), in her early thirties. A lot of what Danny saw in amazement, Rose takes for granted; his experience is her history. (We—I—don't have to run a catalog for Rose as I did for Danny; making her twenty years younger creates a basic cultural and social background that is obvious.) But where he is from New York City, Rose is from somewhere in Middle America, part of what he would remember as "the silent majority." Still, while she's more liberal than he is in most things, she's carrying baggage that makes a difference to her: two children and a husband. They may have an affair (shades of Peg and David in "The Dream That Follows Darkness"; as a writer, I tend to explore many of the same issues, and relationships play a major role in my fiction).

So, we now have some sense of the characters we're watching act something out. If the scene is in the story, it must have a reason for being there, ergo, it's worth sharing with the reader. If the scene between Danny and Rose were to appear in "The Dream That Follows Darkness," it would be there to comment on David and Peg's relationship; it might be used for contrast or for emphasis, to foreshadow or warn. If it takes place during the party, for example, either David or Peg might be witness to it and recognize themselves (or not recognize themselves) in what's happening. And the point of view would be his or hers; by this point in their story, we know them well enough that the use of the word "angrily" could be accepted at face value or, at worst, the meaning and sense of the word would be filtered through the mind-set of the point-of-view character.

Since revision is rewriting, let's add Danny and Rose to one of the scenes in the story: There are parties in the next draft of the story— but since you haven't seen them yet, we'll adapt the scene at the rendez-vous. It will require some adjustments, but that's why we revise—to make those adjustments.

"The Dream That Follows Darkness"—second draft, excerpt

And then the uncomfortable small talk began and ended, the where have you been, what've you been doing, where are you going next kind of talk. Wright made certain to always be between his wife and David, to hover. On the last night of the end of the beginning, there was a dance and prizes awarded to the best marksmen at the meeting. Logan Wright won in the pistol category. And on the dance floor, with Peg in David's arms, lightly and gracefully, Logan Wright started to lose.

"David," she asked during one dance, "did you happen to . . . ?"

"To what?"

"Get any pictures of me at the lake." Her grace fell in front of her discomfort.

"Yes." And that's all he said, and released Peg to let her walk away, back to her husband. With nothing to do now but watch, David stood with his back to the flames of the bonfire, framing what he saw as if he were looking through a viewfinder.

How would he take the shot of the woman he had come to think he loved with the man he was certain she didn't. Logan would have to be in shadows, the leaping flames highlighting bits and pieces, making him demonic, threatening. Peg would be . . .

continued on next page

"The Dream That Follows Darkness"—second draft, excerpt, continued

"I think it's time to go." Rose's voice was like the wind.**1**
He looked in her direction, saw her standing in front of Danny,
roughly brushing her bangs off her forehead.**2**

Danny shrugged. What could he do? "If you say so."**3**

"I do say so." Rose crossed her arms, hands on her shoulders, as if
she were suddenly chilled.

"Okay, okay. You have everything?" Danny started to walk toward
her, then stopped.

Rose looked down toward her left hand, where a thin gold band
reflected firelight. "Of course. I've got everything I need." Her arms
dropped to her side, the thumb of her left hand playing with the ring.

Danny's shoulders slumped and he sighed. "Yeah, I know you do.
That's the problem, isn't it? You do have everything, more than enough.
So, why'd you meet me here?"

David thought he knew, knew that he shouldn't be listening to this.
He'd met them earlier, when he asked to take a picture of Rose, loving
the way her black hair fell thickly almost like a cape, hoping to capture
whatever it was that had Danny looking at her so softly, so much a
prisoner. Probably the way Logan saw him looking at Peg.

They walked past him toward the parking lot, into what was going
to be an endless, chilly ride. "If you'd only pay more attention, we
wouldn't have these arguments all the time." Rose was looking straight
ahead, seeing the same cold night.**4**

"You're the one who's arguing, Rose. I'm just trying to give you—"

continued on next page

1. This is David's thinking; because of the opening scene, his feelings about wind are clear
   to us. It means change.
2. Again, David's impression of the action; we're seeing it through his eyes. But, there is
   a problem: Danny and David—both begin with the letter D, both have two syllables.
   Should Danny's named be changed?)
3. A problem here. What could he do is in Danny's thoughts, but we're seeing the scene
   through David. Better would be: Danny shrugged. "If you say so." David knew exactly
   what he was thinking, *What could he do?* Faced with that kind of anger, resistance is
   futile.
4. Again, we can't know what Rose is seeing, only what David supposes she's looking at.

"The Dream That Follows Darkness"—second draft, excerpt, continued

> "Give me what? I don't want you to *give* me anything, I just want you to . . ."
>
> Her voice trailed off, lost in the sounds of the party going on around them, the party they weren't part of, not now. David looked around, trying to find Peg. What did she want? What could he give her? What was he doing here? ◆

Don't fall into the trap of thinking that you can have only one character relating events. If Rose and Danny were to play a more important role in the story, if their relationship was more important, we could end the above scene with David responding to a wave from Peg and moving off toward her. Then, after a line break, we could join Danny and Rose in their car, and listen to them. As long as we stay in the perspective of only one of them, there's no problem. However, if there's only that one further scene with them, occurring because you, as the writer, want to see what's going to happen, you'd be well advised to cut it from the manuscript.

The rule is this: If you're not using an omniscient voice, you can present only one set of impressions in a scene. You don't have to stay with those impressions for the entire story (unless it's being told in first person), but you can't shift between two or more points of view in any given scene. E.M. Forster, in *Aspects of the Novel*, put it this way:

> A novelist can shift view-point *if it comes off.* . . . Indeed, this power to expand and contract perception (of which the shifting view-point is a symptom), this right to intermittent knowledge— I find one of the great advantages of the novel-form . . . this intermittence lends in the long run variety and colour to the experiences we receive. (Emphasis added.)

"If it comes off"—you'll never discover what you can do until you try. With that thought in mind, I decided to experiment within the context of another experiment: a novella told in second person, present tense, from the point of view of two different characters. In alternating scenes, Rachel and Jonathan are the "you," whose thoughts and actions we experience. I decided that certain scenes would work more effectively if we were in the heads of both characters at the same time. It reads like this:

> You look and wonder what your look is saying. Sleep well? Yes, thank you. And you? Yes: and the smiles that say I can rest later say also you're here/you're here, I hoped . . . but the words are swallowed like honey, a savored sweet in return for being there.
>
> What do you say, do you speak first, what was that, excuse me: the tumble of words is awkward and you trip over them finding yourselves finally in the same place at the same time and wait together for the tests about to happen. . . .
>
> And now the growing distance, footsteps heard, then swallowed by this day. Will he write? Will she answer?
>
> What is happening to me.
>
> Good bye, Jonathan.
>
> Good bye, Rachel. Soon.
>
> But you know soon is too far away. Know that the night was desperation and bourbon; know that there was another moment born in the night.
>
> Know that you will write.
>
> Know that you will write.
>
> You turn and wave, blinded by the glare of sun on ice.

What is being attempted is the re-creation of a moment, after a meeting, after something has begun, filled with the confusion that two people might experience at that moment. Which character is speaking? Thinking? Does it matter, really, at a moment like that? Either might be; either probably is. (And for the story, "might" and "probably" are definitely.)

◆ The scene with David, Danny and Rose is fair game. I've told it from David's point of view because it served my purposes. Rewrite it, making it Danny's or Rose's, but including all three characters.

◆ Retell this same scene as a first-person scene, choosing any or all of the characters for the voice. Notice the way emphases change and, based on what you know about the characters, the way the perceptions of the entire scene change.

By doing that now, you'll begin to see how you can rewrite your own story to make it more effective by finding the right character to tell it. And don't be surprised if you discover that the story you're telling really belongs to a character other than the one you chose. That doesn't mean that the protagonist or hero was wrongly picked, only that it is more effective to see events through someone else's eyes.

And there's a lot to be seen. And known. That's why we have back story.

CHAPTER 7

Back Story and Detail

The work you did creating characters—people—for your story is actually part of the story. Just because you know certain things about the characters doesn't mean that the reader will. Let's imagine that you're writing an adventure story or a woman-in-jeopardy romantic suspense novel, and will be throwing your average citizen in harm's way. Confronted by a threat, your protagonist reacts, does something that seems completely, well, out of character. Whether it's fighting or creating a bomb out of a piece of pipe and a deck of old playing cards, she does something that the reader has no reason to expect the character to be capable of. The result? Your reader says, "Yeah, right," and the suspension of disbelief is lost.

It doesn't take much to correct that, if you discover it while reading your draft. It does take a lot, however, to choose the right place to correct it. Ninety-nine times out of a hundred, sooner is better than later. When you see the third draft of "The Dream That Follows Darkness," you'll see that I've added a line in the scene at Peg and Logan's campsite, on the day David meets them, that indicates that she had wanted to be a dancer; later in the story, when David leaves to build his cabin, Peg will give him "a piece of pink ribbon, like the one around her neck, holding the gold cross."

"What's this?"
"One of the ribbons from my old toe shoes." She touched the

piece around her neck. "I cut them off when I threw the shoes away. I wanted to keep part of the dream."

Because pink ribbons play a role in the story, I wanted a reason for them to be there. I was also making certain that some of Peg's sense of loss in her life, the sense of something missing—which of course is central to the story in its entirety—was made clear. It wouldn't have worked at all, however, if she mentioned the toe shoes without having first set up the lost dream. Keeping part of the dream, given the nature of the story, is an obvious line.

In Bill Pronzini's *New York Times Book Review* New and Notable Book of 1996, *Blue Lonesome*, he faced a fairly usual situation. Jim Messenger, the central character, is an accountant who becomes obsessed with a missing woman. His search for her is going to bring him into some dangerous situations. While instinct would help save him in some of them, he's going to have to call on skills that one doesn't usually connect with the stereotype readers would bring to the story. So, he put in some lines early, during the introduction of the character, that give Messenger's abilities credibility.

Less polished novelists would (and generally do) add the background at the time of the crisis: "Faced by the seven armed men, Dick remembered his military training and. . . ." The problem with this solution is that the information becomes obvious—and thus contrived and too coincidental. It is no less contrived, actually, when it's mentioned earlier (the character is being created to play a particular role, after all), but it is absorbed by the reader as part of the character and either filed or forgotten until the author uses it.

There's an old saying that one shouldn't show a shotgun over the mantelpiece unless it's going to be used later in the story. I don't agree; theoretically useless information still serves a narrative purpose. So, if you have revealed something that doesn't come into play actively, you don't have to feel compelled to take it out during revision. If you haven't revealed something, though, it has to be put in.

◆ Reread your manuscript, keeping a sharp eye on everything your characters do. Does anything happen that seems "out of character"? Do they react in ways that a reader might question? If so, look back to earlier scenes and find the places where the information that makes those actions possible, realistic, can be added.

The challenge is to add back story seamlessly, to make it part of the narrative and not let the reader (or the editor) see the stitches. I find dialogue useful for that; it doesn't have to be a scene in which the character appears, though. Someone who knows Dick can be telling another player about him. A search of Dick's room (but why are they searching?) can turn up a certificate from a martial arts school, or a diary in which he reveals that he took the classes to build self-confidence, with a later entry indicating that the classes failed. The reader will know that the training took place; the fact that it didn't really "fail" because Dick is able to use what he learned goes toward the evolution of the character, teaches a lesson about self-doubt, or whatever other point you want to make.

It is not just the fine points that come into play; events that have occurred in the past will also affect the characters and the outcome of the story. Another thing to look for: tense changes, particularly when you're using flashbacks. Read aloud: Are you confusing the reader by blending the time line, mixing the past within the context of the story with the tale's "present"?

Contemporary popular fiction steers away from flashback as a storytelling device; the reasons for it don't speak well of how readers approach books these days. Readers today complain that they don't have time to read and may be away from a book for a day or two between chapters; therefore, they want things short enough to gulp and simple enough that when they begin reading again, they don't have to reread a few pages to get back up to speed. Or they're listening to audio books while driving. Personally, I don't want them concentrating on the story they're listening to while changing lanes in front of me. That means, again, that the story has to be linear—flashbacks will be confusing unless the listeners are paying strict attention—and relatively more simple. While the flashback is now held in disrepute by many teachers, especially of those concentrating on popular, mass-market fiction, it is a tool that's available to you if you want to use it.

As a storyteller, you have to give the reader all the information necessary to understand the story, to accept the events as they're unfolding. Just as in life, a story doesn't happen in a vacuum. The past affects the present—psychologically (why is someone afraid of heights?) as well as directly (why are the people in town afraid of strangers?)—and if you shortchange us on the reasons, you've failed. The opening pages of Stephen Dobyns's *The Church of Dead Girls*, not only shows how it can be done, but also explains the principle beautifully. The novel starts with a prologue, the opening sentence of which is

> This is how they looked: three dead girls propped up in three straight chairs.

After several pages describing the scene—and establishing the narrator (everything of value in a story should serve more than one purpose, remember)—chapter one begins. Keep in mind that we know that a serial murderer has been at work and our expectation would be that now the search will begin. However:

> Afterward everyone said it began with the disappearance of the first girl, but it began earlier than that. There are always incidents that precede an outrage and that seem unconnected or otherwise innocent, a whole web of incidents, each imperceptibly connected to the next. Take the case of a man who cuts his throat. Isn't it a fact that the medical examiner finds several practice nicks, as if the deceased were trying to discover how much it might hurt? And in the case of our town, even before the first girl's disappearance, there were undoubtedly several events comparable to two or three nicks on the skin above the jugular.

> For example, on a Tuesday morning in early September, just
> after school began, a bomb was found on a window ledge outside
> a seventh grade classroom. . . .

Today's most commonly accepted way of dealing with the situation is the prologue, a chapter or section preceding the beginning of the action of the story proper, used to give the reader information that either the characters already have—because they've experienced it—or that will be discovered (most usually in a crime or suspense novel). It's a manipulative device when presented that way because the reader knows something the characters don't. It's like seeing the bad guy hiding in the basement, rather than letting us stumble on him along with the protagonist. What Dobyns does in the previous example is begin after the events, and then the novel itself is a flashback, bringing us up to the events "today." He also creates further tension: Not only are the readers worrying about the serial killer, but they have to consider the bombing: How are the two related? Will more bombs be found?

Robertson Davies's The Cornish Trilogy contains an entire volume—book two, *What's Bred in the Bone*—that serves as a flashback, the story of the life of the pivotal character. An extreme approach, but it shows what can be done.

What *you* have to do when establishing back story is to make certain the "whole web of incidents" is part of the narrative you're spinning. While motives and motivation are the common reasons, the texture and richness of your story are enhanced by presenting only what's *necessary*. It's possible to get carried away, and you want to find those places before an editor does. You can't do that effectively if you're trying to revise on the fly, rather than dealing with the work in its entirety. Later, when I show the third draft manuscript pages of "The Dream That Follows Darkness," you'll see notes in the margin: "Add: . . ." If I'd tried to revise sectionally, I might not have known that the scene or lines to be added were needed. And it pays to explain here why I'm showing entire manuscripts: The revision process can, for me, be best seen through synoptic readings of versions, rather than simply looking at one out-of-context piece, one paragraph or scene. Reviewing the entire work is especially critical when you're writing a series; in those that are worth reading, the events in one book are going to change, however minimally, the central character. Reactions may change, knowledge is gained, the character has been caught in a web of incidents. Readers should be aware of that, and part of the narrative of subsequent books will consist of that information.

The question for you during revision is, Does the reader know everything that should be known, at the time she should know it? If you have a character referring to a past event that the reader hasn't experienced be certain that enough about that occasion is shared. We might be dealing with a love or business affair gone sour, an earlier criminal incident, a vacation. Whatever it is, if it is important enough to mention in the course of dialogue in the story, it is important enough that the happening be known to the reader.

You have two ways of going about revealing back story: Characters can talk about it, or you can create the flashback, telling the story through the eyes of the point-of-view character as if it were happening. In short, give us the scene. I prefer the second approach.

Relating the story through a conversation tends toward flatness: All the color of a scene, all the showing, disappears, because when folks are talking they tend to simply relate facts. If the important facts in this instance can be summed up in a line or two, you're okay. But if it is, to use Dobyns's words, a web of incidents, you will bore your readers to the point that they'll either skip the passages (and thus miss the point) or skip the rest of the story—a fate you clearly want to avoid.

In most instances, however, you can create the scene, using all the storytelling tricks you've learned. Your protagonist might be musing about a situation and that will cause him to remember.

As with subplots (the other things that are going on in your characters' lives while the main action is also occurring; we don't live one thing at a time), you have to be careful not to let these peripheral but nonetheless key scenes overwhelm the story. If the reader becomes more interested in this other "stuff," you take the chance of having her pay too much attention to it and lose the main story.

While reading for revision, ask yourself the following questions:

◆ Is the reader sharing, completely, your knowledge? Does he know enough to follow and accept the action as properly motivated in terms of the history of your characters? At the same time, look to see if you're offering too much, causing stoppages in the forward motion of the novel. A saga or epic allows you more leeway; an adventure story, dependent so much on pace and a headlong rush toward the denouement, gives you less.

◆ Are your flashbacks integrated into the story, part of an otherwise unbroken scene and related to the action that is being described in the story's "present"? If they're thrown in helter-skelter, or if there are too many of them, the flow of the narrative is interrupted. You're better off having a longer flashback that offers everything, rather than ten flashbacks. (As always, there are exceptions: the form of the story itself may call lots of smaller flashback scenes; that will probably be the case when you're dealing closely with the psychological impact of events.)

CHAPTER 8
Plot

What have all of these changes done to your plot?

By convention, we use the word "plot" to mean what's happening in the story. If you ask someone to tell you the plot of his newest novel in progress, you'll hear about what happens first and what happens next, and then this happens, and then . . .

I think of it a little differently, with plot being more about how things happen, cause and effect resulting in the story line of the novel. It is about *purpose*, the purpose of the story itself, of the action, of the scene. Without purpose, after all, what's left?

Every scene is following logically on the scene before; one thing leads to another. There's a rationale behind what you're doing, even if life itself is not rational and chaotic events cause us to turn in other directions. It isn't too much of a push, in fact, to think of the structure of the story in much the same way that we think of a mathematical formula or proof. There are givens, as in logic (if A, then B); you establish them when you start, and your reader is going to trust you to adhere to those statements of fact.

The process of creative writing, however, is more subject to the chaos of quantum mechanics than the old logic. An idea comes to you, as the result of something you've just written or because a cardinal has just landed on your window sill and cardinals are not native to where you live. You continue typing, following the natural flow of your imagination: You've still got the same characters; the same thing—whatever it was—is still happening, but it's happening in a way you didn't expect. The good news is that unexpected plot developments are exciting; the bad news is that you have to change what came before.

And even if a creative frenzy isn't the reason, stories still tend to twist on themselves. Revision is when you unknot them or find ways to use the knots. Most of the time, you save the tangles for another story and begin to participate in an act of authorial murder: You have to kill your darlings. Trust me: It hurts you far worse than it will ever harm the story.

A bit more about how "The Dream That Follows Darkness" came about: I'd heard Charles Grant, a preeminent horror writer and anthologist, speaking at a conference. He talked about ghost stories (a form he was particularly fond of), and he mentioned that he wanted to do an anthology of ghost stories. Perfect! I had this reincarnation story in mind, listening to him served as the last bit of impetus I needed to get going on the story. Ghosts would be easy: With all the dreams and fantasies I was mixing together already, that was the hook I needed to begin.

The opening lines, about the wind and the rain, had been with me all along; even before I knew what the story was, I had the line in my notes. Now I knew exactly where they were going. Here, then, is the penultimate draft of the story, reproduced with all my marks and notations. It is virtually complete, beginning, middle and end.

"The Dream That Follows Darkness"—revised draft

"The Dream That Follows Darkness"—Revised Draft

And later that night, after the rain stopped, the wind began, cold

and scouring the sky of clouds. It was a strong wind that blew in

circles and people curled into their sleeping bags and under blan-

Their sleep was restless disturbed by dreams
kets, in tents and campers and lean-tos. The wind would stop, of
of running horses.

course, and then the dawn would begin, a mad palette followed

by a sky so clear and blue and high that it would almost hurt to

look at it. It would be a beautiful day. A perfect day.

continued on next page

For an accident. That's how Malek thought of it, anyway. An accidental meeting. They happen, they're forgotten. Just one of those things. It would be years before he learned the reality of accidents, the truth of things.

He had gone to his blind next to the lake between the moments when the wind died and the dawn began; a grey time. He put his camera onto the tripod, focused on the spot where he knew the deer would come to drink; trusted his instinct for the exposure settings. He wondered, but just for a moment, about what he was doing there. His fame, such as it was, came from photographs of the bizarre, ~~wreckage thrown in and left behind by~~ **the out of the ordinary.** ~~**&** add: photos caught moments...~~ ~~humans~~. Pictures framed to reflect pain. Now he was next to a mountain lake, cold and wet—his own pain personified—waiting to take photographs of a herd of deer drinking water. He had been asked, once, when his work would stop being so "tortured." So he was going to test himself. A silly effort, he knew, doomed to failure. He wondered about self-fulfilling prophecies, but just for a moment; then slept and missed the dawn **but dreamed a dream he never recalled**.

~~Peg Vogel Wright~~. How did she come to be there, be in that place and time? ~~Another accident~~ What brought her from her

continued on next page

beginnings in Billings in the north to Beaumont in the

south, and finally to the night of rain and wind on the

edge of a mountain lake? ~~She didn't think about it at all, then~~ *It might have been an*

accident, if there are accidents. It
~~or later. For all that it mattered, it didn't call for thought. What~~

was w/purpose, though,

~~mattered, finally, is~~ that she rose from her husband's side, saw

the play of color in the sky, walked unseeing past David Malek's

blind, removed her clothes and, taking a deep breath, dove from

a rock into the icy embrace of the water.

David woke to the sound. Automatically, ~~eyes still closed~~,

he released the shutter; ~~T~~hen he looked out. Tendrils of mist

whispered up out of the lake as if seeking purchase; finding

none, they faded into the air. Small ripples played on the surface

of the water, then disappeared. There were no deer. A fish, he

though, jumping for a fly. A rock loosened and tumbling into

the lake.

~~But he was awake now, and he crawled to the front of the~~

~~blind and looked at the day.~~ He turned the camera's motor

drive on, and watched what was in front of him as if he were

peering through the camera, framing each shot. His thumb

played idly against the button on the cable release. The lake's

continued on next page

now still again surface began to pulse, the tension preparing to break.

She rose from the water in a straight line, up gleaming, droplets of water prisming on her skin. She was facing him as she came up and then swam toward him. Even strokes, strong, as if she had been born to water. Vaguely, he heard the sound of the camera as frame after frame was exposed.

Her towel was thirty feet from where he hid and he watched as she dried herself, as she wrapped the towel about her and ran her fingers through her hair, short light brown shading to blonde locks that began to curl. She stood at the edge of the lake then, and stretched; the lean lines of a dancer silhoutted against the blue of sky and water's gleam.

Dry and warmed, she dropped the towel and moved at the lakes edge. To her right, a buck peered out from the trees, watching, waiting to see if it would be safe to come to drink. She saw the deer and smiled, knowing that this place was his. She wrapped the towel around herself again, gathered her clothes, and walked away, passing the blind, passing David Malek, and humming to herself.

continued on next page

"The Dream That Follows Darkness"—revised draft, continued

The photographer sat silently, still, and watched the
herd
deer moving. This is what he was here for, not naked

sprites. He kept his camera going, the sound of the moving
camera's

mirror was loud in his ears. The buck lifted his head, sniffed the air,

and went back to his drinking.

Now Malek's thoughts went to the woman, to the grace with

which she moved, to the play of light on her body. And he

wondered. Behind him, somewhere, he heard sounds carried on
their
the still air. The deer turned and walked with dignity back into

the woods. This part of the day was done.

Malek packed his equipment and began to walk toward the

sounds he had heard. He smelled smoke and sausages cooking.

He saw the woman, dressed and lounging against a tree while a
hard-edged
tall man with white hair crouched by the fire. The man was

smoking a cigarette, and as he tended to the food, ash fell into

skillet. The woman was looking directly at him, at David, as he

walked into the clearing, and she smiled in greeting. then her

voice followed the smile and she said, "Hello."

The man looked up, cold eyes assessing the intruder; they

were questioning eyes, jealous, vengeful. David looked into

continued on next page

feeling ice and vacuum,

✓ them, through him, and said, "Hi. Sorry to disturb you.

I was on my way back," he pointed into an indefined

distance, "to my car." He held up his equipment case. "Just

down at the lake, taking some pictures of the deer."

"They were beautiful, weren't they?" Her voice danced in

his ears. She turned to the man, to her husband. "I saw them,

too, when I went down to wash." She looked at David. "My

name is Peg Wright. And this is my husband, Logan."

"David Malek." He paused, uncertain. She knew that he

had seen her. Must know. He looked at her—into her, per-

haps—and found her within herself. He remembered the sound

and feel of the wind in the night. "Well," he said, and started to

walk away.

"No, wait. Why don't you join us. We have enough." David

heard her voice coming from far away. He looked at her as she

stood up, kicking at a stick that had been stuck in the ground

at her side; she rubbed her left shoulder, just above the breast.

"Please." Logan Wright grunted.

They sat and talked and ate. Wright was quiet, watchful. A

psychiatrist with a thriving practice in Beaumont, Texas and a

continued on next page

collector: Black powder weapons, bronze miniatures, books, art. Peg had wanted to dance, but time had gotten away from her; now she was a social creature, fulfiling the demands her role as wife of Logan Wright presented. In the moments she could steal she sketched scenes of native American folklore and tradition.

Soon, food finished and conversation straining, David watched Peg watched the sky, saw her again rub her shoulder. He pushed himself up. "Thanks for everything, you guys. I think I'd better get going. Logan. Peg. So long."

He started walking along the path, passing Peg. She smiled at him. "I hope you got some nice pictures, David."

Yes, he thought, she knew. "Thanks. Listen," he turned so that he was facing both of them, "why don't you give me your address, and I'll send you a print. Who knows, you may start collecting ma."

"How mu—," Wright started to say, but Peg interrupted him. "Thank you, David. That's very kind." She gave him their address and then, as he started to light a cigarette, she added, "If you cared about yourself, you wouldn't do that."

continued on next page

"I guess you're right." He ~~ground the unsmoked~~ put the match to the cigarette and ~~cigarette underfoot~~ took a drag, "See ya around, folks. And, oh, Lo- smiling sheepishly and shrugging.} gan, the print's on me. This time."

Wright smiled uncertainly, then waved.

He didn't wave three months later, though, when Malek met them for a second time. And Malek knew this time was not an accident. He had gone home to New Orleans and worked and thought and looked at the prints of the photographs he had taken next to the lake and realized that he didn't have to con- askew tinue shooting ~~pain~~, but that he was comfortable with it. And then he learned of the convocation of black powder enthusiasts, the recreation of the old fur trappers' rendezvous, and knew that it was time to travel again. On the Mississippi, the whistle shrieked of the steamboat *Natchez* ~~screamed~~ and echoed and sheet light- ning played against the sky. The sky was not blue as malek flew into it. In a bar on a corner of Bourbon street, a stripper sighed.

It was not a perfect day. There are no accidents. ~~There is a hunt.~~

"David, how nice to see you again." Peg's voice was filled with joy, the words danced from her lips. "Logan, you remem-

continued on next page

"The Dream That Follows Darkness"—revised draft, continued

ber David Malek, don't you."

"Of course." David heard a mountain wind in Wright's voice. "I seem to remember you saying you were going to send us a copy of one of the pictures you took up at the lake. What happened, forget to load your camera?"

David smelled the beast protecting his lair. "As a matter of fact, I have them with me. Hi, Peg."

"What made you think we'd be here?" Wright's voice didn't dance, it attacked, cracked. He looked at his wife, appraising her infidelities, seeing what was behind his eyes and not in front of them. She brought her hand to her neck, fondled the pink ribbon there; a small gold cross hung from it and sparked in the hollow of her throat. She rubbed her shoulder.

"I didn't know. My agent told me you'd been in touch, though, that ~~you'd bought~~ You're considering a couple of my portraits. And when I heard about this gathering, I just figured I'd take a chance that an enthusiast like you would be here. If you hadn't been, I'd have mailed them on to you.

"~~How do you like the ones you got?~~ What do you think about you've been looking at? Interested?"

Wright smiled for the first time. "Well, I'll tell you, they're

continued on next page

certainly different. I don't know that I'd want to display

them, but as a psychiatrist, they certainly intrigue me.

They look like some of the nightmares my patients describe." *We'll see.*

He reached out and took the envelope David had given Peg

from her hand. "Let's see what we have here." *look at we've got*

There were three prints. Two showed the herd of deer at the

edge of the lake, mist around their hooves, as if they were walk-

ing on clouds. The third was just the lake and a sky of blue

clarity. The surface of the lake was rippled, as if a rock had

loosened and tumbled into it. Peg looked at David and back at

the last photograph, knowing just where her form was hidden

by the water, willing herself to see. David touched the spot deli-

cately, casually. "Like them?"

"David, they're beautiful. And so different. Do these look

like your patients' nightmares, Logan?"

"No. No, not at all. Why the change in style, Dave?"

"Like I told you, that was the purpose of the shoot. My work

hasn't really changed, though."

No, his work hadn't changed; his life had. Now, each mo-

ment took him further away and closer. Wright hovered, David

continued on next page

"The Dream That Follows Darkness"—revised draft, continued

or Peg was always in sight; perhaps in his sights during the pistol shooting even. On the final night of the rendezvous, there was a dance—the prizes were going to be awarded there and Logan had won. And begun to lose: On the dance floor Peg moved gracefully in David's arms.

"David," she said, "did you happen to . . . ?"

"To what?"

"~~To get any pictures of me at the lake." Her grace fell in front of her discomfort.~~

"To get any pictures of me at the lake." Her grace fell in front of her discomfort.

"Yes." And that's all he said.

And she asked no more about them.

Until a year later, when Malek had has first showing in Houston. They weren't on display, but on the afternoon of the opening, Peg came to the gallery and he showed them to her, and shook his head when her eyes asked the question.

"They're mine. Alone. Maybe yours. Someday." He put a cigarette in his mouth, but before he could light it, she too, it from his lips.

continued on next page

"I told you," she said, "that if you—"

"—cared, I wouldn't do that. And if you cared . . . ."

She broke the cigarette, dropping the pieces on the floor.

"One of us has to." Then she left, to go home and change her

clothes. The Wrights were hosting a party in Malek's honor and

celebrating Logan's latest acquisition—a stud farm.

That evening, with the stars as witness and the wind for

company, David kissed Peg, and they began to dance around

a relationship developed, an affair waited,

the edges of what was happening to them; ~~touching~~ when they

^ They touched

could. Then came the time when they couldn't: David Malek

went away.

"There's domething I have to do," he had told her one eve-

ing at the farm. "It means I'll have to go away for a while, maybe

four months."

"An assignment? What is it?" There was excitement in Peg's

tone, a shared pride in his accomplishments. They talked about

their work often, of his growing reputation, of the contracts she

was beginning to get from publishers to produce cover art for

their books. One company, renowned for their editorial accu-

add: Her

racy, insisted that she paint *all* their covers.

drawings captured the moments...

continued on next page

"The Dream That Follows Darkness"—revised draft, continued

"No . . . well, I'll probably do some shooting. But this is something else. A surprise."

Peg laughed. "I love surprises. When can I know?" She spun around the room, her skirt flaring.

"Soon enough. Now, come, kiss me good-bye."

They embraced. "You'll call me, won't you?" Her voice became serious.

"I don't know; it may be difficult. I also think it would be a good idea if I didn't. Logan's getting colder and colder. I don't trust him."

"Don't worry, David. He's jealous as all get out, but he really doesn't give a tinker's dam about me as a person. I'm just another possession, something to list like the Porsche, the boat, the collections. He doesn't love anything, doesn't respect anything." Peg shook her head and stepped ~~back~~ away from ~~her lover~~ him. ✔

"He's screwing anything that will hold still long enough, and some that won't. I keep waiting for some patient to file suit against him for some kind of sex therapy scam.

"But don't worry about him, sweetheart. He's not going to do anything. He doesn't have the soul; he traded it for enough

continued on next page

95

"The Dream That Follows Darkness"—revised draft, continued

new patients to give him the money to buy the ranch."

David kissed her. "So you keep saying. And you keep staying—"

"Yes, I stay. This is how it has to be. For now. The time is wrong. We've talked about it, David. I'm here, you're here. Trust me." She kissed him gently, then reached into her pocket. "Here," she said, "take this with you. It will tie us when we're apart."

David looked at what she had given him—a piece of pink ribbon, like the one around her neck, holding the gold cross. "What's this?"

"One of the ribbons from my old toe shoes." She touched the piece around her neck. "I cut them off when I threw the shoes away. I wanted to keep part of the dream, though."

"Now, you take this one with you, wherever you're going." She tied it loosely around his neck, over the gold chain holding his Star of David. She kissed him again, quickly, hearing Logan's footsteps as he approached the room, finally missing them. "Go. And come back."

There is a nameless mountain growing from the side of a

continued on next page

creek near a place called Three Mile Curve in the middle of West Virginia. On the side of the mountain is a table of land, and a cave. Across the creek there was a mining camp, ramshackle homes, a beer hall, the company store. Malek had come there first twenty five years earlier, with his first camera and his life ahead of him—a time of beginnings. On hot summer nights, he slept in front of the cave and heard ghosts whisper. Or the wind in the trees. And there came a time when he had to leave. Or thought he did.

Now he came to a place that used to have a name; after the dam broke and the water swept through in a rage, it was considered dead. But it wasn't deserted. Like Lazarus, a spirit moved within it. Some of those who had survived the flood tracked back through the mud as the water receded, reclaiming what was theirs. The mining company had left with the waters; the company store was no more, of course, but the beer hall, Paulie Boy's, was there.

And Malek's cave was there, too high to have been touched by disaster. That is where he returned to, pitching a tent at the beginning of a summer and causing the hollow to echo the

continued on next page

sounds of his axe.

As Malek built, the spirit brought the town back to life and he was accepted as part of it . . . the strange man with the ribbon around his neck, the Jew, building his place, but always being part of what was being reborn, pitching in when they needed him even though he refused all offers of help in his own work. Some of them were just as happy that he turned them down. While the offers were made in good faith, many of the people remembered the legends of the haunted cave. The strangest thing about this stranger was that he didn't seem to care about the stories. In the evening, after he had finished the work of the day, he went to Paulie Boy's and drank beer, and ate spiced jerky and from the jars of pickled items lined up like specimens in a lab. He knew he belonged, they knew he belonged. That was all anyone really cared about.

As the October chill began to creep, he finished his work: A four room cabin using the living rock of the mountain as the back wall, the cave a fifth room. The home was warm, already felt lived in. He pictured Peg sitting in the front room, the one with light, turning her sketches into oils. One that she had given

continued on next page

him before he left, ~~depicted an Indian warrior standing~~ before an attacking enemy; a sash was draped around ~~his body and a lance pinned the material to the ground. Malek~~ hung ~~the picture~~ on the wall of the bedroom so that the morning light would strike it. All that was missing was Peg. He felt alone, but not lonely. He felt good.

And went down the road to Paulie Boy's, to have a few last beers, to say good-bye and arrange to have someone keep an eye on his house until he could get back to move in. He was sitting at the counter, watching the room behind him as it was reflected in the stained backbar mirror. He couldn't be sure, then, whether it was the drinking or the imperfections in the glass that made the scene so blurred. Not that it mattered, much.

Except that he would like to have had a clearer view of the
have /d
woman who had walked in about five minutes earlier, bringing the cold in from outside where the rain came down, hard. So hard, it brought memories and tears to the people who had survived the last flood. Thunder banged down the mountainside, rumbling with the sound of a mine collapse. Men stopped their banter and looked anxiously through the rain-stained

continued on next page

windows and conversation died for a moment or two, then slowly resumed.

He hadn't seen her before, or heard of her, and given the reactions of the other people in Paulie Boy's, neither had they. She sat in the corner, where he had sat when he first came to the town, and ordered a beer. Men turned to stare at the woman in white, women to glare, but she paid no attention, made no movement until she got up and went to the juke box, an old Wurlitzer salvaged from somewhere, and stood with her back to the room, reading the playlist. She made her selection, and as she sat again Willie Nelson's "Don't Get Around Much Any-more" filled the room with bourbon mellow sound. David wanted to go to her, a feeling he hadn't had since meeting Peg.

(Tactile fantasy scene?)

Instead, he watched her in the mirror, stared into her violet-dark eyes and felt the touch of her look on the back of his neck. He called to Mollie, who was working the stick, and ordered another beer.

And felt the cold again, as the door opened. When he looked around, into the mirror, into the room, the woman in white was gone. Malek shrugged, drank his beer and said his goodbyes.

continued on next page

The arrangements had been made. It was time to leave again.

That night, for the first time, he slept in his new bed, built that afternoon. The cabin walls glowed red and orange and yellow with the flames reflecting from the fireplace.

Outside, wind curled around the cabin, looking for places to enter. Rain pounded against the roof and windows. Malek dreamed—of a woman running east, of horses. The woman wore a buckskin dress, white in the moonlight, a dark stain over the left breast. Her hair was black, and in braids. He had lost the dream by the time he awoke, **but remembered dreaming.** ✓

In the morning, he left the mountainside, first for New Orleans, to close his home there. Then for Houston, where he had a showing of new work, including some pictures of people building a town.

"Where's the surprise? What did you bring me?" Peg laughed.

David gestured at the wall, where a black and white photograph of a half-built house hung alone. Printed in high contrast, you could see the skeleton of the building, and the dark mouth

continued on next page

of the cave behind it. "I don't have a photograph of the finished cabin. You'll have to come and see it for yourself."

Peg smiled, and waved to Logan, calling him over. See what David's building, Logan. Isn't it nice?"

"Might be. Can't tell yet. Where is it? Doesn't look like anywhere around here."

"It's not. It's in West Virginia, up in the mountains. A place I found years ago. Always wanted to go back; now I have."

"Well, whatever turns you on. I'd've thought that you'd stop trying to run away by now, though. Settle down." He looked at Peg. "Find a good woman and start livin'.'"

"Soon Logan, I've me someone; just waiting a bit longer."

Standing behind her husband, Peg stared at David. She touched the ribbon at her neck, touched her shoulder. ~~It was the time of beginning to end.~~

And told Logan she wanted a divorce, later, as he sat on the edge of their bed. "Never," he said, and laughed. Peg stared down at him, and shook her head.

"That's the wrong answer, Logan." She turned and went into her studio, and studied some of the sketches on the walls.

continued on next page

"The Dream That Follows Darkness"—revised draft, continued

She moved with small, almost skipping steps around

the room, then slumped to the thick rug, and slept. **Thus the**
beginning ends; the end begins.
That night, in his hotel room, David dreamed of a battle

and of a warrior woman wearing ~~pink ribbons~~ **her hair** in her braids, and

he felt the rush of wind and noise and the trembling of the

earth. He forgot the dream when the sunlight pierced the light

drapes. **and spent the day in silence.** **(transition ?)**

But he heard the sound and felt the trembling again at the
at night
ranch, after yelling "Fire," and watching the glow build behind

the barn and move toward the stables and finally pushing Tom

under the thrashing legs of the panicking horses, hearing the

thuds and whinnies and the rushing sound of the hands coming

to fight the fire, save the horses, and the shrill sirens of emer-

gency vehicles; in the middle of the concerto of fear David killed

Logan Wright ~~and claimed Peg as his prize~~

~~The sky was so clear and blue and high that it hurt to~~

The sky was so clear and blue and high that it hurt to look
~~And thus the beginning ends, David Malek~~
at it. It was a beautiful day. A perfect day for a wedding.

Yisgadal v'yiskadash shemay rabo . . . David Malek mouthed

the ancient Aramaic words of the sacred mourner's prayer and

continued on next page

shivered in the chill of the late autumn West Virginia

Clouds began to mount,

morning. Snow was possible. *Two years,* he thought

with that part of himself that had split away and was watching

the group at the gravesite. He had never felt more lonely. Or

less alone.

They had travelled to the places that had been special to

them separately: Moose Creek, Idaho and Santa Fe, a deserted

cay somewhere between Florida and the South Pole and San

Francisco, a corner of Oklahoma and the edge of Maine, and

made them something to share. And they found new things that

were theirs alone: The headwaters of the Mississippi and the

moonbow at Cumberland Falls, the Vietnam War Memorial

and Little Big Horn. They travelled and grew together until it

was time to go home.

"We've been moving a long time, David," she said one night

as they drove away from the lake where they had first met, a

~~visit both had wanted to make.~~ They had watched the deer

drink in the morning, and he had stood on the shore, skipping

rocks across the surface of the water as she swan and dove,

emerged and danced along the rocks. "It feels like forever, like

continued on next page

"The Dream That Follows Darkness"—revised draft, continued

it's time to stop."

Yisborach v'yish-tab-bach, v'yispoar . . . David shiv-

ered and smelled the change in the weather. He'd learned so

much from Peg. ~~He'd learned how to dream, and how to re-~~

~~member the dreams.~~

their wedding.

They reached the cabin six months after ~~he left.~~ There was

snow all around, and fresh cords of wood stacked under tarps

in a little shed that he hadn't built. The rooms smelled fresh;

wood was laid for fires in the bedroom and the front room. The

sliding door he'd installed across the mouth of the cave was

closed.

"Oh, David, it's everything I thought it would be." She

moved through the rooms, touching the furniture he'd built,

looking into the cabinets as if she knew what would be in them.

Her voice was a song, her movements a dance. "Thank you,

David, for bringing me home."

"Thank you, Peg, for bringing me home." He took the pink

ribbon from around his neck and tied it to a hook over the bed.

"This is where we are tied to, now. I love you, Peg."

"And I, you, David." She removed the ribbon she wore, and

continued on next page

tied it next to his. "Make love to me."

Later, they slept, and David dreamed: A warrior stood surrounded by a battle. He wore a sash—dull red, with four horizontal bands of yellow quills spaced eight inches apart on its lower half. His hooked lance, wrapped with otter fur, tied with buckskin in four places and decorated with small eagle feathers, was driven into the ground, through the sash.

Even as he dreamed, David recognized the painting hanging across from the bed, recognized ~~that he was~~ the warrior, that his name was Raven's Eye. He brought his eagle bone whistle to his lips and then sang, soundlessly. He knew he was about to die.

David
~~He~~ awoke with a start, drenched with sweat even though the fire had gone out and the room was cold. He reached for Peg and found only her pillow. He wrapped the quilt around himself, then reached for the matches on the table next to the bed and lit the Coleman lantern. "Peg? Peg, where are you?" There was no sound but the hiss of the burning mantle.

Still shivering, David walked through the cabin to the back, where the sliding door ~~blocking the mouth of the cave~~ was open. "Peg, are you in there?" He moved more quickly, now,

continued on next page

"The Dream That Follows Darkness"—revised draft, continued

not quite running, feeling the weight of the lantern as

He saw a flash of white

it preceded him into the cave. The woman in white?

(? delete itals !)

Peg turned in her sleep, her nightgown gleaming in the lan-

tern's harsh light. "Peg. Peg, wake up."

She awoke slowly, dazedly. "David? Oh . . . ." She smiled

wanly. "I woke up and you looked so peaceful; you smile in

your sleep, did you know that? Anyway," she stretched and

yawned, stood up, "I wanted to see the cave and I just came

back here—You've done a nice job, you know, turning it ito

your darkroom. So, it's so warm and cozy, and the cot was there,

kind of waiting for me, like, and I lay down for a minute . . . ."

She stretched up to put her arms around his neck, kissed him,

and pulled him down onto the cot, holding him tightly. He felt

her warmth and strength and they drifted off into sleep to-

gether. He didn't dream again that night, though he did think

to ask for just a second what she had used for light, since he

hadn't turned on the power yet. But sleep came too quickly and

too fully.

And life was full. The little town grew below them on the

other side of the frozen creek. They worked and walked, played

continued on next page

and talked. It was if they had always known one another, sensing needs before the other felt them, filling
empty spaces before the gaps were discovered. Then, one night
in summer, while the sky lowered and lightning played on their
mountain's peak, they went down to Paulie Boy's for a party.

Outside thunder rattled, shaking the windows. The creek
rose, slowly. Inside, the tables had been pushed back against the
walls and the thirty or so people who made up the community
danced to the jukebox, finding steps they'd lost when the '50s
became the '60s and the '70s and the '80s; the older folks leading the youngsters, everyone drinking too much and trying not
to pay attention to what was happening outside where the creek
continued to rise and the darkness of the storm seemed to
stretch into infinity. *And yesterday.*

Finally, sweating and footsore, David stopped dancing and
stood at the window, a bottle of beer moving from his lips to
his forehead as he tried to cool down. He watched Peg sketching
something on a paper napkin and laughing with Mollie's daughter, as if they were sharing secrets. Lightning stroked down with
deadly intent; in the sudden blue and ozone-smelling light,

continued on next page

"The Dream That Follows Darkness"—revised draft, continued

he saw the woman in white standing in the parking lot

out front, her black hair streaming down her back.

He ran to the door and threw it open, feeling the rain pelt

against him. The shock forced him to close his eyes; when he

opened them, there was no ~~one standing in the storm.~~ only the night before him. Behind

him someone yelled, "Dave, damnit, ~~close~~ shut the door, your lettin'

the chips get wet."

"Okay, okay," he called over his shoulder, waving upraised

arms as it in surrender, "just gettin' a breath of air." He looked

as far into night as he could, but saw nothing. He stepped back

into the room and pullled the door closed against the storm.

Sitting at the counter, David watched Peg in the backbar

mirror, and sipped at his beer. She danced with one and then

another, flirting with the men, but in the harmless fashion of

someone who knows that no one will take it seriously; she wore

innocence. And finally, breathless and glowing, she came to him

at the bar, put her lips to his ear, and whispered, 'Take me

home. I need you." ~~He felt a fearful exaltation.~~ This

They ran to their Jeep, heads covered by rubberized pon-

chos. He had put the canvas top on, and the sides, and they sat for

continued on next page

a moment in the cloth cocoon and listened to the rain

while the windows fogged over. "C'mon, big boy, you

takin' me home or ain't you? 'Cause there's lotsa guys in there

who will if you ain't man enough."

"Done and done, woman." He started the engine, backed

around into the road. In gear, David drove with one hand, the

other resting on Peg's ~~right~~ *left* thigh, feeling ~~the~~ *her* heat and muscle *and*

strength against his palm. He looked at her looking at him, looked up

and swerved, jamming on the brakes.

"What's wrong, David?" Peg bounced off his shoulder,

against the door of the Jeep, ~~swinging~~ *forcing* it open ~~and looking~~

~~around~~. There was a catch of fear in her voice.

"I thought I saw someone in the road, running across.

Didn't you see anything?" Please, he thought, say yes.

"No. Are you okay, David? You look as if you've seen a

ghost." Peg pulled the door closed again, settled back in her

seat. "Do you want me to drive; you had a lot to drink."

He shook his head. "Nah, I'm okay. Ready?" He began to

drive again, but the image of a black-haired woman in clothes

too white to be sensible on a night like this was burned into his

continued on next page

mind. They drove silently the rest of the way home. It was not a time to talk, Peg knew, only to touch. Her hand, gently, undemanding, on his leg. Thumb gently stroking, easing, soothing.

Even though it was a summer evening, the rain had brought a chill, and as soon as they were in the cabin, David set a fire in the bedroom and they lay on top of the covers, whispering whatever it is lovers whisper and other things: "Is it a good time, Peg?"

More than anything, the only thing, they wanted was a child. "I hope so, David." She giggled into his shoulder. "But what the heck, right?"

David dreamed. ~~It was the same dream~~, Raven's Eye standing in front of his enemies, surrounded by other members of the Dog-men society, each with his sash lanced to the earth. Wherever the lance was, that was Arapaho land. Raven's Eye could not remove the lance; that had to be done by another member of the society. There could be no retreat until the Dog-men ordered it. He was defenseless, then.

As he stood, he heard the scream behind him, Steps High

continued on next page

Fawn's scream; his wife. Her back was to him, to the battle, and he could see blood seeping through her buckskin dress. Dream Speaker, a man of great magic, a leader of the Sweat Lodge society, held her, seemed to be whispering to her. Dream Speaker would not fight on this day or any other; he was there to bring power. *with his medicine* He wanted Steps High Fawn and while Raven's Eye would have allowed her to go with another member of the Dog-men—because that was their privilege— none had ever asked—because that was their honor. Dream Speaker was a man of power, a strong dreamer to whom all the spirits talked, but he was *now* ~~without~~ *sacrificing his* honor. And Raven's Eye's lance stood through his sash and *this* piece of land was home. And he could not move.

Al yisroel v'al tsa-de-ka-yo, v'al kol man . . . David looked over his shoulder at his friends who had come down for this strange rite of burial, who came in support of him to participate in something which, for many of them, smacked of heresy. He was sure that more than one minister would have something to say about this. He knew the young rabbi would, but he wouldn't be there to hear it. The cold reached into him. He could feel

continued on next page

the piece of pink ribbon lying loosely against his throat.

"David, you have to promise me something."

"Anything, my love. Just name it."

"I'm serious, David. No joking."

It was a beautiful day in late Septemer. The mountain had begun to wear it's autumn coat of flaming colors; the mornings found a light frost on the grass in front of the cabin. As the temperature shifted, mist and fog dressed the land before them. David's photographs began to take on a new quality, one of unspecific ceriness. There were times he could swear that there were things in the pictures that weren't in his viewfinder when he snapped the scenes. Peg told him it was only the mist, only the play of light, only his imagination. It was perfect day for making promises, the kinds of promises meant to be kept.

"Okay," he said solemnly. "I swear. Now, what am I swearing to?"

"Right. Now listen. And stop smirking. I'm working on a painting. It's very special and I don't want you to peek. When I'm at the easel, stay out of the room; when you're in the room, leave ~~leaving~~ the drop cloth over the canvas. You can't see it until I

continued on next page

say so. That clear?"

"Yeah, clear. And easy enough."

"Good. Now, get out of here and let me get to work."

For the next month, Peg worked. Whatever it was she was doing, she was happy with it. On those evenings when she was preparing dinner, she whistled and sang as she cut and cooked and served. No matter how David cajoled or begged, teased or whine, she would say nothing about it; she would just reach up and place a finger on his lips. "There's time enough," she might say, "we have all the time there is. You'll see." That was her promise, and she always kept her promises.

Then, one night in bed, Peg pulled the covers back and rolled close to David. "I have a surprise for you, my beloved," she whispered.

He felt a fearful exaltation

David put his arms around his wife. Her breath smelled of mint, her hair of herbs, her body of the world after rain. In the moonlight, here eyes darkened from gray to violet. He'd never noticed that before.

"I have a wonderful surprise and gift for you, David," Peg whispered against his throat. And then she ~~sighed and~~ died in **?**

dele ox?

continued on next page

his arms.

They came and took her to the hospital and asked

him about arrangements. Reverend Morris offered to conduct

a service, but David shook his head.

"No, thank you, Jim. But I think I have to bury her in a

tradition I understand—"

"But—"

"Please, no. I know how you feel but, well, burial is for the

living, right? Wherever Peg is, she'll approve. And she'll wel-

come your prayers, I know. But this will have to be done my

way.

"What you could do for me though, if you would, is intro-

duce me to a rabbi around here. Is there one, even?"

The minister shook his head in dismay. "Of course there is,

down in the city. If it all means so much to you, you'd think

that you'd have found out about . . . ."

"I'm sorry, David. This isn't the time for lectures. I'll call

him for you, his name is Sobol, Eric Sobol. He's young, a nice

man. It's a shame you didn't know him before this."

"Thank you, Jim. Very much. ~~And, uh, I think it might be~~

continued on next page

best if ~~you didn't say anything to him about any possi-~~

~~ble religious quandries we might be facing.~~

The shaking head again. "David, David, I don't know what I'm gong to do about you. But, okay, again."

Rabbi Sobol welcomed David, offering him the aid of the small, dying synagogue. "You'll need a *minyan*, people to help while you're sitting *shiva.* Whatever, we'll do what we can."

The service was held in a small chapel that the congregation reserved for these needs. David had been standing over the casket, and didn't hear the rabbi walk in behind him.

"What . . .?" the word sounded as if the speaker had just been hit in the stomach. David had been tying the ribbon with the cross around Peg's neck.

Sobol looked at David, sternly. "I think we should close the casket, Mr. Malek. It's traditional."

David looked calmly into the rabbi's eyes, saw the questions, the problems. He could think of nothing to say that would put this poor man at ease. "Yes, I think you're right." David leaned down again, straightened the cross in the hollow of Peg's throat, kissed her on the forehead and lips, and brought the lid down.

continued on next page

"The Dream That Follows Darkness"—revised draft, continued

Behind the men, the people of the town that used to have a name began to enter the chapel, coughing nervously.

O'seh sholom bim'-ro-mov, hu ya-a-seh sholom, olenu v'al kol yisroel, v'imru: Amen. The Kaddish was done. David looked into the grave, at the reflections of the weak sun on the highly polished pine. He knelt to pick up a handful of coarse earth and threw it onto the coffin, heard the hollow bounce. He took a deep breath and turned away, toward the east, toward the entrance to the small cemetery.

Two years, h/e thought, and the time before that. *Peg, you said we had nothing but time*, the words were a cry in his heart, *and now* . . . . And now, he thought, I will go on or I will die, but sometime I will join you.

"Mr. Malek . . . ." David felt the rabbi's hand on his shoulder. "Is there anything I can do for you now?"

"No, thank you, Rabbi Sobol. You've done more than I could have asked for. Thank you. I think I'll just go home, now."

"We'll come to visit you, for the prayers." David couldn't

continued on next page

tell whether it was a statement or a question.

"Yes, that would be nice. You know where my cabin
is, up on the mountain?"

"We'll find it. Tomorrow?"

"Yes, No, no, make it the day after. That would be better.
Okay?"

"Ad you like. Your friends will take you home now?"

David looked down at the quickly filling grave and up at the
trees bending bare branches in the wind. He was warm now,
and felt no more lonleliness, felt no longer alone. "Yes, my
friends will take me home."

Malek walked through the cabin, feeling the different feel of
the rooms. In Peg's studio, he looked at the covered easel, at the
painting which might or might not be finished. He went to it
slowly, touching the cloth draped over it on a frame so that it
would not come into contact the the canvas while the paint was
wet. He lifted a corner, then dropped it slowly. No. Maybe
tomorrow.

He heard his neighbors coming in, bringing food for him,
companionship. He didn't want the emptiness now, though

continued on next page

he didn't need the company. He welcomed them, showed the women where the plates were, the silverware. These were people used to wakes, he realized, people who drank and laughed and told stories about those who had died. It was a good tradition.

It was a good evening, considering. When, finally, everyone had left, and he fell into bed, he didn't expect to dream.

Dream Speaker was pulling Steps High Fawn, dragging her away, retreating with her. In front of Raven's Eye, the horsemen were coming, riding right at him. His wife shouted, and he turned, saw the arrow piercing her left shoulder, the blood running down over her breast. Then the horses were on him.

The large, blackbird fluttered its wings as it landed on the tree limb. A cold wind keened across the Plains, causing the People of Our Own Kind—those who had survived the battle with the Utes—to curl in their sleep. They had won, and credit was given to the members of the Sweat Lodge society and to the bravery of the Dog-men and Lance Men. Raven's Eye would be missed; and his woman, Steps High Fawn who had fought bravely beside him and was probably one of those captured.

continued on next page

She lay tied to some trees miles from the village.

Dream Speaker would return for her, she knew that as

she knew that Raven's Eye was dead. She had heard his song

and he had heard her screams. Now, she heard the shaman's

approach, could smell the stink of him. He was a man without

honor, without soul.

He stepped into the grove, and pulled the blanket off his

prize. In the cold light of the moon, her body glowed with her

~~power~~ ~~strength.~~ (stet) She was more powerful than even he, Dream Speaker

knew, but now she was powerless. He stripped himself of his

robes, his manhood before him like the lance of a warrier. Laug-

hing silently, he picked up a knife and cut the ropes holding the

woman's legs together, then dropped between them.

Spent, he slept. The bird in the tree cawed and flew down

from its roost. On the ground, it cocked its head, looking at the

woman covered in blood, here eyes closed, her breathing rag-

ged. He hopped around the body of the man lying next to her

and pecked at the rope holding her left arm to a branch. She felt

the movement and opened her eyes, watched the bird climb and

soar against the circle of the full moon, then lighting on a

continued on next page

branch, pecking at something.

Steps High Fawn pulled with her left arm, weakened by the wounding she had received in the battle, and felt the rope give. She worked at it some more, knowning she could not pass out, that this was not her time to die. As she struggled, the bird returned, two strips of cloth in its beak. He cawed again, ~~dropping the ribbon.~~ ✗ ✔

She didn't realize that her had was free; feeling was gone. It was when she felt it against her body that she knew. The bird hopped excitedly while the woman reached for the knife Dream Speaker had dropped earlier. She cut her other hand free, then stood silently, staring at the man on the ground. With a scream that shook the mountains, she thrust the blade into his heart and then cut his head from his body, impaling it on a naked branch.

✔ The black bird rose with a roar of wings and pecked at the **head's lolling tongue.** ~~dead eyes.~~ Steps High Fawn found her dress and put it on. She braided her hair, tying it with the pieces of ribbon the bird had brought. She looked back—this was her past, now; she couldn't return to the People. She walked out of the copse, untied

continued on next page

Dream Speaker's pony, and began her trek toward the east, toward the morning sun, toward the beginning.

The places she saw, the peoples she encountered, recognized her *medicine* ~~magic~~ and her passage was without incident. Her wound healed well, she ate and had water to drink. She considered taking the name of raven—for her savior and man—but honored instead her spirit.

Which eventually brought her to a land of mountains and rushing waters. She found shelter and waited.

Malek woke to a perfect morning, the clouds threatening the snow of the day before blown clear. The sky blue and high; the sun brighter than it had any right to be in that place and that time. He knew he had dreamed in the night, but he couldn't remember what he had seen. It would come back, he knew. Just as he knew that it was time to look at Peg's painting.

He dressed and made coffee, delaying the moment until it demanded to be answered. Then he pulled the cloth away.

It was the kind of painting she might have done for a book jacket. In the center, a large raven in silhouette against the moon. Surrounding it, scenes: The scenes from his dream. But

continued on next page

he wasn't taken aback, shocked. It made every bit of sense, really, once he stopped to think about it. And he did think about it.

All day, while he went about doing what had to be done, he thought about it, and nodded. And in the evening, he went down to Paulie Boy's, where they were surprised to see him, but he explained that life goes on, that all they had was that and *and time* that Peg would have wanted this.

He drank at the counter for an hour, watching the room in the mirror. When he saw the woman in white come in, he simply nodeed, and ordered another drink. When she left, he waited a mimute, then said goodnight and followed her out.

But she wasn't there. Wasn't waiting. Had he been wrong? Was it all a ridiculous fantasy born out of his grief? Malek didn't know, and now he didn't want to think about it. He wanted only to sleep.

He started a fire in the bedroom fireplace, and crawled into bed. Tendrils of mist whispered up out of the ground and into the cabin as if seeking purchase; finding Malek, they wrapped themselves around him.

continued on next page

They pulled, and he knew he was right. The cave door slid open and the woman in white stepped into the room, her braided hair held by pink ribbons, the stain gone from her breast. She held out her hand and David rose.

"We have only time," ~~she whispered.~~

"Only time."

"Thank you for bringing me home, Raven's Eyes.

The cabin was a heap of ash by the time anyone from the town across the creek could get up to it. They waited for the ruins to cool, joined by the rabbi and the members of the congregation who had come to pray with David Malek. The grey heap was relieved by one spot of color, a piece of pink ribbon caught by one of the rocks that had come sliding down the mountain, blocking the entrance to the cave.

The ribbon waved in the wind, and was torn loose, blowing down into the creek where it floated away, into the river and around Three Mile Curve. ◆

The dreams are centrally featured, offering some connections with the past; the sequences give more than a hint to the reader of what's coming. If someone remembers the story of David and Bathsheba, the scene on page 103, the one that ends with "in the middle of the concerto of fear David killed Logan Wright," will resonate properly: King David sent Bathsheba's husband, Uriah, into battle, in front of the troops, where he was certain to be killed; the dream scenes of Raven's Eye's battle with the Ute, emphasize it—though this time it is "David" who has been put in harm's way. There's a problem, though with the word "killed." While it can be argued that Malek is not a hero in the sense that we use the word when referring to characters, I didn't want to make him a murderer per se. That was one thing that had to be dealt with as I read the draft.

And the ghost: She appears three times in the story, once on pages 99-100 (having been set up on page 98, with mention of the legend) and again on pages 109 and 110 (with foreshadowing on pages 106-107).

I loved those scenes; shivered as I wrote them as I hoped the reader would. This was what storytelling is all about; I'd written the story, finally, because I had those scenes. The only problem was that they didn't belong in it; they were as unnecessary as a fig leaf on Michelangelo's statue. Ultimately, the mention of the legend of the woman in white who lived in the cave was enough; as with the shotgun on the mantel, letting the reader know of the myth was enough; she'd be "fired" at the right time and place; showing her again and again wasn't serving the purposes of the story at all.

You'll also notice that instead of going to New Orleans and renting a small room, as the early draft indicated, he now goes home to New Orleans. Why, I'd wondered, would he go there, of all the places in the country? There was no reason at all; in fact, there's no reason for the scene at all; in this case, we were dealing with a darling I couldn't kill, a paragraph left in because I liked the steamboat and the stripper sighing, a transition, allowing him time to think and then to travel. Removing it would make no difference whatsoever. (The job of revision is never done. If the story were to be reprinted, I'd make the change. Probably.) But there is no purpose: Nothing is said, the reader learns nothing beyond the fact that David thought things over.

Purpose. Your plot, how things are happening, why they're happening, is served by everything you choose to do. If you don't know why an event is taking place, why a bit of dialogue occurs, if they are not moving things forward, they should be cut. There shouldn't be anything, anywhere, that doesn't serve a purpose. The plot is the purpose of the action, the action develops from the scenes, the scenes are made up of actions (movement, dialogue) . . . pull any thread and the tapestry changes.

When you do your revision, consider the purpose of every scene (actually, consider the purpose of every word; we'll get to that later). Does this have a familiar ring to it, sound like something you may have read earlier? Well . . . that's the purpose of the advice: to drive home the fact that everything in your story counts.

As you read, then, consider these factors as part of the purpose of the scene serving the story:

◆ Is there a conflict in the scene, something that will force a character into action? If not, what's happening? Can you foreshadow the scene's relevance to the plot?

◆ Does the scene serve to further character development and evolution (which is part of the plot; the characters' changes cause things to happen)? If not, what are the characters doing that will interest the reader?

◆ Does the character consider the events you're showing important? Or is something going to happen later that surprises her because she wasn't paying attention?

If nothing of value is happening, if some purpose isn't served, cut the scene, or add something to it that might make a difference. In my ghost scenes, the woman in white is a harbinger of the scene in which David finds Peg asleep in the cave. However, his dreams serve that purpose already. He's also seen her rubbing her shoulder; it's important enough for me to mention, but not important enough for him to comment on, to ask if she hurt herself diving. Adding that dialogue, and having her respond ("Yes, I hit a rock," or, "A branch snapped back and smacked me" [or, "stabbed me"]) would play into Steps High Fawn's injury. For my purposes, enough was enough.

Could the scene be made more important, somehow advancing the story? Look at everything more than once, consider it from various angles, as we just did with Peg. Remember: The race isn't won by the swiftest, but the one who knows the landscape best; it makes far more sense to spend an extra week or two in the creation of your work and getting it right. There isn't going to be one, definitive answer; a good story has a personal element that helps shape it, that makes it something identifiable with you and only you. If it might be written by anyone, why would anyone want to read it?

Because the scenes are the foundation of how things are happening, they don't stand alone; each is followed by what it causes. Are your scenes directly linked: Do you have transitions, lines (or something more) showing the reader the passage of time? In a more complex work, if you're doing a flashback or following two separate lines of action that will merge on the horizon of your story, have you made it clear to the reader that we're in a different time and/or place?

And have you resolved a character's conflict? If you have, you've made a mistake—broken the tension too soon. So, as you're studying your story line and plot, you'll want to be certain that you've left the reader wondering about what's going to happen next.

Go back and look at the major shift in "The Dream That Follow Darkness": Peg and David have gotten married—it was a perfect day for a wedding. Because of the events that have preceded Logan's death (page 102, Peg telling him that "never" is the wrong answer when she asks for the divorce), the reader is aware of something else at work; to emphasize that, a line was added in the final version: ". . . everyone expressed sadness at the accident, Malek knew there were no accidents."

A short story is one thing, a novel another. But the principle is the same: Scenes (or, more usually, chapters) have to leave the reader anxious. That doesn't mean you have to assuage that tension immediately. In a novel, with the tapestry of characters, the next chapter might, as we've just indicated, be set elsewhere; you can leave your reader dangling (along with your character) while setting up another set of tensions. If I'd told the story of Peg and David by following them each separately, letting the reader know what Peg was doing while David was building the cabin, most of their separate scenes would have needed some kind of incomplete ending.

Experiment with different ways of introducing tension. As important as the discovery of the body, the bomb, the vampire's tomb or the cheating spouse is the manner in which it is discovered. Tension builds, but it also comes from shock, from the element that's out of place in the context of the scene.

Avoid having anything happen "suddenly." The moment the reader sees that word, the surprise is lessened; it's a giveaway that something is occurring. Devote some time to thinking of the paragraph *before* the event, leading the reader to jump to a conclusion, and then . . . Look at the way Peg's death is introduced on page 114 in the "The Dream That Follows Darkness" revised draft: She's talking about the time they have; the reader knows they want a child; David and Peg are in bed; he's aware only of her scent, her eyes. And: " 'I have a wonderful surprise and gift for you, David,' Peg whispered against his throat. And then she died in his arms." I can't speak to the reactions of readers alone in their chairs when they come to that line, but based on the reactions when I present the scene during readings, and even though they've known Peg is dead, there's an audible intake of breath. When I heard that the first time—during a reading while it was still a work in progress—I knew that scene, anyway, was finished; like riders on a roller coaster, they'd been taken slowly up an incline and now were rushed to the bottom. What was on the other side of the next upgrade?

Don't confuse the idea of the cliff-hanger with the old movie serials in which the hero was left, literally, dangling; that works in thrillers and much genre fiction, but it doesn't fit too well with a mainstream novel. There, the tension can just as easily be created by an emotional concern for the character(s). Chapter four of John Irving's *The Cider House Rules* opens with Wilbur Larch, an OB-GYN who runs the St.

Cloud's orphanage, thinking about one of his charges, the central character of the novel, Homer Wells. Homer's been there too long; his fate, in Larch's view, is pretty much sealed. He's a young man now, knowing nothing of the world. Larch has been training him to assist him:

> What Wilbur Larch was thinking of, regarding "options," was that Homer Wells had no choice concerning either his apprenticeship or Melony. He and Melony were doomed to become a kind of couple because there was no one else for them to couple with.

The chapter ends with Larch and Wells standing outside the orphanage. Homer's been walking in the darkness and Larch, wondering what's wrong, goes out to talk to him:

> "I couldn't sleep," Homer told Larch.
>
> "What is it this time?" Dr. Larch asked Homer.
>
> "Maybe it's just an owl," said Homer Wells. The oil lamp didn't project very far into the darkness, and the wind was strong, which was unusual for St. Cloud's. When the wind blew out the lamp, the doctor and his assistant saw that they were backlit by the light shining from the window of Nurse Angela's office. It was the only light for miles around, and it made their shadows gigantic. Larch's shadow reached across the stripped, unplanted plot of ground, up the barren hillside, all the way into the black woods. Homer Wells's shadow touched the dark sky. It was only then that both men noticed: Homer had grown taller than Dr. Larch.
>
> "I'll be damned," Larch muttered, spreading his arms, so that his shadow looked like a magician about to reveal something. Larch flapped his arms like a big bat. "Look!" he said to Homer. "I'm a sorcerer."
>
> Homer Wells, the sorcerer's apprentice, flapped his arms, too.
>
> The wind was very strong and fresh. The usual density in the

air above St. Cloud's had lifted; the stars shone bright and cold; the memory of cigar smoke and sawdust was missing from the new air.

"Feel that wind," said Homer Wells; maybe the wind was keeping him up.

"It's a wind coming from the coast," Wilbur Larch said; he sniffed, deeply, for traces of salt. It was a rare sea breeze, Larch was sure.

Wherever it's from, it's nice, Homer Wells decided.

Both men stood sniffing the wind. Each man thought: What is going to happen to me?

So simple: The chapter begins with the doctor certain of what's going to happen and ends with both characters wondering about the future. As important, study the language used: the image of the sorcerer (with the simile of the bat); the "plot of ground, up the barren hillside," carrying with it the sense of death and loss. Then: Homer's growth, the sense of something rare; the air above St. Cloud's—fresh, "new air."

Each man thought: "What is going to happen to me?" And by then, the reader wants to know, too, forced into it by Irving's use of language.

When revising your work, consider these questions:

• Do your scenes have a point in terms of the story? Do they leave the reader wanting more because you've established a danger, a concern or a question that matters, to the characters and to the audience?

• Have the scenes remained consistent in terms of point of view? And is it the *right* point of view?

• Have you accomplished what you set out to do in the scene: resolved a conflict and begun a new one? Have the characters grown, changed, reacted?

• Does the scene lead naturally to another one, even if it isn't the next in terms of telling the story?

• Can the scene be made stronger by adding dialogue or action? Can it be made stronger by taking something out, chipping away things that don't matter?

• Does the scene read too slowly? Is it slowing the pace in a place where it should be faster?

Those last two questions, variations on the question of the pace of the story, lead to the next set of things we have to consider when revising. They aren't story elements, but they are part of storytelling as an art and craft and, like everything else involved, also deal with engaging the reader.

We begin, naturally, with the opening.

CHAPTER 9

The Opening

The importance of the opening of your story cannot be underplayed; many (if not most) competitions sponsored by writing conferences have a category devoted to great beginnings. Unfortunately, the majority of them are judged on the amount of action present in the submission—the idea of hitting the ground running is repeated so often that mystery writers, for instance, are led to believe that the murder must happen within the first chapter, that something "exciting" has to occur immediately. I don't agree, and in my editing and working with writers generally, I emphasize that it isn't a matter of action, but of drawing the reader in, giving her something to care about, something to intrigue or entice, something to pull her in and make her wonder.

Watch people buying books—or consider what you do when you're browsing in the bookstore—and you'll begin to understand one of the fallacies. If you are to take off immediately, you would have to have the action in the first three paragraphs because that's about all anyone reads while standing in front of the shelves. It is your language, your style—the way you speak to the reader—that makes much of the difference. Can your reader "hear" a distinct "you" as he scans the words on the page? Is there a sound there, or just a series of words? If your action scene is flat, if it's told and not shown, if your language doesn't lead your reader toward a visualization of whatever is happening, it doesn't matter how much action you have.

So, call it action, call it conflict, call it a situation; the label is unimportant. The writing and how it's presented make the difference.

If you're like most writers, you've given a lot of effort to your opening scene because, well, that's what we do. It's not rare, however, to discover that once you've gotten into the flow of your story, the real beginning finally appears. Here's an example of one instance, from my story "Gridlock." I'd submitted it to my usual markets and wasn't getting an interest. This is what the editors saw:

> She thought she saw him again for the first time on April 1, 1980, the recognition coming simultaneously with a splinter of pain just below and to the right of her left breast.
>
> She had stepped over his outstretched legs as he sat on the sidewalk, his back against a building near Columbus Circle. His face was pale, scabbed and scarred. His hair, once thick and styled, hung in greasey spikes, spearing the air around his head.
>
> The burning dart in her chest caused her to reel, to grab at the lamppost at her side. She threw her arm around it, clutching as she would the waist of a sturdy lover leading her to bed. His waist, perhaps; his waist, untouched for ten years.
>
> She shook her head, hearing laughter. . . .

Five pages later, I had an italicized section, three paragraphs, that described what was going on in the city at the time. Given the failures so far, I moved that up to the beginning, so the story now begins:

> *"Okay, c'mon, move it." Throughout the city, the underground city, the police moved, clearing out the shopping bag ladies and homeless men who made the subways—the trains and stations, the platforms and hidden corners—their home.*
>
> *They walked in a stupor. Some knew about the strike; others, too far gone to be aware of much of anything, wondered where the trains had gone. A few, not too many, were taken out on stretchers and gurneys, in body bags. They would have had to leave anyway. Some of them would be missed, eventually.*
>
> *The ones who left moved onto the streets, finding walls and alleys, rediscovering their legs, walking, tasting the springtime city and becoming part of the traffic.*
>
> She thought she saw him on April 1, 1980. . . .

There were some changes in language in subsequent drafts—the first sentence of the second paragraph became "They walked slowly, entranced," and other tweaks—but by putting the underground people on the street, I gave the man who has shocked the woman some context. My thought, as I was writing, was that immediately offering a close-up of Lorraine and her shock was going to grab the reader: a woman in some kind of danger or dismay. As it happened, though, the editors were caught by the image of the homeless becoming part of the traffic (remember: the story is titled "Gridlock") and that made the difference. It also happened that putting the information about them being dislodged came too late in terms of the story line, of the *when*, of the cause and effect. Moving the three paragraphs, making them a prologue, if you will, kept the linear progression correct, strengthened the story and got the sale.

Here's another example of a small rearrangement that made the difference. The piece, "Lust and Process: A Rumination," is a narrative essay—creative nonfiction, a form that's gaining in popularity (memoir is an extention of it)—and it uses the same techniques honed by storytellers. The essay considers the parallels between lust and the writing process.

As it was first written, it began with some thoughts about writing itself, the heat of creativity.

> Heat . . .
>
> It was decided once on a morning like this or different, there in the humid nastiness of the back hallway to which you retire to smoke, that with the right first sentence, the rest of the copy simply flows.
>
> . . . humidity . . .
>
> (It's not the heat but . . . Unless, of course, it is.)
>
> . . . the air as still as a dead man's lips. (Lips: *Clara-Bowed; thin and tight, pursed to kiss you hello or off.*) . . .
>
> . . . and noise: The #1 pushes in from the Bronx . . .
>
> You stand pushed together on the train . . .

The train ride that's about to begin is central to the questions being investigated in the piece, but it's coming too late when considered as part of a story. So, things were shifted and it appeared in *Fourth Genre* magazine this way:

Heat . . .

. . . and noise: The #1 pushes in from the Bronx on its way to Battery Park, this a stop on the literary Upper West Side; pushing in, it punches hot winds before it, into the station where you stand and wait in the noise and heat, clothes, even at this early hour, already sticking to backs and legs, beads of sweat rolling like crystal lava tearing bits of mascara away from eyes and rolling them down, raving the landscape of a face used to icy calm.

(Lava flows downward to the sea, burning brush and homes, adding layers to the layers already there, flows to the sea where it sizzles and steams and cools, extending beaches, building something other than what was . . . *creating.*)

It was decided once on a morning like this or different, there in the humid nastiness of the back hallway to which you retired to smoke, that with the right first sentence, the rest of the copy simply flows.

. . . humidity . . .

(It's not the heat but . . . Unless, of course, it is.)

. . . the air as still as a dead man's lips. (Lips: *Clara-Bowed, thin and tight, pursed to kiss you hello or off.* Eyes: *Brown-eyed blonde; blue-eyed brunette, redhead with trite emerald saved by flecks of honey. Oh, honey.*) Faces. Sweat . . .

You stand pushed together on the train, the sudden almost-cool of the air conditioner bringing chills, drying sweat, and try not to look each other in the eyes. . . .

What's been accomplished?

We begin with the one word, "heat." Lust, the heat of the creative process, passion: they're all present immediately.

And then the train comes "pushing" in: an overt sexual connotation, more heat. A scene, characters (the "face used to icy calm"; later, these images are expanded) and then the metaphor of lava creating, rather than the more usual destruction connected with it.

Now we add the humidity and the copy flowing, like the lava, already established as creating. Lips, eyes, faces . . . sweat. And after having studied the eyes, trying not to look at them: conflict. And contrast: the "almost-cool . . . bringing chills," a sense of fever.

 ◆ Reread the beginning of your story. What is your opening accomplishing? Is it establishing a place, a mind-set, a character; conflict, questions, situations? It should be.

The beginning of "The Dream That Follows Darkness" presents a storm, a clearing and some strange dreams being shared by a group of people. And then, after saying that everything is perfect with the day, "For an accident. That's how Malek thought of it." Something is going to happen; the reader knows that and is made to wonder. What happens? Why does this person think of it as an accident? Does it say something about Malek's attitudes? "It would be years before he learned the reality of accidents." Well, if he thinks it's an accident, something that happens and is forgotten, just one of those things, but then learns the reality, what is that reality? What happens to change his mind?

Questions . . .

What we're going to do now is study some successful openings—successful, anyway, in the sense that they're taken from published books—and look at what made them work and where, even though the book was accepted, they fail. The examples are taken from a broad range of books, and some of them clearly break the "rules" we repeatedly hear and read. Whether they work for you or whether the changes or complaints I may voice here are agreed with is really beside the point; the point is that there is such diversity that no one approach works for everyone—reader, writer . . . or editor. (And we're all editors.)

A last note: In most cases we're going to examine only a couple of paragraphs, not entire chapters. If those first words don't do it, what follows them won't, either.

One of the classics of science fiction is Walter M. Miller Jr.'s *A Canticle for Leibowitz*:

> Brother Francis Gerard of Utah might never have discovered the blessed documents, had it not been for the pilgrim with girded loins who appeared during that young novice's Lenten fast in the desert.
>
> Never before had Brother Francis actually seen a pilgrim with girded loins, but that this one was the bona fide article he was convinced as soon as he had recovered from the spine-chilling effect of the pilgrim's advent on the far horizon, as a wiggling iota of black caught in a shimmering haze of heat. Legless, but wearing a tiny head, the iota materialized out of the mirror glaze on the broken roadway and seemed more to writhe than to walk into view, causing Brother Francis to clutch the crucifix of his rosary and mutter an Ave or two. The iota suggest a tiny apparition spawned by the heat demons who tortured the land at high noon, when any creature capable of motion on the desert (except the buzzards and a few monastic hermits such as Francis) lay motionless in its burrow or hid beneath a rock from the ferocity of the sun. Only a thing monstrous, a thing preternatural, or a thing with addled wits would hike purposefully down the trail at noon this way.
>
> Brother Francis added a hasty prayer to Saint Raul the Cyclopean, patron of the misborn, for protection against the Saint's unhappy proteges. (For who did not then know that there were monsters in the earth in those days?)

What are the blessed documents, and why are they important enough to be the first discovery of the story we're about to hear? When is the story taking place? Most of us know that there is no Saint Raul the Cyclopean, so what world is this, even if Brother Francis is from Utah? And we know there are monsters.

The storyteller announces that he has a sense of humor: "Never before had Brother Francis actually seen a pilgrim with girded loins . . ." And we also learn that the author is a keen observer: Through his description, the apparition, this figure coming over the horizon and seen through the haze of desert heat, is instantly visible to us.

Through the use of language, engaging the senses, creating a puzzle, Miller instantly engages a careful reader's interest and imagination.

Barry Unsworth, a British historical novelist (living in Italy) and Booker Award winner, has written a couple of books that fall, generally, into the mystery category. His *Stone Virgin* appears on several lists as one of the best hundred mysteries ever written. *Morality Play* was short-listed for the Booker Award and was a best-seller in both the United States and Great Britain. One of his more recent novels, *After Hannibal*, is a contemporary story.

Stone Virgin is set in both contemporary and historical Venice, beginning in 1432. It's a murder mystery, an investigation of love, death, creation, faith and evil. It begins:

> He brings me writing materials without asking for money but he does not speak, I cannot be sure what his motives are, whether he has seen my worth and wishes sincerely to help me or whether he is merely acting on orders from his superiors or it is possible he has believed my promises to reward him when I get out of this hole, but whatever the truth of it I take this chance of reaching you, noble lord. I beg you to find out who are my enemies and speak for me; I mean those behind my accusers. From you a few words would be enough. I am innocent of the girl's death. I swear it by all the saints. Ask me to make any solemn oath and I will do it. I was in another part of the town when she was drowned. Those who say I was with her are lying; they have been paid to lie. You are my generous patron, you are one of the Three Hundred, you obtained for me the commission from the Supplicanti,

having seen my work at Bologna. My lord, please help me now
or I will sink under this weight of false witness. Why would I kill
a girl for no reason? Besides, she was a whore. I will tell you
everything I can about Bianca and the carving of the Madonna.

Unsworth has given us a character in trouble, told us of the murder
that's at the heart (or, at least, one of the ventricles) of the novel. Is the
narrator lying? Is he being set up? Why? An attitude is expressed: Why
would I kill a girl for no reason, and what difference does her death
make? She's just a whore. But if that's the case, why is her death so
important to the powers that be?

In addition to the questions Unsworth presents directly, his choice
of language is worth noting. He's created a sound that we can accept as
being of the period, without challenging understanding, and tied us to
the title of the novel with the last sentence. With 232 words, Unsworth
has drawn us into a story.

Morality Play is a medieval tale, centered around a troupe of traveling players. Unsworth lets us know what's happening immediately:

> It was death that began it all and another death that led us on.
> The first was of the man called Brendan and I saw the moment
> of it. I saw them gather round and crouch over him in the bitter
> cold, then start back to give the soul passage. It was as if they
> played his death for me and this was a strange thing, as they did
> not know I watched, and I did not then know what they were.
>
> Strange too that I should have been led to them, whether by
> angels or demons, at a time when my folly had brought me to
> such great need. I will not hide my sins, or what is the worth of
> absolution? That very day hunger had brought me to adultery
> and through adultery I had lost my cloak.

Readers are expected to know the meaning of the title; the idea of
morality is extended immediately—adultery, absolution, death. Bitter

cold, hunger: a situation, not clearly spelled out, but hinted at, teasing the reader. And two deaths, at least.

That tease also plays out on the first page of *After Hannibal*, set in modern Umbria (Unsworth's home):

> They are called *strade vicinali*, neighborhood roads. They are not intended to join places, only to give access to scattered houses. Dusty in summer, muddy in winter, there are thousands of miles of them wandering over the face of rural Italy. When such a road has reached your door it has no necessary further existence; it may straggle along somewhere else or it may not. You can trace their courses on the survey maps kept in the offices of the local *comune*; but no map will tell you what you most need to know about them: whether they are passable or ruinous or have ceased altogether to exist in any sense but the notional. Their upkeep falls to those who depend on them, a fact that often leads to quarrels. The important thing, really, about roads like this, is not where they end but the lives they touch on the way.

The title comes from the fact that Hannibal, in his attack on Rome, slaughtered a legion here and the place names recall that event. Again, crime and secrets abound. And Unsworth defines a novel in the last sentence: It's not the destination that counts, but the journey. All the reader can be certain of, reading this paragraph, is that something is going to happen. Does it matter what those events are? Not to a sophisticated reader, understanding the purpose of storytelling.

Three different openings, three completely different novels, bound together by the most important thing a writer brings to the table: ability and use of language. All done with a minimum of words: 140 for *Morality Play*; 157 for *After Hannibal*.

None of those openings gives a sense of place. Many of the manuscripts editors and agents see start with a description that accomplishes nothing; it seems to be there to give a sense of place, but it isn't integrated into the story. If it weren't there, it wouldn't be missed.

Lev Raphael, a crime writer known for his brilliant academic satires (yes, you can combine genres), begins the third novel in his Nick Hoffman series this way:

> It was Stefan's idea that I eat lunch now and then by the Administration Building bridge—despite the murder.
>
> Well, actually, it was *because* of the murder.
>
> Two years ago, the body of my officemate Perry Cross had turned up in the Michigan River, snagged on some rocks right near the bridge. It wasn't a diving accident.
>
> At the part of the shallow river where they had found Cross's body, artfully scattered boulders created a tiny rapids, and ducks gather year-round to be fed by children and their parents. The sloping lawns on either side of the river were always full of contented-looking students when the weather was even remotely warm enough: reading, tanning, eating, dreaming. An inviting terrace lined with benches stretched along the sound bank, down three wide granite steps from the walk paralleling the river.
>
> All kinds of things showed up in the Michigan River: notebooks, beer cans, sneakers, condoms. But there'd never been a body before.
>
> And even after two years, Cross's murder was still very much alive at SUM's verdant Michiganapolis campus. You could often see students stopped on the wide bridge with its rounded steel rails, pointing down to where they thought Cross's body had been found. Some leaned far over the rail as if pretending to plunge to a battered, wet death. It was ghoulish playacting that got uglier when they shrieked or laughed and made loud jokes or choking noises, then staggered away from the rail crying, "Help! Help!"
>
> The murder hadn't done my career at the State University of Michigan any good, even though I wasn't the killer. . . .

Raphael gives us a sense of place, of the characters: Anyone who has been near a campus of any kind will immediately begin to see and know the where and who of the story. Readers picking up the novel know that it is a mystery; we are also prepared for the contrast that soon comes: the peace of the place, the murder and the cruelty of the students. We learn something about the protagonist immediately—a bit of back story, without need of a prologue—and know that the narrator should not be there. Without saying anything directly, the author has put a threatening shadow on the wall, and the reader waits for the other shoe to fall. All in 267 words.

Margaret Atwood's best-seller *Alias Grace* also begins with description:

> Out of the gravel there are peonies growing. They come up through the loose grey pebbles, their buds testing the air like snails' eyes, then swelling and opening, huge dark-red flowers all shining and glossy like satin. Then they burst and fall to the ground.
>
> In the one instant before they come apart they are like the peonies in the front garden at Mr. Kinnear's that first day, only those were white. Nancy was cutting them. She wore a pale dress with pink rosebuds and a triple-flounced skirt, and a straw bonnet that hid her face. She carried a flat basket, to put the flowers in; she bent from the hips like a lady, holding her waist straight. When she heard us and turned to look, she put her hand up to her throat as if startled.
>
> I tuck my head down while I walk, keeping step with the rest, eyes lowered, silently two by two around the yard, inside the square made by the high stone walls. My hands are clasped in front of me; they're chapped, the knuckles reddened. I can't remember a time when they were not like that. The toes of my shoes go in and out under the hem of my skirt, blue and white, blue and white, crunching on the pathway. These shoes fit me better than any I've ever had before.
>
> It's 1851. I'll be twenty-four years old next birthday. I've been

shut up in here since the age of sixteen. I'm a model prisoner, and give no trouble.

Atwood uses description for contrast: the stone walls of the prison and the softness of the flowers. We know that our narrator is observant, seeing the details that make a difference. And then we learn that she's a prisoner. Is the scene with Nancy a flashback, a fantasy, a little of both? Why has this obviously intelligent young woman been in prison for eight years? Again, this short passage establishes a question and a character, something to give a reader reason to turn the page.

Of course, with the exception of *After Hannibal,* at least as far as we know from what we've read, crime plays a role in these stories, though only the Raphael was marketed as a mystery. Here are a couple of openings from other mainstream novels, ones that don't focus on criminal activity in some way.

David Bradley's second novel, *The Chaneysville Incident,* won the PEN/Faulkner Award, and though it was published in 1981, it remains a staple of the trade paperback shelves. It is about a man's search for the past, for the truth behind a legend and what that truth holds for him.

> Sometimes you can hear the wire, hear it reaching out across the miles; whining with its own weight, crying from the cold, panting at the distance, humming with the phantom sounds of someone else's conversation. You cannot always hear it—only sometimes; when the night is deep and the room is dark and the sound of the phone's ringing has come slicing through uneasy sleep; when you are lying there, shivering, with the cold plastic of the receiver pressed tight against your ear. Then, as the rasping of your breathing fades and the hammering of your heartbeat slows, you can hear the wire: whining, crying, panting, humming, moaning like a live thing.
>
> "John?" she said. She had said it before, just after she had

finished giving me the message, but then I had said nothing, had not even grunted in response, so now her voice had a little bite in it: "John, did you hear me?"

"I heard you," I said. I let it go at that, and lay there, listening to the wire.

"Well," she said finally. She wouldn't say any more than that; I knew that.

"If he's all that sick, he ought to be in the hospital."

"Then you come take him. The man is asking for *you*, John; are you coming or not?"

I listened to the wire.

"*John*." A real bite in it this time.

"Tell him I'll be there in the morning," I said.

"You can tell him yourself," she said. "I'm not going over there."

"Who's seen him, then?" I said, but she had already hung up.

But I did not hang up. Not right away. Instead I lay there, shivering, and listened to the wire.

Atmosphere is created immediately, through the use of language: moaning, whining, crying; something ominous, perhaps evil, something difficult is happening. We don't have to be told that or what, not immediately—everyone has received *that* call in the middle of the night.

We don't know who's talking, what their relationship is, who is sick. But we know that the news is disturbing to John, upsetting: He shivers and listens to the wire.

Bradley's also begun to give us some small insight into the character of John, the man we're clearly going to be following; he's given the reader reason to turn the page.

Pete Hamill's best-seller *Snow in August* is a coming-of-age story, set in Brooklyn, New York, in the late 1940s. Here are his first words to the reader:

Once upon a cold and luminous Saturday morning, in an urban hamlet of tenements, factories, and trolley cars on the western slopes of the borough of Brooklyn, a boy named Michael Devlin woke in the dark.

He was eleven years and three months old in this final week of the year 1946, and because he had slept in this room for as long as he could remember, the darkness provoked neither mystery nor fear. He did not have to see the red wooden chair that stood against the windowsill; he knew it was there. He knew his winter clothes were hanging on a hook on the door and that his three good shirts and his clean underclothes were neatly stacked in the two drawers of the low green bureau. The *Captain Marvel* comic book he'd been reading before falling asleep was certain to be on the floor beside the narrow bed. And he knew that when he turned on the light he would pick up the comic book and stack it with the other *Captain Marvels* on the top shelf of the metal cabinet beside the door. Then he would rise in a flash, holding his breath to keep from shivering in his underwear, grab for clothes, and head for the warmth of the kitchen. That was what he did on every dark winter morning of his life.

But this morning was different.

Because of the light.

. . . From the bed, Michael could see a radiant paleness beyond the black window shade and gashes of hard white light along its sides. He lay there under the covers, his eyes filled with the bright darkness. A holy light, he thought. The light of Fatima. Or the Garden of Eden. Or the magic places in storybooks. . . .

There's a classic story beginning; rather than once upon a time, we're given a specific time, but the sense of fable is immediate. Michael's a normal boy of and for his age. His first instinct on seeing the light is to think in terms of the lessons of the church; only after that does he think in terms of the storybooks he reads. We're charmed by the boy, his neatness and knowledge of where everything in the room is; and then we worry—this morning was different. Where is Hamill taking us? Is Michael in trouble?

I'd imagine that every reader in the country knows John Irving, whose novels all hit the best-seller lists. He's a consummate storyteller, as evidenced by the opening of *A Widow for One Year.*

> One night when she was four and sleeping in the bottom bunk of her bunk bed, Ruth Cole woke to the sound of lovemaking—it was coming from her parents' bedroom. It was a totally unfamiliar sound to her. Ruth had recently been ill with a stomach flu; when she first heard her mother making love, Ruth thought that her mother was throwing up.
>
> It was not as simple a matter as her parents having separate bedrooms; that summer they had separate houses, although Ruth never saw the other house. Her parents spent alternate nights in the family house with Ruth; there was a rental house nearby, where Ruth's mother or father stayed when they weren't staying with Ruth. It was one of those ridiculous arrangements that couples make when they are separating, but before they are divorced—when they still imagine that children and property can be shared with more magnanimity than recrimination.
>
> When Ruth woke to the foreign sound, she at first wasn't sure if it was her mother or her father who was throwing up; then, despite the unfamiliarity of the disturbance, Ruth recognized that measure of melancholy and contained hysteria which was often detectable in her mother's voice. Ruth also remembered that it was her mother's turn to stay with her.
>
> The master bathroom separated Ruth's room from the master bedroom. When the four-year-old padded barefoot through the bathroom, she took a towel with her. (When she'd been sick with the stomach flu, her father had encouraged her to vomit in a towel.) Poor Mommy! Ruth thought, bringing her the towel.
>
> In the dim moonlight, and in the even dimmer and erratic light from the night-light that Ruth's father had installed in the

bathroom, Ruth saw the pale faces of her dead brothers in the photographs on the bathroom wall. There were photos of her dead brothers throughout the house, on all the walls. . . .

Consider all that Irving accomplishes in this excerpt: the sight of Ruth bringing a towel to Mommy—and we, as adults, know what she's going to see when she gets to the bedroom, though we're concentrating so much on the image of the child that we may have put the cause of the noise to the side. Then we get the dead brothers, the house as an altar to them: Something here might not be quite right.

Roland Merullo's *Revere Beach Boulevard* is not as well known as any of the other examples we've looked at, not that it matters.

It was a Revere night, the night the life I been holding together all these years started pulling apart. A nice Revere night near the end of August, with salt in the air and garden smells floating over to us where we sat, and the sky above Proctor Avenue lit up with a light that was like paradise breaking open and pouring down all over you.

Before the phone call came that would take my life and turn her inside out like the sleeve on a jacket, I was sitting in the yard with the woman I been husband and wife with forty-nine years, the woman who was the other half of my body. We were waiting for the moon to come up over Patsy Antonelli's roof. Big, she would be coming up. You could tell by the light between the houses that she would be coming up big on that night, the full circle of her, the full, perfect face.

"Do you have any pain, Lucy?" I asked my wife.

And she said, "No," quiet, in a voice that meant Don't keep asking, Vito. So I didn't.

What's been accomplished here? A dialect has been established; we get the sense of an Italian neighborhood (Vito, Patsy Antonelli). We know something tragic is going to happen, but is it Lucy who's in pain or someone else—something in the phone call? (Remember Bradley's call?)

But the thing I want you to notice particularly is the last sentence of the second paragraph, those last words: ". . . the full circle of her, the full, perfect face." And then: "Do you have any pain, Lucy?" The connection Merullo draws between the perfect beauty of the moon and Vito's feelings about his wife are subtle, a resonance that the reader isn't going to think about, but will sense and take with her as she discovers what it is that turns Vito's life "inside out like the sleeve on a jacket."

How many words are you using, and what are you accomplishing with them? Keeping in mind the idea that everything in your fiction should serve multiple purposes, look again at what you've written, consider how long it's taking you to make your points and then begin thinking of how you will tighten for effect and impact.

CHAPTER 10

Editing the Basic Elements: Three Case Studies

Revision Case Study #1

This is the first page of a manuscript submitted for consideration (as with other examples that will follow, the author is aware of the fact that the material is being used here).

Revision Case Study #1—first draft

The sun's rays already baked the stones that marked the path to Golgotha. The man from Cyrene watched as the parade came nearer. He loved parades. The crowds pushing, cheering, laughing; they told him there would be some of the best in Jerusalem, but, so far, this was the first he had seen. He held up his hand to shade his eyes from the bright sunshine. Would there be wild animals? No. There was a man and a bunch of Roman soldiers. They were whipping him. Several women followed behind him. They were crying. What kind of parade was this?

continued on next page

"Who is that man?" Simon asked the people standing next to him.

"That is the famous prophet, Jesus of Nazareth," came the answer.

"What are they doing to him? Why is he carrying that heavy tree?"

"He has been sentenced to death. He has to carry his cross to the place of execution."

"Oh," Simon answered. Why was this prophet being executed? Who were those women? A million questions flooded into his brain as they came nearer. They had put a purple robe on him and a crown of thorns on his head. The man looked exhausted. It was uphill all the way, and the cross was obviously too heavy for him. He stumbled under its weight twice before he got to the place where Simon was standing. The second time Jesus got up, he turned and spoke to the grieving women behind him. Simon was close enough to hear his words:

"Do not grieve for me, daughters of Jerusalem, but for yourselves."

"We'll never get there, at this rate," one of the soldiers grumbled. "He's stalling for time."

"We already lost time with all the politics between Pilate and Herod. We need to speed things up a bit," said another. He scanned the crowd and his eye fell upon Simon.

"Here, young man," he said. "Would you mind helping out with the heavy lifting?"

Simon stepped out into the street and picked up the cross. As he carried it, he heard hisses and catcalls from the crowd. This was civilization? How did these Romans have the nerve to call people from his country barbarians when they, themselves behaved in such a shameful manner? No one from his village would treat even a criminal like this. By the time they reached Golgotha, he was resolved never to visit Jerusalem again. ◆

The first question, for me, is, What's the purpose of this story? As a reader coming to it cold—as an editor does—I see a retelling of a story most of us in the West know well and assume that the novel is about Simon the Cyrenian: This is going to be his perspective on the events, Simon's story. If that's the case, the first question we have to consider is whether he calls out to us: Is there anything here to make us care about him, beyond what we know of the period through conventional knowledge? (The question of marketability is not going to be considered; whatever is of interest to a writer should be explored. I'm also not going to waste time correcting spelling, punctuation or typos.)

Let's consider the page (about 400 words) in sections.

> The sun's rays already baked the stones that marked the path to Golgotha.

In the course of the narrative, we learn that Simon has no idea of what's going on; would he then know that these stones lead to Golgotha? (We know from the Gospels that Simon has just arrived from the country—Africa—and his other comments here mark him as a stranger.) That being the case, does the word belong in the sentence?

Think about the descriptive words: "The sun's rays already baked the stones. . . ." Does that mean it's hot or that it's late in the day? If the heat and conditions are important in some way (or is it enough to know, later, that Simon has to shade his eyes from the bright sunshine?), would the author here serve the narrative, and thus the reader, better by being more descriptive? The potential is there to give a sense of place. What are the streets like? Offering the smells, the feeling of the noise, dust, heat will place the reader in the scene. As it is (and it may be valid, but not for me), we are left with having to draw completely from our own experience, as lived through movies, to "see" the events. The author has lost control of the audience: We are in our individual places, not the writer's.

> The man from Cyrene watched as the parade came nearer. He
> loved parades. The crowds pushing, cheering, laughing; they told
> him there would be some of the best in Jerusalem, but, so far, this
> was the first he had seen.

Seeing the word "parade" stopped me for a moment; it's an anachronism, I knew that, then I looked it up. The first recorded use of this
word, from the French, in this sense, is in the seventeenth century (c.
1673–74). There was no Latin equivalent; the event doesn't seem to
have existed (though a case might be made for "circus"). That being
the case, what was Simon looking for in Jerusalem when he was told
some of the best would be there? Were there celebrations of the nature
that we understand as a parade; is the word appropriately used, a contemporary, vulgate translation of an ancient event?

The third sentence presents more difficulties: The crowds are presented to us first and then, linked by a semicolon, "they told him there
would be some of the best in Jerusalem." Is the crowd pushing, cheering, laughing that tells him that? Do those three gerunds describe the
people surrounding Simon, or are they his thoughts about what a parade crowd is like? Who are "they" who are informing him?

And the last clause: "so far, this was the first he had seen." How
long has he been in the city? We don't know.

> He held up his hand to shade his eyes from the bright sunshine.
> Would there be wild animals? No. There was a man and a bunch
> of Roman soldiers. They were whipping him. Several women fol-
> lowed behind him. They were crying. What kind of parade was
> this?

This begs the question: Were wild animals regularly exhibited
through the streets of this city, even under Roman occupation?

What is a bunch of Roman soldiers? Why use that unspecific word?
Here is a stranger, looking for something in particular; instead, he's
watching a man being whipped. And, accepting that Simon would be

so caught up that he wasn't counting, why use "bunch" rather than "group"? Is it to give the sense of disorder about the legionaries? Do we have any reason to believe that those troops were disorganized and undisciplined at that point?

With all that is being observed, is it reasonable that Simon—from whose perspective we're seeing this unfold, remember—would see a man and a bunch of soldiers whipping him and the crying women, and not remark immediately on the cross and crown of thorns?

> "Who is that man?" Simon asked the people standing next to him.
>
> "That is the famous prophet, Jesus of Nazareth," came the answer.
>
> "What are they doing to him? Why is he carrying that heavy tree?"
>
> "He has been sentenced to death. He has to carry his cross to the place of execution."
>
> "Oh," Simon answered. Why was this prophet being executed? Who were those women? A million questions flooded into his brain as they came nearer.

What are the people next to Simon doing? Are they part of a laughing, cheering, crowd? Silent watchers? Are they crying, too? Do you, as the reader, care? (As a writer, you're the first reader.)

"Came the answer." That's an awkward locution. Is any tag necessary there? Wouldn't it be better to write, "someone said"?

Given the nature of crowds, and of the event, do you think there would be short answers of that sort? Isn't it more reasonable to think that the answer would be more inclusive, that Simon wouldn't have to ask what was being done? And as long as he's been in Jerusalem as indicated in the previous paragraph, do we think Simon might have heard about the trial and execution? It's something that would have been talked about in the taverns and inns, in the streets. Do you think that Simon might know about the Roman methods of execution and recognize what's happening?

Consider this as well: That crowd would not have called the man Jesus; that's the Greek translation, and it came later. His name was Jeshua ben Joseph—the writers of the Gospels would not have known him as Jesus. Now, that leaves the writer with an interesting problem: historical accuracy or easy understanding? I'd choose the former; after all, as the scene is played out, any reader will make the connection. Does it matter, finally? Not really; by convention, after all, we know him by that name and most novels would use the Greek. As a writer, I wouldn't; as an editor, I'd discuss it with the author.

"A million questions" (rather than "a bunch"—a million is rather specific, not to mention hyperbolic), but we don't get to share those questions. Is the phrase necessary?

> They had put a purple robe on him and a crown of thorns on his head. The man looked exhausted. It was uphill all the way, and the cross was obviously too heavy for him. He stumbled under its weight, twice before he got to the place where Simon was standing. The second time Jesus got up, he turned spoke to the grieving women behind him. Simon was close enough to hear his words:
>
> "Do not grieve for me, daughters of Jerusalem, but for yourselves."

How does Simon know that "they" put a purple robe on him? Wouldn't it make more sense to say, instead, "He wore a purple robe and a crown of thorns"?

The next two sentences fall into the "duh" category, don't they? While the man undoubtedly looked exhausted, I'd suggest to the writer that we get a bit more descriptive: Is the man bleeding? Are there tears? Is the word "looked" important, or does the sentence work without it? Does the exhaustion even have to be mentioned as a separate statement?

Study the order in which we're getting the information in this paragraph:

> "Oh," Simon answered. Why was this prophet being executed? Who were those women? A million questions flooded into his brain as they came nearer. They had put a purple robe on him and a crown of thorns on his head. The man looked exhausted. It was uphill, all the way and the cross was obviously too heavy for him. He stumbled under its weight, twice before he got to the place where Simon was standing. The second time Jesus got up, he turned spoke to the grieving women behind him. Simon was close enough to hear his words:
>
> "Do not grieve for me, daughters of Jerusalem, but for yourselves."

First fix: Begin another paragraph with "They had put . . ."

Then, reorder the information so that what's most important comes first: The robe and crown don't matter here; indeed, they would be more appropriate in the preceding paragraphs, as Simon is seeing Jesus for the first time, seeing the Romans whip him. The crucial point here, far more urgent in terms of story than the "millions" of questions, is that this paragraph leads to Simon being forced to help carry the cross: exhaustion, pain, struggle and Simon's reaction to those things.

The quote from Jesus is also important, but Simon doesn't question the meaning of the words. So, now, near the end, would be the time for the Cyrenian to have his questions about the women and about what Jesus is saying. Instead, the author shifts.

> "We'll never get there, at this rate," one of the soldiers grumbled. "He's stalling for time."
>
> "We already lost time with all the politics between Pilate and Herod. We need to speed things up a bit," said another. He scanned the crowd and his eye fell upon Simon.

"Here, young man," he said. "Would you mind helping out with the heavy lifting?"

No question in my mind that soldiers grumble and complain, but I don't believe that they'd comment on the politics; in a sense, that's a way of adding some back story, but in this case, it's redundant. If the novel will deal with those aspects of the crucifixion, it's better to save it; otherwise, it should serve to cause more questions for our protagonist. Who are the people the soldiers are talking about? What politics are involved? Simon is, as he's been presented to us, totally unaware of what's going on.

And then: a polite request from the soldier (men not known for being polite in terms of conquered peoples) that Simon help with the heavy lifting. A little revisionism isn't bad in a historical novel, but according to the eyewitness sources, Simon was forced to help. In any event, without a second thought, the author continues.

> Simon stepped out into the street and picked up the cross. As he carried it, he heard hisses and catcalls from the crowd. This was civilization? How did these Romans have the nerve to call people from his country barbarians when they, themselves behaved in such a shameful manner? No one from his village would treat even a criminal like this. By the time they reached Golgotha, he was resolved never to visit Jerusalem again.

Does he struggle with the cross? How far does he have to carry it? Would his question, now, be about whether this is civilization or not?

". . . he heard hisses and catcalls from the crowd. . . . How did these Romans have the nerve to call people from his country barbarians when they, themselves behaved in such a shameful manner?" Are the watchers civilized? That's the question a contemporary reader brings to the statement. However, "barbarian" is from the Greek and was used at that time to mean someone whose language and culture was different than the speaker's. Since conquering people all thought their civilization was better, our definition finally became usage. So, this is another anachronism.

It, and the use of "parade," can be gotten around easily; in the instance of "barbarian," changing that word to "uncivilized" or "savages" would be sufficient.

If the author were sitting with us, I know from bitter experience that arguments would be presented, ranging from, "It's my interpretation," to, "I'm trying to make the language contemporary." But you are not with me when I'm sitting at my desk reading the manuscript. You're not with the readers when they consider buying your book. All any of us have are the words on the page, and we'll consider language later.

Okay, based on my complaints, how would you rewrite the scene? I'll show you my take on it now; what you have to remember is that the choices of language (that word again) are based on my style and approach to writing. Yours will undoubtedly be different (yours *had better* be different). What is of concern is whether the new version has more appeal.

Revision Case Study #1—revised

Simon felt the sweat begin to soak through his robe; Jerusalem was as hot as Cyrene, and the crowds battering him as they pushed for a better view of whatever it was that was going on didn't help matters any.

They'd told him before he left that this was a city filled with fine demonstrations, that the streets were always filled with people going somewhere, watching something, but this demonstration . . . this was like nothing he'd seen before.

He held up his hand to shield his eyes from the bright afternoon sun, but the glare shining back from the stone street and the clean, white buildings lining the roadway made it an almost useless gesture. He wiped the sweat from his eyes, trying to maintain his balance as the screaming mass around him, some crying, some jeering, shoved forward

continued on next page

to see more. Someone tried to reach around him, move him out of the way so he could get closer to the approaching procession. Simon pushed back, but whoever was trying to displace him just slipped past him, screaming unintelligible words.

"What's going on?" he asked of no one in particular, not sure that his words were even heard. As he spoke, four Roman soldiers muscled their way toward him, clearing a path for a thin man struggling under the weight of a large, wooden cross. That answered part of his question: Rome's habit of crucifying its enemies was known even in his hometown.

"They're murdering the messiah," someone near him said. Simon looked at the man and then back at the ragged person falling beneath his heavy load. He was wearing a diadem of some sort, a twisted ring of thorns that had scratched cuts into his forehead, and blood was running into his eyes. He stumbled and fell and one of the women following behind reached out, crying.

"Do not grieve for me, daughters of Jerusalem, but for yourselves." Simon understood the words, but not what they meant. There was no misunderstanding the grumbling from the legionaries. They looked around, and it was clear that they were worried; no telling what would happen in a rabble like this.

"Ha!" a woman behind the Cyrenian shouted. "C'mon, fool. You've come to save us and you can't even help yourself, fool." She tapped Simon on the shoulder. "That's the rabbi from Nazareth, the one who calls himself our king, our messiah. They're taking him to Golgotha, to execute him." The woman who answered spit, and Simon felt the spray splatter on his hands. He tried to step away and, unbalanced, was pushed into the path of the soldiers.

That's when Simon knew that coming to Jerusalem wasn't the best idea he'd ever had.

"You," one of the soldiers shouted, grabbing him. "Help the King of the Jews carry his scepter. Hurry." He pushed Simon toward

continued on next page

the prisoner, who looked up at him and smiled gently.

Simon lifted the cross and began to trudge toward the place of skulls, his mind filling with questions that he couldn't hope to answer. No help came from the crowd, just jeers and catcalls. ◆

This approach is a little longer but, for me, is more vivid, involves the reader more. It maintains the author's intent of a contemporary voice but avoids anachronisms. If you don't feel like rewriting the scene yourself, play with this version. Can it be improved?

Revision Case Study #2

Here's another example, from a novel in progress titled *The Accuser*. It's a straightforward genre piece:

The limo screeched to a halt at the side entrance of the court house. A man surrounded by police ran towards it. They had only seconds before the reporters would be on them. The door flung open and Dennis ducked into the back, slamming the door behind him. As he peered out the smoke glass windows a sick smile spread across his face. "He'd done it!", he thought, "Gotten away with murder." There were a few tough moments during the trial but in the end when the verdict was read he knew he was the victor.

He shrugged out of his coat, loosened his tie and let his body relax into the soft, black leather seat. Closing his eyes he thought back over the past few years. He had known Tina since college. At 6'5, he was the best rebounder the college ever had and Tina at 5'2 was a women [sic] to be reckoned with. He had known he wanted her from the moment he had laid eyes on her. She'd played hard to get for a while, but he

continued on next page

knew it was only a game. That's what women did . . . played games. She soon gave in and they became the college odd couple. Their friends called them Davy and Goliath, laughingly warning him not to be taken down by her. Well, this time, Goliath had won. Tina wouldn't be playing any more games.

Dennis wasn't sure when things had started to go bad for them. When he'd made the pros everything seemed to be going his way. He knew Tina wanted children. That's why he'd put off marrying her. He knew once he did he'd be saddled down with one kid after another. Hadn't she realized he wasn't ready for that big a responsibility? Here he was in the prime of his life, making incredible money, women making him offers in every town. He'd had a right to a little fun first. Besides, what Tina didn't know didn't hurt her . . . but she had known.

Just remembering the hurt and shock he'd felt walking in to find her things gone from the house they'd shared made his hands sweat. She had returned all his gifts and flowers but not his phone calls. He'd followed her day after day, missing important practices with the team. People started to take notice. It was then that he'd learned to put a pleasant mask on his face while inside he seethed with anger.

He hadn't actually planned on killing her; He'd thought that if he scared her bad enough . . . what, that she'd come back to him? Now he realized how stupid that was. But that's how crazy she'd made him. He'd covered his tracks well. He knew people would suspect him, but he hadn't left enough evidence for them to prove anything.

Dennis exhaled slowly, leaning forward he pushed the button on the liqueur console. As the bar slid forward a picture fell to the floor. As Dennis reached to pick up the picture, his fingers started to feel numb. Staring back at him was a picture of Tina. It looked like it must have been taken at the crime scene. The numbness spread to his arm. He turned the picture over, and there written in the beautiful calligraphy that Tina always used was one word, "Why?" Dennis couldn't breathe. The numbness had spread over his entire body.

continued on next page

The limo slid to a stop, the door opened and Dennis could hear Marcus' deep voice before he could see him. "It's over Dennis . . . thank God it's over." He smiled at Dennis as he leaned into the car. "What's wrong?" Marcus asked as he caught sight of Dennis' face. Seeing the picture, he took it from Dennis' hand. "My gosh," he exclaimed, "Where did you get this?" Dennis could only shake his head. His eyes seeing things that had happened months before. Things only he knew of. "Get out of the car," Marcus demanded. The sharpness of his voice brought Dennis back to the present. He got Dennis into the house and poured him some coffee. The feeling started to come back into his arms and hands. As usual Marcus was there.

Dennis woke up Monday morning with anticipation. He couldn't wait to get back to the gym. He'd missed playing. It looked like the team would be in the playoffs. One game to go. He showered and dressed quickly, and grabbing a bagel made his way to the garage. It felt good to have his life back. He had decided to drive himself today. A high profile trial didn't leave much time for solitude. As the garage door slid open, Dennis quickly backed down the drive and through the gates. He slammed on brakes as a car pulled across his path. Suddenly people were everywhere. A loud thump could be heard as a soda can hit the roof and rolled off. A sign was shoved across his window. "Murderer" written in large letters. Several people were aiming cameras, others just shouting. Dennis didn't know what to do, people were in front of the car, behind the car, he couldn't tell how many. He put the car in drive and inched forward slowly. If he could just make it back through the gates. Another thump was heard on the roof, he couldn't tell what it was. He started beeping the horn, finally he made it through the gate. As it started to close people were still shouting and throwing things. Some just pushed through following him up the drive. He pulled into the garage, allowing the door to shut behind him. Dennis turned the car off and just sat. He felt trapped. As the shock wore off he became

continued on next page

angry. Slamming the door of the car he went into the house. He called Jay, his driver, and told him to pick him up, then he called Marcus.

By the time Jay pulled out of the driveway, the police had pushed the people back from the gates. "They'll forget about you soon enough," Marcus said. Dennis sat staring out of the window. When they pulled up outside the gym the situation was the same, except this time Marcus had called ahead. The police kept everyone away from the entrance so the limo could get by.

As Dennis entered the locker room he could hear the guys shouting things to each other. The voices ceased as the first one, then another caught sight of him. "Hey Dennis, welcome back," Jimmy, their forward said. As ice starts to crack, slowly first then gaining momentum, the others spoke. Dennis wasn't sure which bothered him most, the ones who looked at him with outright suspicion, or those that wouldn't look at him at all.

Dennis suited up and made his way to the court. Coach Lenox shook his hand, and brought him up to speed on the plays. The tension was noticeable as the guys started warming up, but soon Dennis forgot as they got into the plays. Everything else faded away as they all concentrated on perfecting their jump shots, picks, and worked on defense.

Jimmy caught up with Dennis as they headed back to the locker room. "It's going to take the guys awhile. If you want someone to talk to, just give me a call." He clapped Dennis on the shoulder as he walked on ahead. Dennis stared after him.

Marcus and Jay were waiting when Dennis emerged from the gym. He quickly got in the limo. "Are you stopping somewhere for lunch?" Jay asked. "No, just go home." The crowd was still outside his home when they arrived. Dennis stared straight ahead. "Maybe this was the same as prison." he thought. "Trapped in your home, your car, not even being able to go out in public." ◆

The first question, a cold, cruel one: How many of the 1,400 words offered did you read before you cut to here, figuring that you didn't need to read much more to know that the author was in deep trouble? Did you even finish the first three paragraphs (350 words)? How is an editor going to react?

Let's take it paragraph by paragraph.

> The limo screeched to a halt at the side entrance of the court house. A man surrounded by police ran towards it. They had only seconds before the reporters would be on them. The door flung open and Dennis ducked into the back, slamming the door behind him. As he peered out the smoke glass windows a sick smile spread across his face. "He'd done it!" he thought, "Gotten away with murder." There were a few tough moments during the trial but in the end when the verdict was read he knew he was the victor.

First, the sentences in quotation marks. Strictly a format issue, but thoughts are not placed in quotes. That's going to stick out as the editor reads the page, and he's going to be warned immediately that the author isn't aware of the basics.

What is the author trying to accomplish with this paragraph? Tension—someone trying to get away. Presentation to the reader of a bad guy, obviously—he's gloating about getting away with murder.

By the time we've finished the scenes (we're being offered several in this opening sequence), we know the murderer is a star athlete. Would he be running for the car alone, or would he have an entourage? Would the limo come screeching up, or already be in place? Based on your answers to those questions, you can start the rewrite.

The limo's door is flung open. Are we ever aware of anyone else in the car (though there must be a driver)? Dennis gets in the back, but it would be impossible for the driver to fling that door open. We have to add someone, have one of the police officers open the door, or have Dennis do it.

"A sick smile." Is that an editorial comment, in that the smile is perverse? Or an indication that even though Dennis has won, he feels sick about it? What is a sick smile? So, the last four lines, rewritten:

> He'd done it. He smiled through the smoked glass at the receding crowd. He'd won; that's all that counted.

Those lines were easy. Now, let's get Dennis into the car. What do we know? He's a basketball star who just got off on a murder rap (think O.J. Simpson, whether that was the author's intent or not; anyone looking at the manuscript is going to consider it that way). That means he's got an entourage with him; he's not going to be running to the car alone. So, the car's there, waiting; there's at least one or two people—his attorneys, friends—either with him or already in the car. It's not only reporters who're waiting to catch up with him: fans, supporters, detractors (maybe members of Tina's family?) will be there, too. In a sense, the crowd scene parallels the one we examined previously: a rabble mixing cheers and jeers. Dennis is going to have to run that gauntlet.

It would help if we knew where the story was set; in the material we have there's no indication at all. But if it were New York or Los Angeles, depending on the courthouse, there might very well be underground parking, which will change the nature of the action: Rather than the man running, we'd be dealing with a car trying to maneuver through a mass of people. Since we don't know, we're going to have to work with the information at hand. It would also help to know Dennis's last name. For our needs, right now, it's Macintosh.

> Dennis Macintosh stared through the small window in the courthouse door at the crowd milling in the street. Running toward the basket through the Knicks was one thing; this . . . He turned to his attorney; Cortland had gotten him through the trial, now he counted on him to get him to the waiting limo, to his home and peace and quiet.

"No sweat, Denny. The cops'll clear a path for you. Remember, don't stop for anyone or anything, don't say a word . . . just run for the car."

Macintosh nodded. "Whatever. I just wanna get outta here, man." He smiled, something he hadn't done for the last few weeks, not since the trial began and everyone seemed to turn against him. What did they know? Nuthin'.

"Ready?" Detective Bill Smith, the cop who'd busted him, who tried to take his life away, probably because he was jealous, like everyone else, put one hand on the door's pushbar and the other in the middle of Dennis's back. "On three."

Macintosh took a deep breath and nodded, wondering if Smith was going to try to push him down the stairs. Wouldn't surprise him at all. The door swung open, he felt a light touch on his shoulder, and it was fast break time, all alone, heading for the layup. The limo's door was open; he could see a shadow in the backseat. He ran, hearing the noise, a wall of sound like the one that went up when he took the rebound that took them to the NBA finals.

"Murderer." "Asshole." "Way to go, man." "It ain't over yet." Words . . . someone swung a sign on a stick toward him and he ducked, a reflex, no way it was gonna hit him. Reflexes—name of the game. He slid into the back of the limo, Cortland right behind him, and heard the door slam shut, blocking the noise. What did any of them know? Nuthin'.

He'd done it. He smiled through the smoked glass at the crowd, flinching when someone threw something that crashed against the rear window. Let 'em scream. He'd won; that's all that counted.

Do we want to know, that soon, that this guy's gotten away with murder, or is it better to tease the reader? What did he win? How? That's part of the story; the rest, probably, is his comeuppance.

Our version takes care of most of the flashback that follows: His attitudes, everything the author wants us to know, except the relationship with Tina, is there, integrated into action.

That should also be the end of chapter one; the flashback material that follows should be cut. For the exercise, however, we'll study it before making it go away.

> He shrugged out of his coat, loosened his tie and let his body relax into the soft, black leather seat. Closing his eyes he thought back over the past few years. He had known Tina since college. At 6'5, he was the best rebounder the college ever had and Tina at 5'2 was a women [sic] to be reckoned with. He had known he wanted her from the moment he had laid eyes on her. She'd played hard to get for a while, but he knew it was only a game. That's what women did . . . played games. She soon gave in and they became the college odd couple. Their friends called them Davy and Goliath, laughingly warning him not to be taken down by her. Well, this time, Goliath had won. Tina wouldn't be playing any more games.

Ignoring things like spelling and punctuation, the most important thing—for me, at any rate—in this paragraph is the information that women played games. So, in addition to wanting Dennis to lose because he's just gotten away with murder, we also have the natural distaste for a misogynist. He's ugly, okay, but do we hate him enough to want to read a book about his downfall?

That's emphasized in the last sentence: "Tina wouldn't be playing any more games." Fine, but how many more times are we going to be told that she's dead and that he's responsible?

> Dennis wasn't sure when things had started to go bad for them. When he'd made the pros everything seemed to be going his way. He knew Tina wanted children. That's why he'd put off marrying her. He knew once he did he'd be saddled down with one kid after another. Hadn't she realized he wasn't ready for that big a

responsibility? Here he was in the prime of his life, making incredible money, women making him offers in every town. He'd had a right to a little fun first. Besides, what Tina didn't know didn't hurt her . . . but she had known.

The story isn't going forward; because this is all interior, we're being told everything and shown nothing but Dennis's ugliness—something we've learned . . . and accepted.

Just remembering the hurt and shock he'd felt walking in to find her things gone from the house they'd shared, made his hands sweat. She had returned all his gifts and flowers but not his phone calls. He'd followed her day after day, missing important practices with the team. People started to take notice. It was then that he'd learned to put a pleasant mask on his face while inside he seethed with anger.

He hadn't actually planned on killing her; He'd thought that if he scared her bad enough . . . what, that she'd come back to him? Now he realized how stupid that was. but that's how crazy she'd made him. He'd covered his tracks well. He knew people would suspect him, but he hadn't left enough evidence for them to prove anything.

The flashback ends here. The important information for the reader is that Tina left him because she knew he was not quite the person she wanted to spend her life with and that he killed her, accidentally in his mind, but then had the presence of mind to clean up after himself. The four paragraphs can be reduced to one if we want to save the information:

He shrugged out of his coat, loosened his tie and relaxed for the first time in months. [I'd be specific if I had any idea of what the timing is.] He was a star, always had been, ever since college, when he'd met Tina: the basketball whiz and the beautiful cheerleader. It was all so perfect. Was it his fault that he'd wanted to live a little before they had kids? Was it his fault all those women were throwing themselves at him? Why'd she have to ruin it all by walking out? He hadn't wanted it to work out this way; she wasn't supposed to have died, but that wasn't his fault, either. But now it was over, all over, and he could get on with the business at hand: winning the championship.

All the details of the relationship can and should be brought out later, not as narrative but as scenes in which we participate, if they're important enough. As it is, our paragraph tells the reader enough about Dennis's attitude. That accomplished, the story picks up again.

Dennis exhaled slowly, leaning forward he pushed the button on the liqueur console. As the bar slid forward a picture fell to the floor. As Dennis reached to pickup the picture, is fingers started to feel numb. Staring back at him was a picture of Tina. It looked like it must have been taken at the crime scene. The numbness spread to his arm. He turned the picture over, and there written in the beautiful calligraphy that Tina always used was one word, "Why?" Dennis couldn't breathe. The numbness had spread over his entire body.

Now something is beginning to happen: forward momentum is being created, and there's a surprise for the reader: We've gone from what has been a straightforward crime novel to something else. Maybe. Is the appearance of the photograph a supernatural phenomenon, or was it planted by someone? The comment about the handwriting would indicate the former, but anything is possible. Because we've added some hangers-on, other things will now have to be added: conversation in the car and everyone's reactions to the photograph. By adding that material, we've also added suspects: Any of the folks in the limo (including the driver) might have planted the picture. Or not.

The limo slid to a stop, the door opened and Dennis could hear Marcus' deep voice before he could see him. "It's over Dennis . . . thank God it's over." He smiled at Dennis as he leaned into the car. "What's wrong?" Marcus asked as he caught sight of Dennis' face. Seeing the picture, he took it from Dennis' hand. "My gosh," he exclaimed, "Where did you get this?" Dennis could only shake his head. His eyes seeing things that had happened months before. Things only he knew of. "Get out of the car," Marcus demanded. The sharpness of his voice brought Dennis back to the present. He got Dennis into the house and poured him some coffee. The feeling started to come back into his arms and hands. As usual Marcus was there.

This paragraph is reproduced for one reason: the opportunity for you to rewrite it, regardless of context. First question: Is this one paragraph, or several? Where would you break it? And what words would you change? Do you think, even without knowing Marcus, that he would exclaim, "My gosh"? If we say "Marcus demanded," is it necessary to say "The sharpness of his voice"? Knowing Dennis as we do—remember, he was going to pour a drink when he found the photo—would Marcus serve him coffee . . . or a stiff bourbon?

No question about one thing: Marcus is a sycophant. What else do we know about him? I'd like to know who he is, what his relationship to Dennis is. As we reveal this, keep in mind that the bit would have to be changed completely because of the changes that precede it.

The door seemed to open even before the limo came to a stop, and Dennis heard Marcus's deep voice breaking through the fog he'd been in since picking up the photograph.

"What?" Dennis looked up at his old friend's face. Marcus. Been with him since the beginning, always there.

"I said, thank God it's over, Dennis." His smile disappeared. "What's wrong, man?"

Dennis held the photograph out to him.

"Jesus, where did this come from?" Marcus took it, staring at the word. "C'mon, get out of the car." He reached in to help Dennis out, feeling the cold fingers lifeless against his hand. "Let's get into the house. I'll pour you a drink." He shoved the photograph into his back pocket with his right hand, his left reaching around and supporting Dennis, leading him up the steps to the front door.

That's the end of the first scene, of what would be chapter one. Looking at the rest of the chapter as it exists, we see that it's now Monday. Fine, except we don't know what day it was when the trial ended. We don't know what's happened since Dennis got home. But there are some very reasonable questions to be asked: Were there no demonstrations outside the house, since there is a crowd on Monday morning? Did Marcus and Dennis (or Dennis and the others we've put in the car) talk about that picture? You bet they did—and it allows the author to present the information about the relationship between Tina and Dennis.

A more serious difficulty: Is it reasonable to expect Dennis to just show up at practice and be ready to play? How long's the trial gone on? A murder trial of this nature, based only on the information we have, might have lasted months.

Would all the players have welcomed him back that quickly, that easily? Would Jimmy (yet another character without a last name) just say "welcome back"; is that the language you expect to hear in a professional locker room?

What team is this? Who are they playing in the championships?

Is any of the material that follows Dennis's arrival home of any importance? The public reaction is, and the last paragraph, with the protagonist's thoughts about the prison created by his celebrity, is. The rest is a sentence or two.

There's more quarrying to be done here; no story exists yet, just an idea.

A last first chapter to look at, chosen at random from the stack on my desk. And, as was the case with the earlier ones, the author is taking far too long to hit stride. It pays to emphasize that that doesn't mean action—Dennis's scenes began with action, and the biblical story had action as well. It means engaging the interest of a general reader: While we all acknowledge that books are marketed to niche audiences, the author who is going to be successful, who has potential to make it to the best-seller lists, is going to have to appeal to more readers. The examples we looked at from the published novels share that broad-based interest.

Revision Case Study #3

Here's part of a mainstream novel; it might be a romance, in the broadest sense, or a psychological study—it could even be a mystery novel. And that's the beauty of general fiction: it doesn't have to be anything but a story that someone cares about.

Revision Case Study #3—first draft

> When he went from being the next Sandy Koufax to just another hard luck story, his friends warned him that self-pity is the world's second favorite indoor sport. He likes it here, with the sweet scent of freshly mowed grass filling the air and the empty bleachers leering at him from the sidelines. He rubs up the cover of an imaginary baseball, scuffs the tightly packed dirt of the pitcher's mound with the toe of his sneaker, and glares at the batter's box. At the Enemy. At the One who never answered his prayers, his desperate pleas for just one more chance.
>
> Now pitching for the New York Yankees . . . number twenty-seven . . . Ken Steinberg. . . .
>
> So close. He came so close.
>
> He starts his windup. The familiar pain comes again, knifing through his elbow, tearing into his heart, permeating every aspect of his being. He sighs and stops in mid-delivery. You win again. You always

continued on next page

win, damn You.

To the parents and spectators who've begun filing into the stands, it's a lovely day for baseball, a brisk spring afternoon. Ken's eyes only see what might have been. He almost made it to Yankee Stadium, almost made the marriage with Carol work.

Almost.

He imagines her sitting there in the bleachers, blonde and petite, drawing admiring looks from the other men. Waiting for him to come back into her life, back into her warm, inviting body.

Yeah, right.

There's a woman sitting in the front row behind first base. But she has dark brown hair swirling gently around her shoulders, a figure that's pleasingly feminine but bordering on zaftig. He takes a closer look, and a decade vanishes as if by magic. The next thing he knows, he's standing in front of her.

"Hi, Jane," he says.

There's an awkward silence. Then her cool, appraising glance gives way to the smile he remembers so well. "Ken. It's been so long. What have you been doing with yourself?"

"Well. I'm on my own again. Got divorced last October." He always could talk to her about anything, everything. With Carol, shared feelings were a foreign country to which neither of them had an entry visa. He sighs. "Marriage is supposed to be forever. Mine lasted a year and a half."

"I'm sorry. I thought you'd be with the Yankees by now."

"So did I. Tore up my arm trying to break off a curve ball."

Her brown eyes are warm, sympathetic. "You must miss it."

Yeah, he misses it. The euphoric rush when he struck out the other team's best hitter, the roar of the crowd, the high fives from his teammates. He'd been a can't miss major league prospect with a hundred-mile-an-hour fast ball and a multimillion-dollar future, until that one moment of lousy luck. "So now I teach psych courses at our local community college."

continued on next page

There's another troublesome silence. Then: "Jane . . . I never meant to hurt you."

She touches his hand gently. "I know. You wanted something I could never give you."

He looks at the kids on the baseball field. He wants one of his own; he always has; he always will. When Jane finally told him she couldn't become pregnant, he had no choice. So why did he keep thinking about her long after he'd called it off? "What brings you here?"

"Someone I have to see."

Her cotton navy suit is somewhat out of place at a municipal athletic field, and there's no wedding ring on her left hand. He should have known. "You have a date."

"Not a date. Business."

Business. What a nice word. He's about to ask what her business is when there's a tug on his arm. It's a wiry fifteen-year-old wearing a jersey with the name Eagles on the front. It's Billy Spencer, Ken's star shortstop.

"Hey, coach. Everyone's here. Let's get going."

The game. How could he have forgotten about the game?

Jane smiles. "Go coach your team. We can talk later."

No guilt trips, no accusations. "It's great to see you," he says, and he's genuinely surprised by how much he means this. Spencer tugs at his arm once more, and the two of them jog back to the field.

Ken's usual intense concentration takes a leave of absence during the game, but it doesn't matter; the Eagles don't need his help today. In the fifth inning Spencer lines a routine single to left, rounds first base without a moment's hesitation, and stretches it into a double with a slide that knocks the opposing second baseman halfway into the outfield.

As Ken helps break up the ensuing fracas, he suggests that such enthusiasm might be a trifle inappropriate with a twelve run lead. Spencer glares at the ground and mutters, "Nobody gives you nothin'. You gotta take what you can get," and Ken musses the boy's hair gently and drops

continued on next page

the subject.

The Eagles celebrate their victory with high fives, and the opposing team troops dejectedly off the field. In the stands behind first base, Jane is talking to a man and woman. She gives the man what appears to be a business card and makes her way down the steps that lead to the field.

Ken asks, "What's that all about?"

"Recruiting some new members." Jane takes a cell phone from her purse and dials a number. "Gotham Cab? I need . . . Uh-oh." She looks at Ken. "They put me on hold. My car won't be ready until Monday."

"Where are you going?"

"Temple Mekrah Shaynei."

The synagogue isn't far from his one-room apartment. "It's on my way. I can drop you off."

She hesitates, then says, "Okay. Thanks."

Ken waves to Spencer and the other Eagles. "We clobbered 'em today."

"I noticed. Your team never lets up."

"Good teams don't. Hey, I put some substitutes in." Hell, he even let Robbie Green play right field in the final inning. Fortunately, nothing was hit in Robbie's direction.

She smiles. "Yes, you did. With the score 16 to 1."

"I teach them to play to win. They'll need that attitude when they grow up."

"There's more than one kind of winning."

"All that matters are the numbers on the scoreboard at the end of the game." She looks away. "What other kind is there?"

She slides into the passenger seat of his Toyota Camry and waits for him to get behind the wheel before she answers. "The most important battles are the ones we fight with ourselves."

He guides the Camry out of the parking lot and into the street. "They're also the toughest. Maybe too tough."

continued on next page

"That's a strange attitude for a psychologist."

"I'm not a shrink. I just teach. And I try to help the kids on my team with their problems."

"What kinds of problems?"

"The kind you'd expect in a society as screwed up as this one. My best hitter lost his father in a drive-by shooting last winter. My short-stop's upset about his parents' divorce. That skinny kid I put in right field for an inning wants to impress the girls by becoming a jock, even though he doesn't have a prayer. Getting through to them isn't easy."

Jane frowns. "Isn't that like practicing without a license?"

"Not if I don't charge for it." She starts to say something, but he cuts her off. "They're like family. Carol wanted to wait and see if the marriage worked, so we didn't have kids. . . . When did you get back to town?"

"Two weeks ago." Her voice is soft. "Have you ever considered prayer?"

Been there, done that, doesn't work. "God won't fix my arm. Or my marriage. If there is a God who cares, which I for one do not believe."

The Camry turns a corner, and there's a white concrete building on the right. "Here we are," Jane announces. "You can let me off in front of the steps. Thanks for the ride."

She gets out, and the warm togetherness he's been enjoying exits with her. He says, "Maybe we could get together some time. Have dinner, talk some more."

"You mean, like old friends? Or like a date?"

Something stirs deep within him, something that's more than just erotic. "Like a date." Wait a minute. What is he starting here?

"Now, Ken. If you and I were stranded on a desert island, you'd prefer one of the palm trees."

He tries on a grin; it almost fits. "Maybe I've changed. And you look a lot better than any palm tree."

She smiles. "Thank you. I think."

continued on next page

> "No promises, no strings. I just want to see you." He looks into her eyes. Her warm, brown eyes. "Please."
>
> She studies his face. "Okay. You can call me at the synagogue."
>
> Which reminds him. "What are you doing here?"
>
> She calls back over her shoulder as she goes up the steps, "I'm the new rabbi." ◆

Again, we're dealing with a lot of words. Let's look just at the first five hundred.

> When he went from being the next Sandy Koufax to just another hard luck story, his friends warned him that self-pity is the world's second favorite indoor sport. He likes it here, with the sweet scent of freshly mowed grass filling the air and the empty bleachers leering at him from the sidelines. He rubs up the cover of an imaginary baseball, scuffs the tightly packed dirt of the pitcher's mound with the toe of his sneaker, and glares at the batter's box. At the Enemy. At the One who never answered his prayers, his desperate pleas for just one more chance.

Do the first and second sentences make sense; wouldn't it be better to reverse them? In fact, consider all the actions, and consider that the author wants us to like this man, to care about him. Starting off by telling us that the man is filled with self-pity is not, to my mind, the way to do it. So, we'll recast the entire paragraph:

> He likes it here, with the sweet scent of freshly mowed grass filling the air and the empty bleachers leering at him from the sidelines. He rubs up the cover of an imaginary baseball, scuffs the tightly packed dirt of the pitcher's mound with the toe of his sneaker, and glares at the batter's box. At the Enemy. At the One who never answered his prayers, his desperate pleas for just one more

chance. When he went from being the next Sandy Koufax to just another hard luck story, his friends warned him that self-pity is the world's second favorite indoor sport.

Okay, he's still self-pitying, but he's doing something, so we have a context for the emotion. But since he's on a baseball diamond, and because there'll be a game soon, wouldn't it be better to have him holding a real ball, rather than an imaginary one?

What about the use of the word "leering"; there's a negative connotation to it and that emphasizes the man's attitude—even inanimate objects seem to have it in for him. Mark Twain said that the difference between the right word and the almost right word is the difference between lightning and the lightning bug. It's a lesson we should all remember.

Finally, this question: Is Ken, that's his name as we learn in the next paragraph, someone who takes responsibility for his actions, or does he place blame—in this case, clearly, on God? How does that make you feel as a reader? Is it something you want to know immediately, or discover as the story goes on?

> Now pitching for the New York Yankees . . . number twenty-seven . . . Ken Steinberg. . . .
>
> So close. He came so close.
>
> He starts his windup. The familiar pain comes again, knifing through his elbow, tearing into his heart, permeating every aspect of his being. He sighs and stops in mid-delivery. You win again. You always win, damn You.

His fantasy continues and we begin to get some idea of what his problem is: injury. And, again, the blame is placed. Whatever happened to Ken has to be someone's fault: There are no accidents. We don't know how close he came, though: Did he make it to Yankee Stadium, or only the minors? I'd like to know, now, otherwise the whole thing could be in his head.

To the parents and spectators who've begun filing into the stands, it's a lovely day for baseball, a brisk spring afternoon. Ken's eyes only see what might have been. He almost made it to Yankee Stadium, almost made the marriage with Carol work.

Almost.

He imagines her sitting there in the bleachers, blonde and petite, drawing admiring looks from the other men. Waiting for him to come back into her life, back into her warm, inviting body.

Yeah, right.

There's a woman sitting in the front row behind first base. But she has dark brown hair swirling gently around her shoulders, a figure that's pleasingly feminine but bordering on zaftig. He takes a closer look, and a decade vanishes as if by magic. The next thing he knows, he's standing in front of her.

"Hi, Jane," he says.

How do we know what the spectators think? The author has gone from Ken's mind and point of view to an omniscient one and then, after one sentence, returns to Ken. How do you fix that? I'd go with something along the lines of:

He watches the stands fill with spectators—parents, friends, people here to enjoy, to cheer—but what he sees is only what might have been.

That's in keeping, of course, with the author's intent.

Another commentary on Ken's failure follows: Carol. And then, a line that probably indicates something about where the story is going to go: "There's a woman . . ." someone who takes his mind of his baseball troubles, someone with whom he seems to have a history. What bothers me here is one word choice; it dooms Ken: "a figure that's pleasingly feminine *but* bordering on zaftig." There's nothing wrong with zaftig, which can range from simply voluptuous to Rubenesque; the word "but," however, is conditional: She's okay but she's a little heavy. That one word spells doom (again) for Ken; of course, he'll blame someone else. Deleting the word would serve to tell us a little about his taste (making the weight a positive rather than a negative; or, at least, meaningless). As the author's editor, I'd delete it.

As someone considering the manuscript, I will begin to have serious doubts about the market possibilities. Ken seems to be a weak person; Jane may be strong, the character the reader will care about and root for, but if that's the case, especially with a setup like this, I would want to see Jane first.

There's an awkward silence. Then her cool, appraising glance gives way to the smile he remembers so well. "Ken. It's been so long. What have you been doing with yourself?"

"Well. I'm on my own again. Got divorced last October." He always could talk to her about anything, everything. With Carol, shared feelings were a foreign country to which neither of them had an entry visa. He sighs. "Marriage is supposed to be forever. Mine lasted a year and a half."

"I'm sorry. I thought you'd be with the Yankees by now."

"So did I. Tore up my arm trying to break off a curve ball."

Her brown eyes are warm, sympathetic. "You must miss it."

Yeah, he misses it. The euphoric rush when he struck out the other team's best hitter, the roar of the crowd, the high fives from his teammates. He'd been a can't miss major league prospect with a hundred-mile-an-hour fast ball and a multimillion-dollar future, until that one moment of lousy luck. "So now I teach psych courses at our local community college."

There's another troublesome silence. Then: "Jane . . . I never meant to hurt you."

She touches his hand gently. "I know. You wanted something I could never give you."

Now I have to wonder: It's been ten years since they've seen each other and, as it turns out, the breakup probably wasn't the most amicable (Ken's apologizing and, finally, accepting responsibility for something). Ken's conversation is self-centered (and again we have to emphasize that this may be the author's point; it would make me the wrong editor for the project if it were submitted to me for publication.)

We also get more insight into Ken: It isn't sufficient that he strike someone out; it has to be "the other team's best hitter." He's still very much focused on himself; he hasn't said something I consider natural: "What are you doing here?" (It would follow, comfortably, his comment about teaching at the community college.) We still have no idea of how long ago his career collapsed. Was it before or after Carol? Questions are good; they're what draw the reader along. But are these the questions the author wants to offer the reader? Are they questions that matter? Or is the ambiguity that permeates the story so far a negative?

Where is it set? Can you get any sense of place, even knowing it's a baseball diamond? Is it on a college campus, well maintained? Is there anything to see?

    ◆ The author of case study #3 has chosen to use third-person present tense. I'm guessing that the voice is supposed to add immediacy—that's the reason most often given for using the form. Does it work? Try rewriting the scene in a standard past tense. Try it in first person (past or present). Does the rewrite force you to notice other things? Can Ken think or say the same things if you switch to first person, or does getting into his head that way force him (and you as the author) to notice other aspects of the world around him?

Several of the successful openings we looked at in the previous chapter dealt with people in some kind of trouble, folks with problems— *Stone Virgin* began with someone awaiting execution and, of course, blameless—so Ken is not, necessarily, a character doomed to failure as the focus of a novel; the danger is in the presentation, in choosing the jumping-off point.

That decision, always, has to tie in to your intent: What are you trying to accomplish and what's the best way of doing that? The answer, always, is a matter of your style . . . yours and yours alone.

Refining and Reworking

CHAPTER 11
Further Revising

We've been working with the things you're going to look at in your early drafts, items for which easy examples exist. Now we're going to consider other aspects, based on what you've done thus far. A bit more talky and less hands-on but just as important. No matter how many examples you've seen of edited material, no matter how many classes you take, no matter how carefully and how often you revise your own work, one fact is going to remain unchanged: You're the only one who can do the work; you're the one who is most intimately aware of what your story is supposed to accomplish.

David Bradley summed it up perfectly in a speech at the Breadloaf Writer's Workshop: "The Compleat Writer is one who has mastered the art of self-manipulation; who can in some manner control the state of mind in which he or she approaches a given writing task." If you cannot, or will not, see the errors in your work, no one will be able to lead you to the corrections that have to be made. It's been my sad experience over the years to sit with writers, show them—as we've been seeing—the things that jar, and have them shrug and deny the problems. I can think of only one who managed to publish. Revision is not advanced physics; it is common sense, patience and a willingness to let go.

Some things to remember as we proceed:
- A first draft is only that—you, the writer, talking to yourself.
- The first draft is your attempt to quarry a stone. The stone has to be large enough to do what you need it to; if your theme is a big one, a small block is not going to suffice. It is out of everything that's in your first draft that you'll pick and choose the material that makes up the second pass. In the second draft, you'll begin to chip away

rough spots and start polishing. In the third, you'll finish the buffing; what you have then may be the finished novel . . . or something that will need some more work. You, and only you, can decide.

- A story is a report of events, a plot is the cause and effect driving those events; the former is *what*, the latter is *how*. Your first draft should contain all of the basics of your story as you know it when you begin. Some items will go, some will be expanded. Don't worry about them as you write, don't edit on the fly, don't rewrite on the run—doing that results not so much in quarrying a stone to be worked but in creating a quarry.

- Begin by having some idea of what you want to write, how you want to treat the subject.

- Continue by writing. What you will be writing are linked scenes. Once you have your scenes, you'll know what belongs and what doesn't belong, what can go and what has to be added.

- Write with a sense of complete freedom. If you are a category writer, familiar with the conventions and needs of your category, that knowledge will guide your hand; if you're writing without consideration of genre restraints, your knowledge will guide your hand. Don't stop to think about what is permitted, forbidden, conventionally demanded or expected. Those considerations can come into play later. For the moment, what you're doing is writing, telling yourself a story. You may think you want to create one thing and instead discover that there's another form buried in your draft. Feel free to go with that one.

- When you're finished with the first draft, when you've written all the scenes that you felt were necessary to tell your story, stop. Put the manuscript away for a week. Read something different. Concentrate on anything but the story you've written. Then, pick it up and read it, pencil in hand, notepad ready.

- Make your changes, put the manuscript away, rest. Pick it up, begin again.

We've looked at scenes and characters and dialogue in a broad sense, fixing them so that they read correctly for presentation to an editor.

Because your first draft is in a sense a form of blocking, putting scenes where you want them to tell the story effectively, the things you're going to look for as you read are those that interfere with a coherent telling.

• Do your scenes contain what's necessary to maintain reader interest? Is there dialogue that serves a purpose other than to show your cleverness? Is there action caused by, or causing, other events?

• Do you have every scene you need? Do things happen that aren't set up by previous action or that present an action that isn't completed? If the scene is not a cause, what function is it serving? If you remove it, what harm is done? If there are effects for which there is no cause, where can you place the missing scene?

• Is a scene too long for the purpose you want it to serve? What can you remove to maintain pacing? Things to look for here: dialogue that goes on long after the point is made; bits of business that may seem cute or telling or reveal how well you know the language of kids in a dorm but that don't advance the story; actions you thought you'd need but that no longer fit because of other changes; events that aren't part of this novel in any way at all, that are really part of something else you're going to write; the introduction of characters that serve no purpose; the beginnings of subplots (secondary stories) that you haven't followed up on or that detract from the main story.

An example of a too-long scene: You're writing a mystery and, wanting well-rounded and complete characters, you've introduced a social interest for your heroine. In doing so, you've created several scenes in which the heroine and her boyfriend are with another couple. So that this other couple (who has nothing to do with your main story) is fully realized, you've taken time to create a back story for the pair, given the two of them a situation or conflict that may be interesting but that, again, serves no story purpose: Your sleuth and her lover do not discover anything about themselves as a result of the interaction; the new couple does not serve as a metaphor of anything else in the novel—the characters are just there, taking up time and space. As much as you may like them, they have to go.

At the same time, consider whether you need a subplot in the novel: By keeping the narrative strictly focused on the central event, have you sacrificed a sense of reality? Do your characters have a life beyond the investigation or the love affair or the battle with the ranchers? These secondary story lines should tie in to the main events, creating conflicts or actions that help form character. Being late for a date because the sleuth is hot on the trail of someone, or missing a meeting with an informant because lunch is just going so well—whatever the events, they should serve to give your characters fully realized lives. Remember: The story is never about the events, but about the events' impact on the people.

Which brings us neatly to characters. (I love it when a plan comes together.)

• Are your characters three-dimensional? Do they have a past and present, and can the reader imagine a future for them, based on how they're acting in the story?

• Because the past shapes the present, do we know enough about the characters' histories? Have you avoided the pitfall of stopping the action to bring the reader up to speed by incorporating what we need to know in the contemporary action? This can be done through dialogue, the use of a prologue or the judicious use of flashback.

• If you're using a flashback, is it integrated into the story? Does it flow naturally from what is happening, or have you simply (and incorrectly) started a new chapter to tell the tale?

• Have you introduced your characters at the right time? Introducing someone too soon, setting the reader up for the appearance, may dilute the impact. Introducing him too late, though, seems like a contrivance: I need a superspy to finally resolve the issue, so I'll throw him in now. As often as not, this may be a judgment call, but part of effective storytelling is maintaining suspense (in the broadest sense of the word), and if the readers know from the beginning that your amateur is going to be receiving help, they won't worry. It's more effective to have readers meet a character who hints at some knowledge and build toward the revelation.

• Are all your characters serving a purpose, or are they there simply as dressing? In the early days of *Star Trek*, we used to joke that if you were not a regular member of the cast and were on an away mission, you were going to die; the same might be said of characters on *Murder, She Wrote*. If you need a character who is going to die, make him important enough that his death means something to the reader. The folks your central characters meet in passing—the checkout clerk at the supermarket, the waitress at a diner stopped at only once—do not need careful delineation. Don't waste time on them.

• Are your characters "real"; is the reader left with the sense that he just might meet this person someday? To accomplish this, the character has to speak in a way that we recognize as appropriate, has to reveal concerns that we might share (and that goes beyond death and taxes). While the hero without failings or warts has been with us for a long time, the classic heroes, people like Odysseus, shared the faults of the people who listened to Homer. (Most of the mythological gods were just common folk writ large, with some powers thrown in for good measure.)

The astute reader will have noticed by now that these questions all seem to be part of a much broader topic: how to write a novel. But that's what revision is about: writing it right. The issues cannot be separated, and the faults we see in submitted manuscripts, the things that cause us to send them back for rewriting, are all the things we've been talking about. Revision is rewriting, doing the writing that wasn't done in the first place.

We've talked about dialogue; let's revisit:

• Do your conversations have a point? Is there a reason for what's being said? Dialogue should serve two purposes: character development—letting the reader learn important things about the story people based on what they say; and advancing the plot—what's said means something in terms of the story.

• Have you avoided overuse of "said bookisms"—words like *hissed, explained* or *observed* used in place of the invisible word *said*—and dialogue tags? The words, and the context in which they're delivered, should carry the weight of *how* they're delivered. Remember, if you have to tell us that Andy said something angrily, it means the words (and the scene itself) don't accomplish the task.

• Is the dialogue true to the character? Does someone we've come to see as uneducated suddenly start speaking like someone defending a doctoral thesis? Is the language appropriate to the scene and situation?

• Are your characters "talking heads," or have you interspersed action, movement of some kind? No one sits perfectly still as he's speaking: There are head and hand movements, facial tics, nervous habits, and they're all part of the development of your character, telling the reader something about what's going on.

• Do you use appropriate slang, idioms and figures of speech to help create a sense of time and place? At the same time, be certain the language isn't anachronistic. If you've used dialect, does it overwhelm the scene, making it impossible for the reader to understand what's happening? A little goes a very long way.

• Read your dialogue aloud, or have someone else read it. Do the words sound natural? Can you hear the conversation as if you were sitting next to the characters? Have you used contractions? Have you avoided the use of contractions when you want the words to have a different emphasis? Can the sentences be spoken, or are the combinations of words difficult to enunciate?

• Do your characters have different voices? Do they speak differently, so that the reader can identify them, even if you don't? We all have patterns to our speech, ways of speaking—tone, language, rhythms—and you want your characters to reflect that.

• Can your reader see your characters? Or your setting? If you've stopped the action to offer the reader a description, find ways of breaking that block of text by inserting actions that lead to something else being seen. Your heroine might walk across the living room, feeling the rug under her feet; another character might walk to a bookshelf and take down a volume. By reporting that, you offer some insight into the owner of the shelves and allow yourself the opportunity to describe those shelves. If the books are old, leather-bound, dog-eared or paperbacks, you've revealed something. If you simply describe the room as having bookshelves, what have you accomplished?

• Have you used all the senses in your descriptions (or, at least, used them as appropriate)? The more you can reasonably use, the more vivid the scene will be. (Remember that the sense of smell is considered the most powerful spur to memory.)

• "Blakely, a short, dark man, was sitting behind the desk." What does that tell you? If Blakely is important, we'll need more; if this is a onetime meeting, and your hero is picking up a package, the short, dark man is beside the point. (I run into that one a lot, which is why I mention it here.)

• Are your descriptions accurate? It really doesn't matter if you put a drugstore at the corner of Forty-ninth Street and Broadway when the business there is actually a boutique. It does matter, though, if you have a character looking at the clock on the Central Savings Bank building while facing south, and though the clock is there, it can't be seen from the south. If you're using an actual place as your setting, you can be sure that some reader, somewhere, is going to know if you have the facts wrong.

• Details come from research. No matter what it is you're writing, odds are you've done at least some hunting for the facts that make the difference. A historical novel needs a sense of the time and place you've set it in. A mystery needs some sense that you know police and/or investigatory procedures. (I think most criminals caught by amateur sleuths would probably get off, with the help of even a mediocre attorney.) Even a mainstream novel, beholden to none of the genre conventions, needs to be accurate in terms of place or behavior—if you have a character who is a pharmacist, some of the action will undoubtedly take place in a drugstore; you have to get it right.

Now's the time to not only check your facts (can you drive from L.A. to Las Vegas in under two hours?) but make sure that you haven't shown all your research. That's easy enough to do: I must have read ten or fifteen books on Plains Indian life before I finished "The Dream That Follows Darkness." If I'd put in all the details I'd learned, the story would have been a novel (and it doesn't deserve to be), and the reader would've gotten bored, bogged down in the detail.

If your character is a heart surgeon, don't give the reader any more detail about transplants than necessary to continue the suspension of disbelief. Don't explain that "stat" means immediately; let the action surrounding the command show that to any of the readers who don't know. (And this is a good time to remind you that you have to give your reader some credit for intelligence, for sufficient worldliness to understand certain things. And just as you own a dictionary, so do your readers.)

If your novel stops for a dissertation on quantum physics, you'll stop dead. The information may be interesting, but if it doesn't advance some aspect of your story—character or plot—take it out.

• Have you *shown*, not *told*? Can you add some kind of action, describe some emotional reaction to events so that the reader sees it happening rather than being told that it does? At the worst, you can always have another character comment on something so that we see it through eyes other than those of the storyteller. Of course, that adds an additional burden for you: The event being commented upon must still be understandable to the reader in the same way it is to the character. If a character says, "Okay, let's go," and he gets up to walk to the door, and someone else says she could feel his excitement, well, I'm going to wonder about that person's powers of observation. That may very well be your point—that the second speaker is unreliable. If it is, fine; if it isn't, chip away the comment.

When dealing with the emotions of the characters, and their observations, make certain that you've maintained point of view.

In most fiction, scenes should remain in one point of view. You can shift, but you have to make it clear that you've done so. Nothing is more disconcerting, especially in popular mass-market fiction, than experiencing a scene through Danny's eyes and then, in the middle of a paragraph, reading, "Rose was upset and said . . ." Whatever she says should let the reader know her emotional state, and it can be followed by Danny saying, "Calm down, Rose." You will have both shown her feelings (through the comment and Danny's reaction) and maintained point of view.

• Is the language and tone, your style and manner, appropriate to what you're trying to accomplish with the story and the market? (We'll be discussing that in more depth in the next section.) While I have personal arguments with the idea that we have to write to the reader's expectation, genres all have their iconographies. Have you, at least, remained true to the form, if not the formula?

• Another time to consider reading the manuscript aloud. How does the story *sound* as you hear it? Think of yourself as an oral story-teller: Does everything scan? As with dialogue, does your voice rise and fall naturally because of the cadence of your sentences? Have you used punctuation to create stops? Are sentences too long, so that you've forgotten the beginning by the time you reach the period?

• With the finished first draft in hand, with your notes in the margins or on a pad, with word changes marked, is this the story you want to tell? Have you created the shape of your story sufficiently that you can now polish and buff and finish?

What's missing? What's been overdone? Does the ending of the piece flow from what came before?

We haven't discussed endings and denouements because they're difficult to show. We'd need an entire manuscript with a faulty ending to do that properly. So, some words of advice.

Some writers say they know the endings before they begin. To a certain degree, they're right: We know that in ninety-nine out of a hundred novels, there'll be a happy ending. (In the contemporary short story, that is no longer a truism; many of them are vignettes that just come to a stop. But if you're writing for newsstand magazines, you have to wrap things up neatly, just as you do in the novel.)

One of the difficulties you may run into if you're writing a story with a convoluted, many-layered plot is that a thread will simply be left hanging, issues will be unresolved. That's fine in mainstream fiction, which is more a mirror of life as we live it—things are unresolved in our lives, and sometimes we worry about them and sometimes we simply shrug. It isn't that way in category fiction, though.

A friend of mine, Robert Randisi, wrote a P.I. novel titled *Separate Cases*. His protagonist, Miles Jacoby, was involved in one case that led to his sticking his nose into another. The first case was solved, the second wasn't; the editor wanted "closure" on that one, because that's what the genre demands. Bob stuck to his guns, I'm happy to say; leaving the matter hanging was his intent from the beginning, because that's how these matters really go. A bright light in an often bleak world.

Here's one way of dealing with possible continuity problem in your fiction: Make a chart—as part of your revision process if you haven't done it as part of your outline—tracing each of the story lines, subplots and peripheral incidents you're relating. Things may have cropped up as you wrote that you weren't planning on—a bit of business leading to another and another—and because they were part of the ending you'd envisioned at the start, you will have lost them as you got back on track.

Think of it as a flow chart or family tree. If you've introduced a character who is supposed to be important on page seven, to create a conflict, for instance, keep a record of the rest of her appearances. Is the conflict resolved? If not, go back and chip her out of the story; she wasn't important. (No, don't add a resolution; clearly your story was going somewhere else. It's a far, far better thing you do to edit her out.)

Frequently a thriller or saga writer, working on a very large canvas, seems to reach a point in the story when it occurs to him that he'd better reach a conclusion soon. Everything gets wrapped up quickly, and the ending seems abrupt. (I have that problem with many of Stephen King's novels.) Motivations, a reasonable sense of cause and effect, are lost and the book ends.

Is that a problem in your book? Does the ending flow naturally from *everything* that's gone before? Have you rushed into the ending because your contract or guideline called for X number of words?

Odds are, there are enough words preceding the ending that can be cut, leaving you the space needed to satisfy the reader—and the characters. And the story is about them, isn't it?

Writing is revision(ing) is rewriting is writing is. . . . That's all you really have to remember. The rest is commentary and practice.

CHAPTER 12

Style

"Style" may be one of the most misunderstood words a writer hears. The simplest way of looking at it is this: Style is the author's approach to subject matter, based on language, knowledge and need.

The search for a style is a fool's errand: You have it, whatever it is, from the day you put the first word on a page. Your style may change as you gain more experience, as you begin to see things differently, as you begin to learn. But even if you spend hours a day trying to write in the "style of Ernest Hemingway," all you're doing is an emulation colored by your background. Hemingway's style had as much to do with his concerns about death as it did with short sentences; Faulkner was a lot more than complex language.

Want proof? When someone becomes popular, be it Stephen King or John Grisham or Danielle Steel, the rush is on to write the same kind of book, and to write it in the same way. We're told to study what they've done and do it ourselves. An interesting way to spend time, but how many other writers succeed? The agents and editors are inundated by manuscripts written in the style of _____, or written in the manner of _____, but if you look at the shelves in the bookstore, you realize that there aren't that many titles competing with the established writers. You may hear that someone is the "new whomever," but how often does he go on to a lasting career? Not often. And in this instance we're not talking about stylistic masters but simply excellent storytellers, whether we, personally, think they're worth the hype they receive. The public supports them . . . and them alone.

Nicholas Delbanco, one of the better writing teachers at work today, gives his classes an assignment to write scenes in emulation of those penned by some of the masters . . . with changes: Instead of a storm, the class may approach the scene from the point of view of what would happen if the day had been bright. As he puts it: "I'm hoping for additional language in the mode of Joyce or Faulkner, for paragraphs that Ford or Woolf might well have drafted and cut."

The value of imitation is in discovering your own voice, your own style. That's one of the reasons I tried not to change language (dramatically) in the works we've been considering. Language is very much a part of style, and so is subject matter. I'd no more suggest to the author of the piece about Simon that she write a different novel than I'd suggest to Ken's creator that he doesn't want to write about a man who appears to be a loser. I'd insist, though, that they consider their words more carefully. (Discussing market is a subject for another book.)

Strunk and White's *Elements of Style* aside, what are the elements of style?

Use of language comes first, at least for me. While there may be a modicum of value to the admonition to stick to Anglo-Saxon words rather than those with a Latinate root, and while abjuring obfuscation makes a certain amount of sense, reducing language to a basic vocabulary is counterproductive. Words are the blocks that add texture and richness, that are the core of metaphor and simile and imagery and the other tricks we use to make our stories come alive. You'll have noticed that throughout the preceding pages, almost every time some change was discussed, I mentioned that language was tweaked, a word changed. The reason that happens is because of the primacy I place on language. That doesn't necessarily mean that you have to (though as your editor, it's something I'm going to do to your work), but language is the tool we use to chip away at our ideas, and I know that a craftsman is only as good as his tools.

Unfortunately, by the time most of us start writing, we've pretty much finished learning language, and finding the words we need becomes something of a struggle. That isn't to say that plain, simple language doesn't work; that isn't the point. It's finding the word that is the only right word, not the one that's close enough. We can use a thesaurus to help us, but the most important thing to do is read enough so that we absorb as much as we can.

Your own approach to your material, no matter what you're writing, comes next. With all the sample material we've studied so far, you can easily tell that the the pieces were written by different people; even my created dialogue for Danny and Rose has a sound that is "me." To extend it further, the various samples of my writing, all radically different as stories, share a common "sound." That's a result of my use of language, my concerns, the things I write about and how I choose to write about them.

My nonfiction for writers also shares a common sound: I write informally, always trying to live up to the review of one of my earlier books that said, "It's like sitting down and having a 200 page drink with the author."

None of that was consciously developed; when I sat down to write the first time, that was the voice I had, and while it's been refined over the years, it hasn't changed. On the other hand, the choice of second-person present, which I showed earlier, isn't a matter of style; that's a choice for storytelling—how the story is told within that choice is the style.

Subject matter and the quests you pick for your characters can be considered stylistic options. Most writers, even those with widely varied bodies of work, tend to examine many of the same issues (or variations on them) in everything they write. The story is different, the more obvious theme may be different, but whatever is at the center of the story for the lead characters echoes from book to book.

If you're writing something that matters to you (and why would you be writing it if it didn't matter?), you bring something of yourself to the work; it cannot be helped. Sometimes it's called worldview, sometimes it's called vision—the label is beside the point. What matters is that you remain true to it within the course of a particular story. It's entirely possible that you'll try to write something "different" someday (because, mayhap, someone in your writing group has told you that this new thing is what everyone is looking for; she knows because she heard an agent say it at a conference somewhere just last week). Let's assume for the moment that this new thing is a western as it might have been written by Hemingway. You can learn the basics of both the form and the formula, but it is the sentence structure that everyone is talking about, so you try a couple of paragraphs, decide you can do it and begin working.

At some point, though, you're going to look at your pages and realize that you've crept back into your work. And when that happens, it's going to be a signal that it's time to revise. You can make everything read the way you always write, or the way you want to be writing, but you don't want to get the two mixed up within a single work.

Style is you—a result of the way you were brought up, educated, lived and live. It is, in its entirety, the most important thing you bring to your work and give to the reader.

Why do you suppose people want to read every book by James Lee Burke or every story by Andre Dubus or every novel by Rebecca Brandewyne? Why does every book by a particular author become a best-seller, but none by some other author ever get to the lists?

There's a bit of luck involved, sure, especially in terms of bestseller-dom, but we go back to some writer because we like her style, the way she tells a story. It doesn't matter one whit that there are a dozen other books on the shelf at the same time that are telling the same kind of story. It doesn't matter to us, as readers, how many copycat, jump-on-the-bandwagon writers are trying to pull off the same trick. We have our favorites because they're doing whatever it is they're doing, fulfilling whatever needs we have as readers, in their own ways. If a large enough public likes what they do, they're deemed successful.

As you reread your manuscript, then, you're going to have to be certain that you've remained true to yourself or, at least, to the self who's writing *that* piece.

There's no right or wrong style—though certain aspects of style will gain and lose popularity over a period of time. Write in the way you find comfortable and stick to that way. It'll give you one less thing to worry about in a world of woes.

CHAPTER 13

Chipping Away, Word by Word

One of the principles of revision is that while words are the building blocks with which we begin storytelling, using too many of them, and unnecessary ones, does not make the structure stronger; they simply create clutter. As you revise, the words, sentences, paragraphs and scenes that are just lying there, accomplishing nothing, should be removed. Harking back to our original conceit, you want to chip away everything that isn't David.

The following scene is taken from Iain Pears's *The Raphael Affair*, an amateur sleuth crime novel set in Italy, where Pears lives. As background: A young Englishman, Jonathan Argyll, has become involved in the search for what is believed to be a missing canvas by Raphael. He's working with a special investigatory squad and is under the care and protection (insofar as that's possible) of a young woman named Flavia. Their search is taking them from Rome to Siena:

> It's a long, five-hour voyage to Siena, even if you drive—as Flavia did—far too fast on the motorway. It's also a very beautiful trip. The autostrada, one of the best in the country and one of the longest in Europe, starts outside Reggio di Calabria at the very tip of the southwestern peninsula. It curls through the parched hills of the south to Naples, then turns up through the poor countryside of Calabria and Latium to Rome. Then it heads for Florence and swings east, through a series of giant tunnels and dizzying climbs, over the Apennines to Bologna. Here it splits, one

arm reaching out to Venice, the other travelling on to Milan.

Even on the relatively small segment between Rome and Siena, it takes the traveler within easy reach of some of the most wonderful places in the world: Orvieto, Montefiascone, Pienza and Montepulciano; the Umbrian hill-towns of Assisi, Perugia, Todi, Gubbio. The stepped hills of vines and lowland pastures of goats and sheep mix perfectly with rivers, the steep drops, and the dozens of often largely ignored medieval fortress-towns, perched on top of their protective hills as if the Medicis still reigned supreme.

It was wonderful. . . .

And pointless. What did the author accomplish with the scene? Unless one has traveled the same roads (or at least been to that part of Italy), it's meaningless. None of the setting plays a role of any kind in the story—no car chases through those hills, no shoot-'em-up in the hills. Can you see any of what's being described, except in the sketchiest of ways? Like my scenes with the ghost of Steps High Fawn in the West Virginia beer hall, this had nothing to add to the story and nothing was lost by leaving it behind.

Two lessons, then: one, a reminder to make sure everything you write into a story belongs in the story and, second, just because something's in a published book doesn't mean it's correct.

It's not just scenes that are out of place; descriptions, dialogue—every word makes a difference. That's why, at the risk of repeating myself, I kept pointing out that words had been changed or deleted.

At this point, I want to look at some sentences and examine how they might be improved, strengthened, by the deletion and changing of words. We can begin by looking at the sentences just completed: Do we need the words "at the risk of repeating myself"? No. We also don't need the words "At this point." Two reasons for that: It's obvious and "point" and "pointing" shouldn't appear there together. (Go ahead, strike the word "there"—unnecessary.)

A couple of sentences from a description of a crime scene:

> Farthingham's insides were now on the outside in a glistening
> pile beside an opening in his abdomen. Someone had eviscerated
> him. The sight was not attractive and my partner reflected my
> aversion in his wide-eyed stare. The coroner seemed unfazed. It
> takes a lot to faze Felicia Hamilton.

"Eviscerated" is a nice strong word, and appropriate. But the sentence in which it appears doesn't have to appear; it adds nothing in the way of information and gets in the way of the next point: that the sight was not attractive. Is "not attractive" the best phrase to use there? Would a metaphor or simile be stronger, more useful?

One thing to consider is the author's intent. This is first-person narrative, and the choice of language reflects the character's way of seeing the world around him. In traditional hard-boiled, private eye fiction, for instance, we would expect some stronger imagery: "His guts lay there like an unwanted reminder of a high school biology class."

But in this case it's enough to say: "My aversion was reflected in my partner's wide-eyed stare. The coroner seemed unfazed."

We know it isn't attractive, and by quick cutting to Felicia's seeming disregard of the sight, we emphasize that the detective and his partner were fazed. With those changes, the paragraph reads:

> Farthingham's insides were now on the outside in a glistening
> pile beside an opening in his abdomen; his guts lay there like an
> unwanted reminder of a high school biology class. My aversion
> was reflected in my partner's wide-eyed stare. The coroner
> seemed unfazed; it takes a lot to faze Felicia Hamilton.

I'm still bothered by "aversion." Lightning or lightning bug? The word sounds forced, too reflective rather than showing the immediacy of the thought. Try it as "feelings" or "disgust." At the same time, the author might very well be upset by my dissection description; if it isn't appropriate to the book and the character, it's wrong. Everything you do is in service to your story.

A sentence, a few lines later:

> Felly rose to get up off the floor and I reached over to offer her a hand. She grinned and grunted as she got to her feet. "Thanks anyway, I have to keep in shape."

The first consideration: We had no idea she was kneeling next to the corpse. Is it important to say that? I think so, given the fact that she was unfazed. She's right down there in the mess; letting us know she was kneeling serves to emphasize that strength of hers.

Establishing that she's on her knees allows us to change the example sentence to: "Felly started to rise and I reached to offer her a hand."

Something else is missing from the scene: the smell. It doesn't have to be discussed here, but any gutted animal, in an enclosed area. . . . No one in the scene we're given is reacting to that aspect; it's only the visual input that's considered. What are the sounds in the room? Only conversation? Is part of the partner's reaction reflected in his breathing? All the senses have to be called into play or, certainly, as many of them as appropriate.

A short scene from my story "Some Reflections on the Death of Robert":

> I stopped talking, and looked down at Sergeant Reilly's hand in mine, the light shining on the clear polish on her nails.
>
> "You're doin' fine, hon. Go on." Her voice was a smile.
>
> "Uh, could I have a cigarette, do you think?"
>
> "Sure. Celowicz?"
>
> The beefy detective groaned, but reached into his shirt pocket to take out a pack of Pall Mall. I could see the strip of leather from his shoulder holster. He tossed the pack onto my lap, and I took one out, tapping it down the way I had seen men do, three sharp raps against the pack, and then put the cigarette in my mouth and looked up at him. He rolled his eyes, but then bent

over, flicking a plastic lighter to life and offering me a light. Reilly squeezed my hand.

I took a deep drag and coughed. I hadn't had an unfiltered cigarette in years and years; I smoked True Green, but mine were in the bedroom. I wiped a tear from the corner of my eye and started talking again.

Some background on the story: The narrator, a young man with some serious problems, is sitting in his living room, being interviewed by the police because of gunshots he's fired; we know they were in the bedroom, after an argument of some kind.

I was trying to hide the gender of the narrator, lead the reader toward the belief that a woman has shot her lover or husband. So in rereading before submitting the story, I stumbled over the lines about tapping the cigarette "the way I had seen men do." It isn't fair play, creates a sense that the narrator either questions his masculinity or is, indeed, a woman. My intent was to have the reader do the misleading. Therefore, the line had to be changed: "the way my father used to do." Perfectly legitimate thought, regardless of sex.

Next: "and then put the cigarette" followed by "eyes, but then." Doesn't sound quite right, does it? The first "then" disappears without a trace, leaving nothing behind.

We change words for meaning, we change them to avoid repetition, and we change them for sound. Reading is, in at least one sense, an aural experience: We "hear" the authors, hear the words we're reading. If a word or combination of them falls harshly, seems hard to pronounce, it jars us. Judson Jerome and other poetry teachers have said that poets have to pay attention to things like rhythm, alliteration and sound, or they might just as well be writing prose. We all have to be concerned with those aspects of language. Look back at the opening of *The Chaneysville Incident* (see page 143). Bradley uses alliteration, rhythm, the sound of the words carry us.

Some sentences from a manuscript:

You see: Rachel nested in her room, contemplating lies you haven't told; Barbara at home waiting for you; Rachel's sons beginning life; your daughter molding hers (but you don't want to see her because she is almost as old as Rachel) and see neon fingers arrowing toward you. You stop looking and feel yourself sinking into the possibilities of a life lived in the moment as it happens.

The first thing that bothered me was the word "arrowing." Try to say it aloud; it's awkward. Changing it to "hacking" not only makes the sentence easier to scan, but it strengthens the image and impact— there's a violence to hacking, a sense of threat, that makes the point stronger.

The parenthetical phrase preceding the neon fingers is a little too long; there are too many syllables there and they shout for attention. Deleting the word "almost" shortens it; taking out "because" and replacing it with a stop, a semicolon or ellipsis, brings the phrase to a workable length: "(but you don't want to see her . . . she is as old as Rachel)." Does the fact that the daughter and Rachel are now the same age, rather than being simply contemporaries make a difference to the story? Perhaps a little; it depends on the ages and the point. From the quoted sentences alone we have a very good idea of what this piece of fiction is about, and in terms of that story (and edits have to be made in terms of what you're dealing with, not some Platonic ideal), it doesn't bother me.

Is that too much attention being paid to what may be a minor point, to refinements that the average reader (or editor or agent for that matter) might not notice? I don't think so, because we don't always notice these things consciously. Have you ever heard someone talking about a novel and saying that it was "flat"? On a subconscious level, that person is reacting to the language; he may not be able to express it, because few of us are trained as critical readers, but he's aware of it. Anything the reader is aware of is something the writer must be aware of, but we have to concentrate on those items.

Another thing you're going to watch for as you read is the sense of the sentence. What might be considered wrong with this?

> Rhea leisurely walked through the meadow polished with dew and moonlight. Darkness and aloneness surrounded her, but Rhea felt no fear, had no concept of it. That freedom from fear represented one of the many weapons she possessed that allowed her to continue weaving the design of her existence.

Say the sentences aloud. We have a woman walking through a meadow. Common sense tells us that it is the field that's polished with dew and moonlight, but it doesn't read that way; it sounds as if Rhea, the subject of the sentence, is polished.

There's a difference between being lonely and being alone, and we have to guess that the author meant to emphasize that sense. Still, aloneness is defined as the state of being alone. Would that surround her? Does the word call attention to itself in a negative way?

If the meadow is polished by moonlight and dew, the impression is of something shining brightly. Where's the darkness?

If Rhea's walk is leisurely, are the three mentions of her lack of fear necessary?

What about the rhythms of the sentences? It's not poetry and is not meant to be, but as you say the words does it feel jerky and awkward? Or do the words flow, bringing you along with them?

The next paragraph:

> She moved easily through this familiar meadow, remembering these woods, that stream, those sounds. She was part of it, and it completed her, she knew all the world intimately. Rhea had lived together with earth for centuries. Tonight she was intensifying her concatenation with the terrestrial and celestial worlds and others of her clan, strengthening herself.

A hint of what's to come: witchcraft of some kind, probably, a

Mother (or Earth) goddess fable (Rhea is the mother of Zeus). Some explanation of why she might not feel fear. The first few sentences flow; the last sounds like editorializing on the part of the author. Even with only one paragraph read, we don't see Rhea thinking in the terms presented. And the sentence immediately shoves the reader out of the mood that's being created.

How would you change those two paragraphs? Here's one approach:

> Rhea strolled comfortably alone through a meadow polished with dew and moonlight. At the edges of the field, the trees shaped a black wall, but even with that darkness, even though she was alone, she felt no fear, a freedom she cherished as one of the tools allowing her to weave the design of her life.
>
> She remembered those dark woods, that serenading stream, all the sounds and shadows. She was part of it all and they completed her; she knew all the world intimately, had lived together with earth for centuries. Tonight she was intensifying her ties with the world and the heavens and the others of her clan, strengthening herself.

Have we changed the author's intent? What was being accomplished? Have we made the paragraphs more comfortable to read? Is there any loss in replacing "concatenation" with "ties"? Does "strolled comfortably" mean the same thing as "leisurely walked"?

Have you resolved the issue of darkness? Reduced the need to mention Rhea's lack of fear? Have you replaced the two words that called attention to themselves, "aloneness" and "concatenation," without changing the sense of the scene?

If you can answer those questions to your satisfaction, you've done the job correctly.

CHAPTER 14

Pace

If you're chipping away, one of the reasons you're doing it is to maintain pace.

There are a couple of ways of looking at that. One is very much intrinsic to the story itself: Does it move forward steadily? This doesn't mean at breakneck speed, one action on top of the other, without giving either the characters or the reader a chance to breathe. It does mean being certain every line advances some aspect of what you're doing. Thinking about it now (because I've been forced to reread "The Dream That Follows Darkness"), I should delete the paragraphs about David going to New Orleans; there's some color, but nothing that happens there makes a difference in the story, nor do I think that those paragraphs add anything to David's character (see page 90). Their presence in the story doesn't hurt, but it doesn't help, either.

In a longer work, where there's a much greater possibility of material like that appearing, the problem is magnified. You get away with one or two of those, but eventually they build up, like a wall. Getting rid of those walls, then, is to your advantage: If you can keep the editor reading, odds are you'll keep the reader's reading.

If they stop, they'll tell their friends that the book was "slow"; they may not know the reason it seems that way, but there's still no reason to cause that kind of reaction.

Anything that isn't part of the story goes out. It's that simple . . . and that complicated.

The second factor when considering pace speaks directly to the way people read today. They don't have (or won't give) time for reading. We're used to receiving information in small doses, things come quickly—thirty-second news reports, quick cuts in movies and television. (Have you noticed how, when a news story gets more than its thirty seconds, we wonder what's so important about it? Maybe we turn away from the television set; after all, we know the important thing, whatever it is. In a sense, we're discussing the same mind-set here.)

One of the things that makes a reader think you're spending too much time on something is a dense paragraph—line after line of type unrelieved by white space. Just seeing a paragraph like that coming, the reader is prepared to start skimming. *There's too much information there.*

Once upon a time this wasn't of as much concern: There are paragraphs in my trade paperback edition of Thomas Mann's *The Magic Mountain* that go on for more than a page. And some contemporary novelists still do that successfully; they have a rightly placed confidence in the power of their words that allows them to not only pen such sentences, but to hold the reader's attention.

Most of us can't do it; that's why teachers today suggest that a sentence not be longer than twelve words, a paragraph not more than eight or nine lines. While I refuse to edit to those parameters, the bleak truth is that we should pay attention to the thought. (And reject the thought at our own peril.)

   ◆ Look at your typed pages (this is something that really can't be done on screen; the "page" is too white and you don't really see the page). Are there areas dense with type? Is it possible to take those long paragraphs and make them two or three? One solution might be to add a couple of lines of dialogue; they inherently create breaks.

Another problem might be chapter length. Readers use chapters as natural stopping points (and they are, after all: A new chapter indicates a new scene, new action, some kind of movement). Again, teachers suggest chapters of no more than about eighteen or twenty pages. (I don't know where all these numbers come from; I doubt that there's ever been a study done, given the fact that demographics in publishing are more often than not seat-of-the-pants considerations.)

◆ Does the action in your chapters, the combination of scenes, allow you to turn a long chapter into two? This might be possible if you're changing point of view, creating a flashback, or in some other way interfering with the otherwise direct linearity of what you've written. If so, you are probably well advised to do so.

Anything that slows the eye, anything that interferes with the pull you want to exert on the reader is going to have an effect on the pace of your story. It can be something as silly as a strange name (the classic complaint about Russian novels is, "I can't keep the names straight; they're so difficult"), complex and unfamiliar language or those blocks of text we've just discussed. That's one of the reasons I recommend to critique groups that someone other than the author read the work aloud; it's much more effective and useful to you, as the writer, to hear the stumbles and the way the pace is affected in someone else's voice.

CHAPTER 15

Revising for Genre

As we've discussed, style is an individual's innate approach to writing (or anything else, for that matter). There are lots of books out there for you, claiming to teach you how to write a best-seller, but if it were that easy, wouldn't many more people break onto the lists? How many books have you acquired that promised to give you the blueprint necessary to sell your mystery, or romance, or scienc fiction novel or whatever? What have the results been?

No one can define what makes a best-seller beyond two things: story and how it is told. If you have those two elements right, nothing else is going to matter. Writing in the style of a famous novelist (not that it's possible, really) is not a guarantee of agent, publisher or reader interest in your work.

That doesn't mean we can ignore what's gone before. Every form of story has certain aspects that readers expect and that, therefore, editors expect. If you're writing in a genre, you know what they are, because you read in it. There are guidelines for some kinds of fiction (the publishers' take on what the readers want based on sales). The publishers can be and have been mistaken and will continue to make mistakes about that; the book that breaks out is, as often as not, one that's gone against conventional wisdom. The "style" for contemporary popular fiction is one of simplicity: short chapters, paragraphs no longer than twelve sentences . . . Umberto Eco's *The Name of the Rose* should not have been a best-seller; Peter Høeg's *Smilla's Sense of Snow* and David Guterson's *Snow Falling on Cedars* should not have captured the imaginations of mystery readers. The list is endless. The exceptions abound. It tells you something about being exceptional, doesn't it?

And your style is exceptional, unique, or it should be. The styles of the authors we've come to respect and study are particular to them: Hemingway's short sentences and straightforward prose and Faulkner's much more complex and convoluted approach have made icons of both writers. Most of the time, though, we cannot begin to pinpoint what the element of style is. Why has Stephen King gone on and on while Robert McCammon (whose stories parallel King's and are at least as good) has pretty much disappeared? Why do Robert B. Parker's private-eye mysteries become best-sellers while those of Robert Crais do not? Why Danielle Steel, why Mary Higgins Clark, why John Grisham, why Patricia Cornwell?

Those are all the writers we're told to study. (See what the best-selling writers are doing, and do it, too. That's the instruction, isn't it?) And we do. And we're not best-sellers.

Each of them tells a story in his or her own way. They bring the insights and knowledge they have to the storytelling. And some indefinable thing in their work appeals to us. We'll never know what it is, will never be able to pinpoint it and duplicate it—"The New Agatha Christie" has yet to sell as well as the original. So all we can do is be ourselves—even if we're writing category fiction with its defined restraints.

All successful novels have an element of suspense: The reader wants to know what's going to happen and hopes to be surprised, hopes to have something happen to a character that wasn't expected. As you read your manuscript for revision, you'll look for that. Are the problems and conflicts you've created for your characters so easily dealt with that there's no tension? Is the situation one for which the average reader will be able to come up with a sensible solution, a solution not made impossible by other incidents in the story?

If that is the case, you have to go back now and twist things in such a way that it appears there is no way out. It may mean creating another character and working her in seamlessly earlier. This is the opposite of the situation we've already discussed: having a character with nothing to do.

Look at the chart you've created to track characters and action, paying attention to what they've done. Instead of having your woman in jeopardy meet the sheriff in chapter three (even though he doesn't appear again until chapter eighteen), consider whether that meeting can take place later so the reader isn't counting on having the knight ride in on cue. Let us worry about whether a knight will even show up. Take care, though, to have the meeting make story sense, and not be a convenience for you.

The antagonist does not have to show up in the first three chapters (nor does the murder have to take place in chapter one): See if you can lull the reader into a false sense of security by making the early conflicts part of a subplot. (And thus offering a surprise: We've been so busy worrying about the petty criminal down the block that we aren't paying attention to the murderer next door.)

In a mystery, particularly of the traditional kind, which is a puzzle and a game between reader and author, clues have to be presented fairly. Does your sleuth have information culled from witnesses that you haven't shared with the reader? Not fair, and it will score points against acceptance. The sleuth may have knowledge that you don't share (basenji dogs don't bark); that's fair. Have the dog appear, mention once that it didn't bark when so-and-so knocked at the door, and leave it at that.

Not all traditions have to be adhered to, and that's where your style comes into play, where your voice begins to make the difference. Parker broke with tradition when he made Susan Silverman, Spencer's girlfriend, a leading character in the novels. Significant others have now become a tradition (which makes sense since most people do have others in their lives).

The important thing is that you remain true to the form, the point if you will, of the genre in which you're writing.

What are the pitfalls to be aware of during the revision process?

Foremost, whatever vision you had of the work before you began should still be there at the end. Did you unaccountably switch from a conscious attempt to write like your favorite author and begin writing in your own voice? Which one is stronger, more compelling? Keep the book unified in voice; if your natural tone is more like John Cheever than John D. MacDonald, maybe that's the way you should be writing.

You know what the audience for your book expects; you've brought the same criteria to your reading for years. Whether it is the level of sexual tension, the amount of violence or the extent of graphic language, the elements have to be there if you want to sell your book more easily into that market. That should not be taken as a command that you follow the conventions rigidly. Remember: It is the form that counts. The writer who utilizes that form but still tells the story her own way is the one more likely to receive attention as a mainstream writer, whose novel will be considered "fiction" rather than "romance" or "mystery" (the two leading categories today). That offers a better chance for reviews, greater opportunity for support from the chain booksellers and the possibility of a broader readership (all of which translate into better advances for later books). If Frederick Busch's novel *Girls* had been published as a mystery rather than fiction, it would not have received half the attention it did get; Danielle Steel's novels are romances, but they can be found in the front of the bookstore, with the other new fiction.

Whatever your decision, whichever risks you want to take, when you read your first draft, pay attention to your voice as it speaks to you from the pages. Whenever it rings false, in terms of what you wanted to accomplish, change it.

If it sounds wrong in terms of what you know of the market, and if that's your primary concern, make the changes.

Everything matters, everything counts.

CHAPTER 16

Language

> She moved easily through this familiar meadow, remembering these woods, that stream, those sounds. She was part of it, and it completed her, she knew all the world intimately. Rhea had lived together with earth for centuries. Tonight she was intensifying her concatenation with the terrestrial and celestial worlds and others of her clan, strengthening herself.

You'll remember that paragraph from the example we looked at earlier. What we want to do now is begin studying the language, the words, that are used.

Language is the essential component of style. By the time we've reached our teen years, our vocabularies are pretty well set. Unless we expend special effort, or unless we have a knack for it, there aren't too many new words that are going to enter our speech beyond the jargon of our professions.

That's a deficiency editors see in manuscripts daily. Does it matter? After all, if you're speaking in the same way as most of your fellow citizens, is there any reason to stretch beyond that? I think so: Our language, drawing from sources that range back as far as, at least, Latin, and as au courant as the latest immigrant group, is wondrously rich, offering a multitude of choices—lightning and lightning bug.

Among your reference books is a thesaurus. The text version is a much better choice than the one built into your word processing application, which doesn't really give you a sense of the word. Case in point: "concatenation" in our sample paragraph. The word means *link* or *tie*; it is perfectly accurate. But is it the right word in the context of the sentence or, really, the several paragraphs we've examined? I'd say not; that's why I changed it to "ties" in the rewrite.

What's wrong with it, if it's correct in terms of definition? First, its very "strangeness" to the eye. There's nothing wrong with that in and of itself; what's wrong is that it stops the eye and, with it, the mind. We may have a sense of the meaning from its place in the rest of the sentence, but the sound of the word is wrong. Unless you know what it means, it resounds a bit too much of commotion or something negative.

The next question to consider: Is it likely that the word would be a normal part of the author's spoken vocabulary? Odds are against it.

Is it part of the vocabulary that most of us use? Again, probably not.

Bringing all the elements together, then—context, previous and subsequent language in the scene, potential for confusion—we're left with no choice but to go for the more common word in this instance. There's no benefit, no subtle connotation that will make a difference to the reader.

Which brings us to books like H.W. Fowler's *Modern English Usage* and the Strunk and White classic, *The Elements of Style*. Both books recommend, strongly, that writers avoid words from the Latinate and use good old Anglo-Saxon language. The problem with rules and instructions like that is that they ignore certain realities. There's a huge difference between having a date with someone and having a rendez-vous with her. Or an assignation. Or a tête-à-tête. At the same time, a knee to the intestines doesn't have quite the same impact (to the reader; the recipient is another matter) as a kick to the guts, which is stronger than a blow to the stomach.

Which means that you, as the writer, have to pay attention to each word you use, and if it isn't the lightning, find what is. Again, if you begin with a limited vocabulary, you aren't going to know the word is wrong; if you're satisfied with a limited range, nothing anyone says is going to budge you. If you want to enrich your language, and thus your writing, the best advice is to read a broad range and when you come up against a word that's unfamiliar, look it up.

You're certainly going to want to look for words when you revise and discover that the same word appears again and again, especially if those appearances are close together. Don't just accept that "link" or "tie" is a synonym for "concatenation," but consider how the words are understood. I chose "ties" in my rewrite because to my mind it is a closer relationship. "Link" may bring the thought of chains, but when we think of people being linked it seems to imply a relationship or connection while "ties" represent a bond. In that paragraph, bond seemed more appropriate.

We've seen other examples of that: In the scene we read about Ken, the pitcher who failed, there were "leering bleachers." Here it is again:

> When he went from being the next Sandy Koufax to just another hard luck story, his friends warned him that self-pity is the world's second favorite indoor sport. He likes it here, with the sweet scent of freshly mowed grass filling the air and the empty bleachers leering at him from the sidelines.

That's a piece of imagery that may or may not work; quite often, it's a matter of taste and the reader's awareness. Examine your images: What do they call to mind when read dispassionately, not as your creation but as cold words on a page? When you are in an empty ballpark or arena and look at the stands, do they (can they?) leer? What does "leer" mean? My dictionary tells me: "to cast a sidelong glance, give a lascivious, knowing, or malicious look." Can a stand of wooden benches do that? Does it matter if the image works? Ken, the man from whose point of view we're seeing the scene, filled with negativity, might just consider them that way, even if he's anthropomorphizing the inanimate.

That brings up another question: If Ken likes it there, as the author tells us he does, why would he enjoy being in a place where things are leering at him?

And if we want to complicate matters further, later Ken envisions

Carol sitting in those bleachers. Given his feelings about her, and his sense of the bleachers, the reader starts receiving mixed signals.

Those are all considerations the author should address before the manuscript goes to an editor, because the editor is going to think about them, and if he's thinking about too many of them, the decision to reject the work becomes easier.

Vivid writing depends on the use of language, not only the lightning bolt but images, metaphors and similes (more things considered part of poetry). I heard a writer once complain that with the deadlines she (and other writers in her category) faced, they didn't have time to "worry" about searching for images. Which tells you something about where her career is going to go. They should, and can, come naturally. And they should be part of your writing. We'll look at them in the next chapter.

CHAPTER 17

Imagery

Imagery is one of the most important aspects of your writing: Used properly, it acts almost as a sixth sense, calling on the intuitive nature of the reader to see something that's being presented in an unusual way. These figures may be simple or complex, and can be extended through several sentences, paragraphs or even entire books: *Moby Dick* is an extended metaphor, not a novel about a whaling expedition.

While there are several forms, the ones important to us are *metaphor* and *simile*, both terms we're familiar with from poetry. Not at all strange: The novel evolved from the songs of the poets, something it pays to remember every now and then.

Simile

Similes are the simplest form of imagery, a comparison between two things, most often using the word "like" or "as." According to *The Oxford Companion to the English Language*, the comparison must be fanciful or unrealistic; if it's simple and straightforward ("the tiger is like a big pussycat"), it doesn't qualify. We're looking for something more figurative.

Many similes are part of everyday language, becoming idiomatic: "like a fish out of water," "run like the wind," "selling like hotcakes." Idioms become trite, as does anything through overuse. If your novel reads like a cliché, editors and agents are going to lose interest very quickly.

Of course, when you're writing the first draft, it makes sense to go with the simpler phrases, the ones that come immediately to mind. What you have to do during the revision process is look for fresh ways of saying old things. What are some other ways of saying what's implied by the examples we've just used, remembering that fanciful language is not only

okay but desired? "Like a fish out of water," which means in an uncomfortable or strange position or situation (with a threat involved: the fish
is going to die), might become, first, "like a tiger in a vegetable patch."
Not a big movement away (it doesn't have to be), but something not
heard as often. Play with it some more: "like a mirror in a blind man's
house." No, that goes too far, changes the implication, carries the idea of
uselessness. "A balloon in a needle factory"? A lot will depend on the
context, on what you're trying to make the reader see and feel.

> Although the tractor's engine made it impossible to hear what
> they were saying, Charley's imagination supplied the strident
> tones of Luverne's voice as she pitched her story to another out-
> of-town bargain hunter. He could hear as if he were walking with
> them, Luverne's voice extolling the hidden virtues of a house ne-
> glected for years.

A very simple statement, probably not meant as a simile but simply
as description, but also bland. The paragraph would not suffer at all by
the deletion of the words "He could hear as if he were walking with
them," because we already know Charley's imagination is supplying
the conversation. (Later in the scene we're told that he's heard Luver-
ne's sales pitch five times.) We've also removed a weak simile.

We have to replace it with something stronger. The first consideration is the type of person we're dealing with: My guess is that Charley
is rustic rather than urban, intelligent (he's portrayed as thinking in
terms of "extolling" and "strident"). So how would he think of hearing
the conversation—it's about Charley's point of view. As if he were
making the pitch? As if he'd written the script? That might be my
choice, backed by that later mention that he's heard it five times. Still
a problem in that it isn't a fanciful comparison, but that probably isn't
needed here; we're simply using the form of the simile to strengthen
the paragraph. Taking it one step further: "He could hear it like the
creak of a locked door at midnight." (Too threatening? We don't know
enough yet to know what Charley's feelings might be.)

And for the exercise we're doing, it doesn't matter: What you've seen is how a simplistic statement can be enriched and made more vivid and so more memorable. That's what you're attempting to do as you look at the images now that the draft is finished.

There's a risk here, too: If you've overwhelmed your manuscript with imagery, making it as rich as a New York cheesecake, it might be too much for the delicate tastes of some readers.

But your style will dictate where the balancing point is.

Metaphor

Metaphors are more difficult, and evolve directly from similes. We might say "he swims like a fish" as a simile; writing "he was a fish or dolphin in the water" moves the image to metaphor. Think of it as a figure of speech that concisely compares two things by saying that one is the other; a metaphor is a condensed simile. A simile makes an explicit comparison: One thing is like another; in a metaphor, the connection is implied through an identification of the two things being compared. (We also try to define the unknown in terms of the known through the use of these figures of speech.)

We've mentioned *Moby Dick* as a metaphor. Another example is George Orwell's *Animal Farm*: The farm is to the state as animals are to citizens is the metaphor at the heart of the allegory.

If you say you "struck out" in an attempt to get publicity for your novel, you're using a metaphor drawn from baseball. Remember, as adolescents, talking about "getting to first base" . . . or farther? A positive metaphor from the same sport.

Metaphor is probably the most common (almost unconscious) use of imagery. It's part of virtually every conversation we have and so it is part of every book.

Sometimes, though, in an attempt to be clever, we use metaphors that don't work. "Striking out" in bowling is something we want to do, but using that as a metaphor for success would be difficult because of the common understanding of the baseball metaphor: It's become part of the language. (And so runs the risk of becoming a cliché.)

The things to look for during revision: the metaphor that rings false, the metaphor that's trite and the metaphor that gets in the way of the story because it calls too much attention to itself by going too far. Saying that a character's eyes are "pieces of a summer sky in her face" might be acceptable; taking it further, saying that they're "pieces of a summer sky borrowed from a painting by Wyeth," while more descriptive, is just too much.

All the other comparatives—allusion, analogy, conceit—are variations on the simile and metaphor (at least for our needs).

But what about oxymorons, that combination of contradictory words that become nicely pointed commentary? We have "deafening silence," which is readily identified by anyone who has experienced one. There are also those that have become jokes: "jumbo shrimp" (which actually does make sense), "military justice" (which also makes sense) and too many others to even consider creating a list.

If you can find one that works, combining opposites to emphasize an emotion or situation, that's fine. The rule, again: If it works, keep it; if it doesn't, make it go away.

There's a school of thought that says the simpler the writing, the better it is. There's something to be said for that, but there's at least as much to be said about clarity, about being precise and about stirring the reader's imagination. Clarity and precision depend on the use of the right word in the right place; the reader's imagination will respond to images. Dealing with language, familiarizing yourself with the vocabularies of the time and place and people you're writing about at least as much as you concern yourself with the language of your readers will create the tapestry of an engaging, readable and strong story.

Every word counts, the ones you add and the ones you delete. Pay attention to each one: Why did you use *that* word instead of any of the others available to you? Why are you using *that* image, making *that* comparison? Are you saying exactly what you want to say?

Revision is a time to question everything you've done. If you're satisfied with the answers, and have made the changes to create satisfaction where necessary, you're ready to begin the second draft.

CHAPTER 18

Grammar and Style: What Can and Can't Be Done

Rules about the use of language come at us from all sides, a barbarian horde storming the gates of originality and creativity. Some of these demands made on us make sense: grammar and punctuation, spelling, all the things our teachers tried to impart when we were in the eighth grade can't be ignored. Even if most of us can no longer quote the rules or explain them, they've become (or should have become) part of the way we think. Because our readers think in the same way, they're going to expect some degree of adherence to those long-ago learned lessons.

The people in your critique group harp on those facts—if you don't have the grammar right, you're going to be rejected; if your manuscript isn't done in *this* format, it's going to be rejected; if, if, if—and you're going to pay attention to what they say. Then you sit down to revise, look at all the commas (or lack of them), look at the semicolons (should they be used or are they now passé?), look at each word and wonder whether it's spelled correctly. . . . You're going to get bogged down in minutiae and start missing the more important issues.

That doesn't mean these rules can be or should be ignored; they are, though, the last of the details with which you're going to be concerned. Most of today's editors are no more skilled at these matters than you; that's one of the jobs of the copyeditor, trained for the work. When editors say they're looking for a clean manuscript, they're talking about a minimum of *obvious* errors.

Style Manuals

Where do you turn for the advice you need? Most publishers use one of several stylebooks: *The New York Times Manual of Style and Usage, The Chicago Manual of Style* and *The Associated Press Stylebook and Libel Manual* are probably the three most consulted. And they differ in their opinions. *The New York Times* newspaper (and stylebook) uses "the 80's" to indicate the events of that decade; the apostrophe before the letter "s" stands—for them and for me, as an editor and writer—as a possessive of events belonging to that decade. Others use "the '80s" because the apostrophe indicates that you've left out "19." That's the kind of thing you can't worry about, or even think about: Each publisher has its own house style and will make the appropriate changes.

The use of punctuation, and each mark has a specific use, however, is not open to quite as much interpretation, beyond the demands of your style. There's a famous story about Joseph Conrad, who after a morning's work said that he'd added a comma, and following the afternoon's efforts said that he'd taken it out.

Each punctuation mark has a use in a grammatical sense as well as sending a signal to the reader about the pace of the sentence in which it appears. There are dozens of handbooks available, and it's worth the investment to get one and glance through it (maybe during that period when you're letting the manuscript sit so that you can gain some distance from it before you begin revision).

There are those who say that semicolons make fiction too formal; others who use the ellipsis with abandon (the author Louis-Ferdinand Céline was infamous for that). Working with your editor and copyeditor, the manuscript, when it goes into production, should reflect what you want to do.

The most important piece of advice here: Know what you're doing and why. It's not enough to think that because it's different it's somehow avant-garde and groundbreaking. (A reminder: if you're aiming for a mass-market audience, writing for the entertainment of a traditional, category market, you'll have less room to maneuver here—with the readers and with the editors. That doesn't mean you can't or shouldn't try something different, just that you have to be more careful as you do it.)

Many of the rules by which writers live come from one of two other stylebooks: Strunk and White's and Fowler's. Even with the updates these volumes receive, they can never keep up with the dynamics of an ever-changing readership. They belong on your reference shelf, and should be read if for no other reason than that they represent conventional wisdom. But neither has the force of law; no editor compares what you've written to a page in Fowler and makes a decision based on that reading. As much as anything, these books represent a sensibility that most of the people with whom you'll be involved recognize and acknowledge. But editors and readers also understand the other needs that drive a writer to work, and we'll give you that leeway . . . as long as it makes sense.

Word Choice

Words enter our language regularly, many becoming part of everyday speech. Some are welcome and useful: Novelist Richard Rosen created the word "psychobabble," which certainly has its place. Some, well, they can be ignored easily.

Many of these words filter up from our children: "duh," "totally," "rad"; some are phrases: "like, ya know," "fugeddaboudit." They creep in from other disciplines: "Parenting" is one that I choke on. Nouns become verbs and through constant use work their way into the dictionary, becoming proper.

They may also date your work. Slang changes.

There are also what Fowler calls "stylish" words, as opposed to "working" words. One of his examples is "viable": perfectly proper when referring to an organism capable of sustaining life, but not proper when talking about a political program . . . although it has come to mean that an idea can possibly be successful. What about "reside" and "live" or "terminate" and "end"? This is another approach to the lightning/lightning bug analogy we considered (Thought about? Discussed? Looked at?) earlier.

The introduction to the Summer 1999 fiction issue of *The New Yorker*, says: " . . . it's revealing that it takes years, decades even, before some writers really begin using language as something to make stories with." One of the reasons for that, I think, is the existence of rules and lists, such as Fowler's.

Here's another example of a published opening:

> The street lay like a snake sleeping; dull-dusty, gray-black in the dingy darkness. At the three-way intersection of Twenty-second Street, Grays Ferry Avenue, and South Street a fountain, erected once-upon-a-year by a ladies' guild in fond remembrance of some dear departed altruist, stood cracked and dry, full of dead leaves and cigarette butts and bent beer cans, forgotten by the city and the ladies' guild, functionless, except as a minor memorial to how They Won't Take Care of Nice Things. On one side of South Street a chain food market displayed neat packages of precooked food sequestered behind thick plate glass—a nose-thumbing temptation to the undernourished. On the other side of South Street the State Liquor Store showed back-lit bottles to tantalizing advantage and proclaimed, on a sign pasted to the inside of the window, just behind the heavy wire screening, that state lottery tickets were on sale, and that you had to play to win.

What, do you think, would be Fowler's reaction to the use of the word "sequestered"? "Confiscated" isn't right. Another definition is "set apart"; but that isn't quite right, either. "Sequestered" is the right word. Should "do-gooder" or "philanthropist" replace "altruist"? In this opening to his first novel, *South Street*, David Bradley used language as something to make a story with.

We've also heard that writers shouldn't use alliteration, but look at that first sentence: "The street lay like a snake sleeping; dull-dusty, gray-black in the dingy darkness." Does that offend your sensibilities in any way? Does the sound and rhythm of the paragraph draw you on? Do you want to know what's going to happen next? Are you willing to at least give the author another paragraph to begin the "action"? That's successful writing, flaunting the rules because the author went back and back again, looking at every word, considering the meaning, the sound, *everything.*

A variation on the theme of stylish words is genteelisms, words we use because they seem more proper, less mundane. How much difficulty do these word choices create? A novel I edited was originally titled *The Bitch Wore Black*; it was a mystery by Carol Lea Benjamin, who uses dogs as central characters. In this case, a black Akita was central to the story. It was published as *A Hell of a Dog*. Fowler decries the use of "lady dog" for bitch. So would I; but I wouldn't be surprised to see "female" used instead of the proper word.

His list includes "lingerie"/"underwear"; obviously, there's a difference there that we all know, but one of his other examples starts creating real difficulties. He advises against "hard of hearing" as a synonym for "deaf." Forgetting about the obvious situation—someone who isn't deaf—we begin, now, to move into that bleak and gray area called political correctness.

People complain about references to overweight characters being called "fat" and, further, to their being portrayed in a negative light. Virtually every group has a term they favor for themselves: Someone I might otherwise think of as handicapped prefers to be called a person with disabilities. Every group resents being portrayed negatively, even when you're not resorting to stereotyping: Women complained that they were too often either the victim or the victimizer in crime novels; others echoed them.

"The 'N' word," as a phrase, has entered the language to such an extent that in a recent brouhaha surrounding an AIDS drug program, people were talking about "the 'F' word" rather than quoting the offending phrase.

Euphemisms have their place in our language, but as writers our duty is to say what has to be said. And therein lies the problem. It's a pervasive one, too: I had a copyeditor remove every instance of "the 'N' word" in a novel set in the period between the Revolutionary War and the Civil War, as well as any reference that she considered sexist. That it was appropriate language, both in dialogue and narrative, since the narrative was from the point of view of a character in the novel, seemed beside the point to her. But it was very much the point to both the author and his editor.

Against that situation, then, you have to read your manuscript during revision and choose between words that you think, based on what you know of the world, will offend someone. A character can do it, but that character will lose the sympathy of the reader. Using the phrases as part of unattributed dialogue, considered the voice of the author, can lose you fans.

It's not only the words and phrases themselves that create problems; attitudes and habits also become magnified. One bookseller complained because a character, whenever confronted with a problem or difficulty (which was about every other page), lighted a cigarette.

    ◆ What do the phrases and attitudes expressed in your novel say about you, about your characters? Forget about the excuse that it's a work of fiction and doesn't have anything to do with what you believe; readers are going to find you and the book inseparable.

That doesn't mean that you have to avoid all negative connotations, nor should your writing veer so far from the world in which it is set that it reads as fantasy (unless, of course, it is).

You've been warned. Make the choice that's right for you.

Passive vs. Active Verbs

Another popular rule is to avoid the use of passive voice or passive verbs, because these de-emphasize the action. I don't know that readers notice the offense all that much; I've never heard editors discussing it as a problem with a manuscript; I've never heard of a manuscript being rejected because the voice was passive. If the sentences themselves are correctly constructed, they make sense, they're *right*.

So what's the problem? It makes the action being described less important at an unconscious level. The simplest way I've found to offer an example combines several sins at once. Let's take a sentence from a tense, action scene:

The grenade was tossed into the pillbox by the youngster.

It describes what happened, and that's all the writer wanted to do—get that grenade into the pillbox and let us know who did it. It doesn't "work" because the grenade is being tossed—it is being acted upon—rather than putting the youngster into the spotlight. It's passive.

The first change is to invert things:

The youngster tossed the grenade into the pillbox.

That's active.

Is tossed the right verb, or is there a stronger one? A toss is a light throw; it might be a lob, it might be underhanded, it might be a hook shot. Was it tossed? Possibly. If that's the lightning word, if that's the action, the author would leave it alone. But it might also have been "hurled", "thrown", "rocketed"; use each of them in the sentence, and study how it changes the impact.

Questions and more questions. Further changes could be made, depending on need. A battle is a sensory experience: there's noise, movement, smells, things flying. Should any of that be included in the sentence? Should the youngster flinch at the noise, throw himself to the ground at the shock? How important is the youngster in the story? Do his reactions to the act matter? Will the action tell us something about him that makes a difference? Part of revision is asking yourself those questions and answering them honestly, so you create impact by getting the words right.

Impact is what you're striving for. That's why you change and rearrange words, sentences, paragraphs, chapters: to make things stronger and more memorable. (Let's add something to the end of that sentence: . . . memorable for the right reasons.)

Concrete Words

Concrete words—nouns and verbs—are memorable. As in our talk about dialogue (why did I use the word "talk"?), and the idea that the words used should carry the weight of how they're used, you want to use nouns and verbs that can carry the story.

◆ Revise the first paragraphs of your fiction by taking out all the modifiers. (The less adventurous may begin by first taking out the adverbs and in a second pass rejecting the adjectives.) Do the paragraphs still make sense, still accomplish what is necessary? Can you change the weaker verbs and nouns so that you don't have to replace the modifiers?

Modifiers are a part of language, a part of speech, and the exercise isn't designed to teach you to do without them, just to keep them under control.

Once you're finished playing with your dangling modifiers, take a close look at your pronouns —"he", "she", "it", "them". Will the reader ask, "He, who?" "It, what?" You'll find that you can not only strike the confusing ones but do without others, too.

The following paragraph is taken from the first edition of Henry James's *Daisy Miller*:

> Winterbourne walked to the middle of the arena, to take a more general glance, intending thereafter to make a hasty retreat. The great cross in the centre was covered with shadow; it was only as he drew near it that he made it out distinctly.

We know what "it" refers to, so an edit here is not for clarity but cleanliness; in the definitive edition (everyone continues to revise, but there comes a time when revision is an excuse not to risk submitting the work), the second sentence reads:

> The great cross in the centre was almost obscured; only as he drew near did he make it out distinctly.

Distinct—that means clear. Have you used any unclear, ambiguous or unspecific words? Did you describe a character as being "about 53 years old" or otherwise hedge on a detail? If the character was being described in dialogue as being about 53, there's no problem; we don't always know how old someone is. But if the description is in narrative, if you're not being specific, it's a mistake. If you don't know how old the character is, you haven't given him enough thought.

"Her hair was brownish." Reddish brownish? Mouse brownish? Brunette?

There are times when approximations are fair: Readers don't need to know, usually, that Danny was $6'2\frac{1}{2}''$ tall or that he weighed in at 237 pounds. "A little over six feet" and "weighing close to 240" are enough. You don't need approximately or exactly, just the fact.

Conversely, there are times when being specific slows things down. If someone's parked a car, you don't have to say that "he opened the front door" or "the driver's side door".

As he's getting out of the car, he picks up a package. Unless the fact that he did it with a particular hand is important (it might be a clue in a mystery), you don't have to specify.

Walking toward his house, he meets a friend. You don't have to say that "he raised his hand and waved"; "he waved" is enough.

Be specific when it makes a difference; remain general when the action describes itself.

There are a lot of words that we use *almost* unconsciously, *practically* scattering them throughout our texts, *then, suddenly* discovering later that removing them makes no difference to the text.

Deleting the italicized words from the previous sentence does nothing but make the sentence better.

> Susan walked up the darkened path. Suddenly, a figure leapt out at her.

We use "suddenly" in an attempt to surprise the reader. But we'll be just as shocked if the figure simply leaps.

> She was truly impressed.

She was either impressed or not. The words you don't use are as important as the ones you do.

Overkill

> He shrugged his shoulders.
> I nodded my head in agreement.
> She pulled the trigger on the gun.
> *I've got to get this manuscript finished*, he thought to himself.
> "I love you," he whispered softly.
> "I n-n-need to n-name him," Joe stammered out.

The problem with each of those sentences is clear, so I'm not going to talk about what's wrong, trusting that having seen them yourself, you'll recognize them on your pages.

Oh, okay: What else is he going to shrug; what else am I going to nod (and since the nod indicates agreement . . .); pulling the trigger is enough; unless you're psychic, you don't think to anyone but yourself; if he's whispering, it is soft; and we've seen the stammer.

Another sentence:

> He'd never been in a crime scene like this before.

Do we need the word "before"? No.

A caveat: In dialogue, the word wouldn't be a problem. People say things that the narrator shouldn't.

As obvious as these errors are, they are among the most commonly made. Because we're so used to them, we don't see them in our own work—only in the work of others. (But it's that way with most of the things we want to revise, isn't it?)

And that's going to be your major stumbling block as you begin revision. Remember Bradley's definition of the Compleat Writer (see page 182): "one who has mastered the art of self-manipulation; who can in some manner control the state of mind in which he or she approaches a given writing task."

It takes more discipline to revise than it does to complete your draft, and it's often a tiring, odious task. With experience and practice, it becomes easier and enjoyable: I look forward to it, look forward to seeing what it is I had to say, look forward to making it better, stronger, more powerful, more entertaining, more accessible, more of everything I think my editors want, more of everything I think my readers want.

And more of what I want as it becomes the finished work that was just an idea when I began.

A Checklist
for Revision

There've been a lot of concepts discussed, a lot of suggestions, some subtle, some obvious. To make life easier, here's a summary in the form of a checklist that will help you keep track of everything.

- Is your novel right for the market to which you want to sell it?

- If you're taking risks, have you maintained the form of the category, even if you're ignoring the formula?

- Is the language appropriate to your market?

- Have you created minor characters and subplots?

- Do you spend too much time on them, distracting the reader from the main story?

- Do you spend too little time on them? If they're not important to the story, should they be removed?

- Are you showing, and not telling?

- Do your characters express their feelings, or do you tell us what they are?

- Do you let your characters and their actions tell the story, or are you stopping to bring the reader up to speed?

◆ Are your characters as clear to the reader as they are to you? Have you maintained their character in dialogue and in actions?

◆ Are all the motivations clear to the reader, or are things happening because you need them to?

◆ Have you spent too much time giving the reader the characters' biographies? At the same time, does the reader know *enough* about the characters?

◆ Are characters telling each other stories simply as a way of giving the reader information? (If a character says to another, "Well, you know Billy did this . . . ," the conversation shouldn't be taking place.)

◆ Do character descriptions come naturally, in the course of dialogue or action?

◆ Are you describing people in terms of icons or idols? Will enough of your readers know what Michael Stipe looks like?

◆ Have you offered full descriptions (naturally) of your major players? There's nothing more aggravating than having a series of characters through the novel introduced by one or two features. It might work once, but by the time we get to the third or fourth "he was a tall man with reddish hair and a brusque voice," it becomes an annoying pattern.

◆ Speaking of iconic descriptions, does your manuscript read like the advertising pages of a magazine, with a product plug on every page? Does it matter that the stereo's an Aiwa rather than a Sony? (It does matter if it's one of the really high priced systems: It tells us something about the character.) Same with most cars, clothes and other products. Unless the brand is a telling detail, leave it out.

- Is interior monologue realistic? Are they thoughts the character would actually have?

- What point of view have you chosen? Why?

- Have you maintained the point of view throughout each scene, or jumped into another character's head in the middle of events?

- If you're writing in first person, is this someone the reader will want to spend time with?

- Unless you're writing in an omniscient point of view, have you made sure you're first-person character does not learn things in the course of the story that the reader didn't become aware of at the same time. (This refers to information; interpretation of the information does not have to be revealed until you're ready.)

- Is your point-of-view character clear from the beginning? If there are shifts, do you make the new point of view obvious soon enough?

- Is narrative in each scene true to the character seeing it? A man and a woman won't see the same room in the same way; they'll describe people differently.

- Have you avoided editorializing, commenting on events in your voice rather than that of the characters?

- Does your dialogue say what you want it to say?

- Are your conversations serving any purpose at all? Are they serving more than one purpose: describing things, adding to character developing, expressing ideas important to the story?

- Does your dialogue stand on its own? If you cut explanations, dialogue tags, and anything else used as a crutch to support the words, does the conversation still hold up, saying what you want it to? If not, change the dialogue, not the tags.

◆ Do adverbs follow quotation marks? This means the dialogue or the scene does not express what you want said.

◆ Does your punctuation work as part of conversation? A dash represents an interruption; an ellipsis, a pause or gap.

◆ Is there any action interspersed through the conversations, or is the dialogue, unnaturally, only words?

◆ Are your characters giving speeches or actually talking to each other?

◆ Have you used dialogue to show off your research, allowing characters to give detailed explanations of things that do not make a difference to the story? (We don't need the principles of rocketry to accept space flight.)

◆ Do the conversations sound natural? Read your work aloud; even better, have someone read it to you. Does the exposition flow easily or does the reader have to stop, either to catch her breath or figure out pronunciation?

◆ Have you used contractions, slang, idioms and regionalisms both to ease reading and to give a sense of character and place?

◆ Does your dialect disrupt the reading? Can you achieve the sense of place without "creative" spelling?

◆ What does your manuscript *look* like? Are there unrelieved blocks of text? Can any of your paragraphs be broken into shorter ones? Long paragraphs can also be broken up with dialogue. It helps the pace and also makes the manuscript (and the printed page in the book) easier to read. As in life, sometimes we're judged by how we look; if a page appears intimidating, the reader is going to be intimidated.

- Does your dialogue look like long paragraphs? Can the talk be broken up by action?

- Are you repeating words, phrases, bits of business because you like them too much or because it was easier to just go with what you know rather than create something new?

- Have you looked at every word, making certain it is the only right word?

- Have you checked for anachronisms, words that weren't in use at the time the novel is set, products and events that are out of time, if not out of place?

- Have you used adverbs and adjectives sparingly? Like italics and exclamation points, these modifiers are fine seasonings and have to be used delicately.

- Are you using trendy words for effect . . . or through habit?

- Have you used "which" incorrectly? Go on a "which" hunt. Nine times out of ten, the word should be "that."

- Have you turned to the dictionary to check spelling and definitions, or simply trusted instinct and a computer program?

- Is your thesaurus near you as you work? Is it well thumbed?

- Did you chart your characters and story lines, to be certain that neither disappears inexplicably?

- Are details all the same at the end of the manuscript as they were at the beginning? Continuity counts, whether it concerns eye color, clothing or reaction to events. If you're working on a series, continuity still counts. Has your character been injured, had an epiphany, taken a lover? Anything that's happened has an effect on the character in the next adventure.

◆ Have you done your fact checking? If you're writing with freedom, you're going to have some details wrong: distances, historical facts, a multitude of problems. With the work finished, and research no longer something to be done to avoid writing, check. Get the details you may have missed: many of the fine points in "The Dream That Follows Darkness" were added once the first (or third) draft was finished. Some corrections were made, some additions, and some extraneous facts cut. No one has to know how much research was done.

◆ Did you make notes as you read, marking the manuscript, so that when you begin to retype, you know what you have to do? Are you going to do it? When?

"The Dream That Follows Darkness"

You've read several drafts and passes of "The Dream That Follows Darkness"; when it appeared in *The Twilight Zone Magazine*, the title was "The Dream That Follows Darkness"—a line taken from the story. Here's the final submitted manuscript.

"The Dream That Follows Darkness"—final draft

The Dream That Follows Darkness

And later that night, after the rain stopped, the wind began, cold and scouring the sky of clouds. It was a strong wind that blew in circles and people curled into their sleeping bags and under blankets, in tents and campers and lean-tos. Their sleep was restless, disturbed by dreams of running horses. The wind would stop, of course, and then the dawn would begin, a mad palette followed by a sky so clear and blue and high that it would almost hurt to look at it. It would be a beautiful day. A perfect day.

For an accident. That's how Malek thought of it, anyway. An acci-

continued on next page

dental meeting. They happen, they're forgotten. Just one of those things.

He had gone to his blind next to the lake between the moments when the wind died and the dawn began; a gray time. He put his camera onto the tripod, focused on the spot where he knew the deer would come to drink; trusted his instinct for the exposure settings. He wondered, but just for a moment, about what he was doing there. His fame, such as it was, came from photographs of the bizarre, the out of the ordinary. Photos which caught the moments people were too busy living through to see themselves; pictures framed to reflect pain. Now he was next to a mountain lake, cold and wet, waiting to capture a herd of drinking deer. He shook his head; he was too old, now, to be taking dares, answering detractors. His was the only judgment that counted and this wasn't his vision. It was wrong, had nothing to do with the lives he knew. It bothered him, then, that he was so at ease in the blind, that there were things to be seen beyond what he saw. And then he slept and missed the dawn, but dreamed the dream that follows darkness, a dream he had seen before:

It is sunrise.

The large, black bird rises gleaming from a pile of driftwood tumbled near the end of a small river. It flies in a widening spiral over a land lush with grasses and game—buffalo and rabbits and deer—together under a clear blue sky and red sun. The river winds like a ribbon of fire. The only sounds are water and wind.

The bird caws.

With a powerful thrust of its wings, the raven circles, riding a thermal, and begins to fly back again. Beneath it, the plain is sere, littered with carcasses and bones. Nothing moves but the river and the bird in the sky. The sun falls behind the mountains to the west. The river winds like a trickle of blood.

The raven lights on the driftwood and caws. A herd of red-painted ponies

continued on next page

thunders by its roost, eyes rolling in panic.
   Then the only sound is the wind.
   The bird caws.

The woman had traveled from Billings in the north to Beaumont in the south and now had come to this place and time, to the night of rain and wind on the edge of a mountain lake. It might have been an accident; it was with purpose, though, that she rose from her husband's side, saw the play of color in the sky, walked unseeing past David Malek's blind, removed her clothes and, taking a deep breath, dove from a rock into the icy embrace of the water.

David woke to the sound. Automatically, he released the shutter; then he looked out. Tendrils of mist whispered up out of the lake as if seeking purchase; finding none, they faded into the air. Small ripples played on the surface of the water, then disappeared. There were no deer. A fish, he thought, jumping for a fly. A rock loosened and tumbling into the lake.

He turned the camera's motor drive on, and watched what was in front of him as if he were peering through the camera, framing each shot. His thumb played idly against the button on the cable release. The lake's stilling surface began to pulse, the tension preparing to break.

She rose from the water in a straight line, up gleaming, droplets of water prisming on her skin. She was facing him as she came up and then swam toward him. Even strokes, strong, as if she had been born to water. Vaguely, he heard the sound of the camera as frame after frame was exposed.

Her towel was thirty feet from where he hid and he watched as she dried herself, as she wrapped the towel about her and ran her fingers through her hair, short light brown shading to blond locks that began to curl. She stood at the edge of the lake then, and stretched; the lean lines of a dancer silhouetted against the blue of sky and water's gleam.

Dry and warmed, she dropped the towel and moved at the lake's

continued on next page

edge. To her right, a buck peered out from the trees, watching, waiting to see if it would be safe to come to drink. She saw the deer and smiled, knowing that this place was his. She wrapped the towel around herself again, gathered her clothes, and walked away, passing the blind, passing David Malek, and humming to herself.

The photographer sat silently, still, and watched the herd moving. This is what he was here for, not naked sprites. The *chack* of the camera's moving mirror was loud in his ears. The buck lifted his head, sniffed the air, and went back to his drinking.

Now Malek's thoughts went to the woman, to the grace with which she moved, to the play of light on her body. And he wondered. Behind him, somewhere, he heard sounds carried on the still air. The deer turned and walked with dignity back into their woods.

Malek packed his equipment and began to walk toward the sounds he had heard. He smelled smoke and sausages cooking. He saw the woman, dressed and lounging against a tree while a tall, hard-edged man with white hair crouched by the fire. He was smoking a cigarette, and as he tended to the food, ash fell into the skillet. The woman was looking directly at him, at David, as he walked into the clearing, and she smiled in greeting. Then her voice followed the smile: "Hello."

The man looked up, cold eyes assessing the intruder; they were questioning eyes, jealous, vengeful. David looked into them, through him, feeling ice and a vacuum and said, "Hi. Sorry to disturb you. I was on my way back," he pointed into an undefined distance, "to my car." He held up his equipment case. "Just down at the lake, taking some pictures of the deer."

"They were beautiful, weren't they?" Her voice danced into his ears. She turned to the man, to her husband. "I saw them too, when I went down to wash." She looked at David. "My name is Peg Wright. And this is my husband, Logan."

"David Malek." He paused, uncertain. She knew that he had seen her. Must know. He looked at her and found her within herself. He

continued on next page

remembered the sound and feel of the wind in the night. "Well," he said, and started to walk away, knowing that she would not let him go, remembering droplets prisming against her skin.

"No, wait. Why don't you join us. We have enough." David heard her voice coming from far away. He looked at her as she stood up, kicking at a stick that had been stuck in the ground at her side; she rubbed her right shoulder, just above the breast, and for a second filled with noise only he heard, he stood unable to move. "Please."

Logan Wright grunted.

They sat and talked and ate. Wright was quiet, watchful. A psychiatrist with a thriving practice in Beaumont, Texas, and a collector: Black powder weapons, bronze miniatures, books, art. Peg had wanted to dance, but time had gotten away from her; now she was a social creature, fulfilling the demands her role as wife of Logan Wright presented. In the moments she could steal she sketched scenes of native American folklore and tradition. As David described what he thought he was trying to do on this shoot, Peg asked if he had sensed himself as an intruder at the lake's edge.

"No," he said, "not intruding so much as mindful of my place, like it wasn't mine but I could use it, you know? That he knew I was there, and approved or something. If I can get that in the prints . . ." His voice trailed away and Peg nodded and looked away down the trail, toward the east.

Soon, food finished and conversation straining, David watched Peg watching the sky, saw her again rub her shoulder. He pushed himself up. "Thanks for everything, you guys. I think I'd better get going. Logan. Peg. So long."

He started walking along the path, passing Peg. She smiled at him. "I hope you got some nice pictures, David."

Yes, he thought, she knew. "Thanks. Listen," he turned so that he was facing both of them, "why don't you give me your address, and I'll send you a print. Who knows, you may start collecting me."

continued on next page

"How mu—" Wright started to say, but Peg interrupted him. "Thank you, David. That's very kind." She gave him their address and then, as he started to light a cigarette, she added, "If you cared about yourself, you wouldn't do that."

"I guess you're right." He put the match to the cigarette and took a drag, smiling sheepishly and shrugging. "See ya around, folks. And, oh, Logan, the print's on me. This time."

Wright smiled uncertainly, then waved.

He didn't wave three months later, though, when Malek met them for a second time. He had gone home to New Orleans and worked and studied the prints of the photographs he had taken next to the lake and realized that he didn't have to continue shooting with pain, but that he was comfortable with it. And then he learned of the convocation of black powder enthusiasts, the recreation of the old fur trappers' rendez-vous. On the Mississippi, the whistle of the steamboat *Natchez* shrieked and echoed and sheet lightning played against the sky. In a bar on a corner of Bourbon Street, a stripper sighed.

Malek knew it was time to travel.

"David, how nice to see you again." Peg's voice was filled with joy, the words danced from her lips. "Logan, you remember David Malek, don't you."

"Of course." David heard a mountain wind in Wright's voice. "I seem to remember you saying you were going to send us a copy of one of the pictures you took up at the lake. What happened, forget to load your camera?"

David smelled the beast protecting his lair. "As a matter of fact, I have them with me. Hi, Peg."

"What made you think we'd be here?" Wright's voice didn't dance, it attacked, cracked. He looked at his wife, appraising her infidelities, seeing what was behind his eyes and not in front of them. She brought her hand to her neck, fondled the pink ribbon there; a small gold cross hung from it

continued on next page

and sparkled in the hollow of her throat. She touched her shoulder.

"I didn't know. My agent told me you'd been in touch, though, that you're considering a couple of my portraits. And when I heard about this gathering, I just figured I'd take a chance that an enthusiast like you would be here. If you hadn't been, I'd have mailed them on to you.

"What do you think about the ones you've been looking at? Interested?"

Wright smiled for the first time. "Well, I'll tell you, they're different. I don't know that I'd want to display them, but as a psychiatrist, they certainly intrigue me. They look like some of the nightmares my patients describe. We'll see." He reached out and took the envelope David had given Peg from her hand. "Let's look at what we've got here."

There were three prints. Two showed the herd of deer at the edge of the lake, mist around their hooves, as if they were walking on clouds. The third was just the lake and a sky of blue clarity. The surface of the lake was rippled, as if a rock had loosened and tumbled into it. Peg looked at David and back at the last photograph, knowing just where her form was hidden by the water, willing herself to see. David touched the spot delicately, casually. "Like them?"

"David, they're beautiful. And so different. Do these look like your patients' nightmares, Logan?"

"No. No. Not at all. Why the change in style, Dave?"

"Like I told you, that was the purpose of the shoot. My work hasn't really changed, though."

His life had. Now, each moment took him further away and closer, as if he were leaving somewhere without going anyplace, finding something he hadn't known he had lost. He wandered through the crowds, camera always ready, and tried to imagine what the real convocations of trappers and Indians had been like, the sounds and smells that lived only in his mind. Focusing on a Creek grandmother sucking a piece of bitterroot, he looked over the camera and saw Peg sitting crosslegged on

continued on next page

the other side of the woman, hand moving rapidly as she sketched the same scene from her angle.

And Wright hovered, David or Peg always in sight; perhaps in his sights during the pistol shooting event. On the final night of the rendezvous, there was a dance—the prizes were going to be awarded there and Logan had won. And begun to lose: On the dance floor Peg moved gracefully in David's arms.

"David," she said, "did you happen to . . .?"

"To what?"

"To get any pictures of me at the lake." Her grace fell in front of her discomfort.

"Yes." And that's all he said.

And though they spoke again, she asked no more about them.

Until a year later, when Malek had his first showing in Houston. They weren't on display, but on the afternoon of the opening, Peg came to the gallery and he showed them to her, and shook his head when her eyes asked the question.

"They're mine. Alone." He put a cigarette in his mouth, but before he could light it, she took it from his lips.

"I told you," she said, "that if you—"

"—cared, I wouldn't do that. And if you cared . . ."

She broke the cigarette, dropping the pieces on the floor. "One of us has to." Then she left to go home and change her clothes. The Wrights were hosting a party in Malek's honor and celebrating Logan's latest acquisition—a stud farm.

That evening, with the sound of Logan's laughing suggestion in their ears, Peg gave David a tour of the ranch. They walked away from the lights and noise of the party and along the winding, gravel paths; soon the glow of the strung lanterns was behind them, the music and conversation buzz swallowed by a Gulf wind.

In the deeper darkness of the stable's shadow, David put his hand on Peg's shoulder, turning her gently toward him. She looked up at him,

continued on next page

stepped backward, and placed a hand lightly on his cheek.

Like dancers following a well-rehearsed choreography they turned, staying face-to-face, waiting for the next beat. David reached out to her, his hands falling gently onto her arms. "Peg, I . . ."

"I know, David." She moved into his embrace, accepted his kiss on her forehead, found his lips with hers for a moment. Then, tenderly, she stepped away from him, from the shadows.

"David, no more." Her hand stayed on his chest. "Please."

He thought of the way she looked in the photographs he had, of the innocence of her every movement, and nodded. Without speaking, they walked back to the party.

But a sharing developed between them. Sometimes, in the seasons that followed that night, they would touch. But not often.

The raven calls.

Dark clouds scud, pushed by howling winds. A warrior alights from his pony next to a painted lodge. The hunting has been neither good nor bad; there are enough rabbits on the string to feed the man and his wife for several days.

He raises the flap and goes into the lodge where his wife is painting a robe with geometric patterns. A large cross, sign of the morning star, dominates the back and repeats along the edges. This will be hers; his robe—as befits a man—has scenes of the hunt and of battle.

The raven circles the lodges of the People, as if shepherding the men into one place with the warrior's lodge at its center. When the pale sun sets, and the bird finds its evening roost, the young men come into the lodge. Their talk, heard by the wind and the raven, is of movement.

Then one evening, David said, "There's something I have to do. It means I'll go away for a while, maybe four months."

"An assignment? What is it?" There was excitement in Peg's tone, a shared pride in his accomplishments. They talked about their work of-

continued on next page

ten, of his growing reputation, of the contracts she was getting from publishers to produce cover art for their books. Her illustrations captured the moments she was born too late to live through.

"No . . . well, I'll probably do some shooting. But this is something else. A surprise."

Peg laughed. "I love surprises. When can I know?" She spun around the room, her skirt flaring.

"Soon enough. Now, come, kiss me good-bye."

They embraced. "You'll call me, won't you?" Her voice became serious.

"I don't know; it may be difficult. I also think it would be a good idea if I didn't. Logan's—"

"Don't worry, David. He's jealous as all get out, but he really doesn't care. We're just more possessions, something to list like the Porsche, the boat, the collections. He doesn't have the soul; he traded it for enough new patients to give him the money to buy the ranch."

David kissed her. "So you keep saying. And you keep staying—"

"Yes, I stay. This is how it has to be. For now. The time is wrong. We've talked about it, David. I'm here, you're here. Trust me." She kissed him gently, then reached into her pocket. "Here," she said, "take this with you. It'll tie us when we're apart."

David looked at what she had given him—a piece of pink ribbon, like the one around her neck, holding the gold cross.

"What's this?"

"One of the ribbons from my old toe shoes." She touched the piece around her neck. "I cut them off when I threw the shoes away. I wanted to keep part of the dream.

"Now, you take this one with you, wherever you're going." She tied it loosely around his neck, over the gold chain holding his Star of David. She kissed him again, quickly, hearing Logan's footsteps as he approached the room, finally missing them. "Go. And come back."

continued on next page

There is a nameless mountain growing from the side of a creek near a place called Three Mile Curve in a corner of West Virginia. On the side of the mountain is a table of land, and a cave. Across the creek there was once a mining camp, ramshackle homes, a beer hall, the company store. Malek had come there first twenty-five years earlier, with his first camera and his life ahead of him—a time of beginnings. On hot summer nights, he slept in front of the cave and heard ghosts whisper. Or the wind in the trees. And there came a time when he had to leave.

And there came a time when he had to return. What drew him to the mountainside was more than wanderlust, more subtle than a search. His first photographs had been of the land around him; it was only slowly, as he became aware of the people on that land, of the slag heaps and of the fear etched into the faces of the men who went into the mines, that he turned his lens away. He had dreamed that it was because they had used the land and not given to it that their lives had been out of joint; that they had learned to fear and that their wives had learned to cry. Finally, having scarred the land once too often, it struck back.

Now he came to a place that used to have a name; after the dam broke and the water swept through in a rage, it was considered dead. But it wasn't deserted. Like Lazarus, a spirit moved within it. Some of those who had survived the flood tracked back through the mud as the water receded, reclaiming what was theirs. The mining company had left with the waters; the company store was no more, but the beer hall, Paulie Boy's, was there.

And Malek's cave was there, too high to have been touched by disaster. That is where he returned, pitching a tent at the beginning of a summer and causing the hollow to echo the sounds of his axe.

As Malek built, the spirit brought the town back to life and he was accepted as a part of it . . . the strange man with the ribbon around his neck, the Jew, building his place, but always being part of what was being reborn, pitching in when they needed him even though he

continued on next page

refused all offers of help in his own work. Some of them were just as happy that he turned them down. Although the offers were made in good faith, a few remembered the legends of the haunted cave. The strangest thing about this stranger was that he didn't seem to care about the stories. It was said that a spirit lived in the cave, that a woman had been left there to die, once too long ago to remember when or why. Those who believed the story said that she wore a white garment stained with blood, that she hypnotized trespassers with violet-dark eyes and then strangled them with her thick, black braids. Malek laughed at the stories, remembering the voice of the ghost, or the wind in the trees, and never dreamed of a woman in white.

As the October chill began to creep, he finished his work: The cabin was built against the mountain's side, three walls of wood, the fourth the living rock. The mouth of the cave was made part of the house, a fifth room opening off what he thought of as the spare room. It was a home: warm, feeling lived in. He pictured Peg sitting in the front room, the one with light, turning her sketches into oils. One that she had given him before he left hung on the bedroom wall so that the morning light would strike it. All that was missing was Peg. He felt alone, but not lonely.

And went down the road to Paulie Boy's, to have a few last beers, to say good-bye and arrange to have someone keep an eye on his house until he could get back to move in. He was sitting at the counter, watching the room behind him as it was reflected in the stained backbar mirror. He couldn't be sure, then, whether it was the drinking or the imperfections in the glass that made the scene so blurred. Not that it mattered much. Except that he would have liked to have had a clearer view of the woman he thought he had seen. Then someone opened the door, bringing the cold in from outside where the rain came down, hard. So hard, it brought memories and tears to the people who had survived the last flood. Thunder banged down the mountainside, rumbling with the sound of a mine collapse. Men stopped their banter and looked anx-

continued on next page

iously through the rain-stained windows and conversation died for a moment or two, then slowly resumed.

Malek turned around and looked at the room, happy with his friends. The arrangements had been made. It was time to leave again.

That night, for the first time, he slept in his new bed, built that afternoon. The bedroom walls glowed red and orange and yellow with the flames reflecting from the fireplace. Outside, wind curled around the cabin, looking for places to enter. Rain pounded against the roof and windows. Malek dreamed—

of a woman running east, of horses.

The woman wore a buckskin dress, white in the moonlight, a dark stain on the bodice. Her hair was black, and in braids . . .

—he had lost the dream by the time he awoke, but remembered dreaming.

In the morning, he left the mountainside, first for New Orleans, to close his home there. Then for Houston, where he had a showing of new work, including some pictures of people building a town.

"Where's the surprise? What did you bring me?" Peg laughed.

David gestured at the wall, where a black-and-white high-contrast photograph of a half-built house hung alone. She could see the skeleton of the building, and the dark mouth of the cave behind it. "I don't have a photograph of the finished cabin. You'll have to come and see it for yourself."

Peg smiled, and traced a finger across the surface of the print, as if to fill in the missing lines of a sketch. She paused when she touched the cave, the way David had once when showing her a photograph of ripples on a lake. Then she waved to Logan, calling him over. "See what David's building, Logan. Isn't it nice?"

"Might be. Can't tell yet. Where is it? Doesn't look like anywhere around here."

continued on next page

"It's not. It's in West Virginia, up in the mountains. A place I found years ago. Always wanted to go back; now I have."

"Well, whatever turns you on. I'd've thought that you'd stop trying to run away by now, though. Settle down." He looked at Peg. "Find a good woman and start livin'."

"Soon, Logan. I've met someone; just waiting a bit longer." Standing behind her husband, Peg stared at David. She touched the ribbon at her neck, touched her shoulder.

And told Logan she wanted a divorce, later, as he sat on the edge of their bed. "Never," he said, and laughed. Peg stared down at him, and shook her head.

"That's the wrong answer, Logan." She turned and went into her studio, and studied some of her sketches on the walls. She moved to her left with small, almost skipping steps, circling the room, then slumped to the thick rug, and slept. Thus the beginning ends; the end begins.

That night, in his hotel room, Malek dreamed of a battle and of a warrior woman with her hair in braids, and he felt a rush of wind and noise and the trembling of the earth and the heat of a fire. He forgot the dream when the sunlight pierced the thin drapes, and spent the day in silence.

But heard the sounds and felt the trembling again at the ranch at night, after yelling "Fire," and watching the glow build behind the barn and move toward the stables. And as the heat grew, Malek rushed toward a stumbling Logan and stopped to watch him fall under the thrashing legs of the panicking horses, and heard the thuds and whinnies and a scream swallowed by the rushing sounds of the hands coming to fight the fire, save the horses, and the shrill sirens of emergency vehicles; in the middle of the concerto of fear, Malek did not save Logan Wright. And though everyone expressed sadness at the accident, Malek knew there were no accidents.

The sky was so clear and blue and high that it hurt to look at it. It was a beautiful day. A perfect day for a wedding.

continued on next page

Yisgadal v'yiskadash shemay rabo . . . David Malek mouthed the ancient Aramaic words of the sacred mourner's prayer and shivered in the chill of the late autumn West Virginia morning. Clouds began to mount, snow was possible. Two years, he thought with that part of himself that had split away and was watching the group at the gravesite. He had never felt more lonely. Or less alone.

They had traveled to the places that had been special to them separately; Moose Creek, Idaho and Santa Fe, San Francisco and a deserted cay somewhere between Florida and the South Pole, a corner of Oklahoma and the edge of Maine, and made them something to share. And they found new things that were theirs alone: The headwaters of the Mississippi and the moonbow at Cumberland Falls, the Vietnam War Memorial and Little Big Horn. They traveled and grew together until it was time to go home.

"We've been moving a long time, David," she said one night as they drove away from the lake where they had first met. They had watched the deer drink in the morning, and he had stood on the shore, skipping stones across the surface of the water as she swam and dove, emerged and danced along the rocks. "It feels like forever, like it's time to stop."

Yisborach v'yish-tab-bach, v'yispoar . . .
David shivered and smelled the change in the weather.

They reached the cabin six months after their wedding. There was snow all around, and fresh cords of wood stacked under tarps in a little shed that he hadn't built. The rooms smelled fresh; wood was laid for fires in the bedroom and the front room. The sliding door he'd installed across the mouth of the cave was closed.

"Oh, David, it's everything I thought it would be." She moved through the rooms, touching the furniture he'd built, looking into the cabinets as if she knew what would be in them. Her voice was a song,

continued on next page

her movements a dance. "Thank you, David, for bringing me home."

"Thank you, Peg, for bringing me home." He took the pink ribbon from around his neck and tied it to a hook over the bed. "This is where we are tied to, now. I love you, Peg."

"And I, you, David." She removed the ribbon she wore, and tied it next to his. "Make love to me."

Later, they slept, and David dreamed:

A warrior stood surrounded by a battle. He wore a sash—dull red, with four horizontal bands of yellow quills spaced eight inches apart on its lower half. His hooked lance, wrapped with otter fur, tied with buckskin in four places and decorated with small eagle feathers, was driven into the ground, through the sash.

Even as he dreamed, David recognized the painting hanging across from the bed, recognized the warrior, knew that his name was Raven Eye. He brought his eagle bone whistle to his lips and then began to sing.

David awoke with a start, drenched with sweat even though the fire had gone out and the room was cold. He reached for Peg and found only her pillow. He wrapped the quilt around himself, then reached for the matches on the table next to the bed and lit the Coleman lantern. "Peg? Peg, where are you?" There was no sound but the hiss of the burning mantle.

Still shivering, David walked through the cabin to the back, to where the cave opened into the house. The sliding door was open. "Peg, are you in there?" He moved more quickly now, not quite running, feeling the weight of the lantern as it preceded him into the cave. He saw a flash of white.

Peg turned in her sleep, her nightgown gleaming in the lantern's harsh light. "Peg. Peg, wake up."

continued on next page

She awoke slowly, dazedly. "David? Oh . . ." She smiled wanly. "I woke up and you looked so peaceful; you smile in your sleep, did you know that? Anyway," she stretched and yawned, stood up, "I wanted to see the cave and I just came back here—You've done a nice job, you know, turning it into your darkroom. So, it's so warm and cozy, and the cot was there, kind of waiting for me, like, and I lay down for a minute . . . ." She stretched up to put her arms around his neck, kissed him, and pulled him down onto a mat of blankets, holding him tightly. He felt her warmth and strength and they drifted off into sleep together. He didn't dream again that night, though he did think to ask for just a second what she had used for light, since he hadn't turned on the power yet. But sleep came too quickly and too fully.

And life was full. The little town grew below them on the other side of the frozen creek. They worked and walked, played and talked. It was as if they had always known one another, sensing needs before the other felt them, filling empty spaces before the gaps were discovered. Then, one night in summer, as the sky lowered and lightning played in their mountain's peak, they went down to Paulie Boy's for a party.

Outside, thunder rattled, shaking the windows. The creek rose, slowly. Inside, the tables had been pushed back against the walls and the thirty or so people who made up the community danced to the jukebox, everyone drinking too much and trying not to pay attention to what was happening outside where the creek continued to rise and darkness of the storm seemed to stretch into infinity. And yesterday.

Finally, sweating and footsore, David stopped dancing and stood at a window, a bottle of beer moving from his lips to his forehead as he tried to cool down. He watched Peg sketching something on a paper napkin and laughing with Mollie's daughter, as if sharing secrets. Lightning stroked down with deadly intent; in the sudden blue and ozone smelling flashes shadows moved.

He went to the door and opened it, feeling the rain pelt against him. Behind him someone yelled, "Dave, damnit, shut the door. You're

continued on next page

lettin' the chips get wet."

"Okay, okay," he called over his shoulder, waving upraised arms as if in surrender, "just gettin' a breath of air." He looked as far into night as he could, but saw nothing. He stepped back into the room and pulled the door closed against the storm.

Sitting at the counter, David watched Peg in the backbar mirror, and sipped at his beer. She danced with one and then another, flirting with the men, but in the harmless fashion of someone who knows that no one will take it seriously; she wore innocence. And finally, breathless and glowing, she came to him at the bar, put her lips to his ear, and whispered, "Take me home. I need you."

Heads covered by rubberized ponchos, they ran to their Jeep. He had put the canvas top on, and the sides, and they sat for a moment in the cloth cocoon and listened to the rain while the windows fogged over. "C'mon, big boy, you takin' me home or ain't you? 'Cause there's lotsa guys in there who will if you ain't man enough."

"Done and done, woman." He started the engine, backed around into the road. In gear, David drove with one hand, the other resting on Peg's left thigh, feeling her heat and muscle and strength against his palm. Peg looked at her husband's face and knew it was not a time to talk, only to touch. Her hand, gentle, undemanding, on his leg. Thumb stroking, easing, soothing.

Even though it was a summer evening, the rain had brought a chill, and as soon as they were in the cabin, David built a fire in the bedroom fireplace and they lay on top of the covers, whispering whatever it is lovers whisper and other things: "Is it a good time, Peg?"

More than anything now, they wanted a child. "I hope so, David." She giggled into his shoulder. "But what the heck, right?"

David dreamed:

Raven Eye standing in front of his enemies—the Ute—surrounded by other members of the Dog-men society, each with his sash lanced to the earth.

continued on next page

254

"The Dream That Follows Darkness"—final draft, continued

Wherever the lance is, that is Arapaho land. Raven Eye could not remove the lance; that had to be done by another member of the society. There could be no retreat until the Dog-men ordered it. He was defenseless, then.

As he stood, he heard the scream behind him, Steps High Fawn's scream: his wife. Her back was to him, to the battle, and he could see blood seeping through her buckskin dress. Dream Speaker, a man of great magic, a leader of the Sweat Lodge society, held her, seemed to be whispering to her. Dream Speaker would not fight on this day or any other; he was there to bring power with his medicine. He wanted Steps High Fawn and although Raven Eye would have allowed her to go with another member of the Dog-men— because that was their privilege—none had ever asked—because that is their honor. Dream Speaker was honored as a man of power, a strong dreamer to whom all the spirits talked, but now he was without honor. And Raven Eye's lance stood through his sash and this piece of land was home. And he could not move.

Al yisroel v'al tsa-de-ka-yo, v'al kol man . . . David looked over his shoulder at his friends who had come down for this strange rite of burial, who came in support of him to participate in something which, for many of them, smacked of heresy. He was sure that more than one minister would have something to say about this. He knew the young rabbi would, but he wouldn't be there to hear it. The cold reached into him. He could feel the piece of pink ribbon lying loosely against his throat.

"David, you have to promise me something."

"Anything, my love. Just name it."

"I'm serious, David. No joking."

It was a beautiful day in late September. The mountain had begun to wear its autumn coat of flaming colors: the mornings found a light frost on the grass in front of the cabin. As the temperature shifted, mist

continued on next page

and fog dressed the land before them. It was a perfect day for making promises, the kind of promises meant to be kept.

"Okay," he said solemnly. "I swear. Now, what am I swearing to?"

"Right. Now listen. And stop smirking. I'm working on a painting. It's very special and I don't want you to peek. When I'm at the easel, stay out of the room; when you're in the room, leave the drop cloth over the canvas. You can't see it until I say so. That clear?"

"Yeah, clear. And easy enough."

"Good. Now, get out of here and let me get to work."

For the next month, they both worked. David rediscovered the power of his first work, as if the land itself were a willing model, and he understood the needs of the model sitting for the portrait. Then the photographs began to take on a new quality, one of unspecific eeriness. There were times he could swear that there were things in the pictures that weren't in his viewfinder when he snapped the scenes. She told him it was only the mist, only the play of light, only his imagination.

Whatever it was Peg was doing, she was happy with it, and no matterhow David cajoled or begged, teased or whined, she would just reach up and place a finger on his lips. "There's time enough," she might say, "we have all the time there is. You'll see." That was her promise, and she always kept her promise.

Then, one night in bed, Peg pulled the covers back and rolled close to David. "I have a surprise for you, my beloved," she whispered.

David put his arms around his wife. He felt a fearful exaltation. Her breath smelled of mint, her hair of herbs, her body of the world after rain. In the moonlight, her eyes darkened from gray to violet. He'd never noticed that before.

"I have a wonderful surprise and gift for you, David," Peg whispered against his throat. And then she died in his arms.

They came and took her to the hospital and he sat as the doctors asked their questions about her health and explained to him about embolisms and cerebrovascular accidents. Remembering how Peg's eyes

continued on next page

had grown violet, he listened and nodded and forgot their words. There are no accidents.

And when Reverend Morris drove him home from the hospital and offered to conduct a service, David shook his head.

"No, thank you, Jim. But, I think I have to bury her in a tradition I understand—"

"But—"

"Please, no. I know how you feel but, well, burial is for the living, right? Wherever Peg is, she'll approve. And she'll welcome your prayers, I know. But this will have to be done my way.

"What you could do for me though, if you would, is introduce me to a rabbi around here. Is there one, even?"

The minister shook his head in dismay. "Of course there is, down in the city. If it all means so much to you, you'd think that you'd have found out about . . .

"I'm sorry, David. This isn't the time for lectures. I'll call him for you, his name is Witt, Eric Witt. It's a shame you didn't know him before this."

"Thank you, Jim. Very much. For everything."

Rabbi Witt welcomed David, offering him the aid of the small, dying synagogue. "You'll need a minyan, people to help while you're sitting shivah. Whatever, we'll do what we can."

The service was held in a small chapel that the congregation reserved for these needs. David, standing over the casket, didn't hear the rabbi walk in behind him.

"What . . .?" The word sounded as if the speaker had just been hit in the stomach. David had been tying the ribbon with the cross around Peg's neck.

Witt looked at David, sternly. "I think we should close the casket, Mr. Malek. It's traditional."

David looked calmly into the young rabbi's eyes, saw the questions. "Yes, I think you're right." David leaned down again, straightened the

continued on next page

cross in the hollow of Peg's throat, kissed her on the forehead and lips, and brought the lid down. Behind the men, the people of the town that used to have a name began to enter the chapel, coughing nervously.

O-seh sholom bim'-ro-mov, hu ya-a-seh sholom, olenu v'al kol yisroel, v'imru: Amen. The Kaddish was done. David looked into the grave, at the reflections of the weak sun on the highly polished pine. He knelt to pick up a handful of coarse earth and threw it onto the coffin, heard the hollow bounce. He took a deep breath and turned away, toward the east, toward the entrance to the small cemetery.

Two years, he thought, and the time before that. Peg, you said we had nothing but time, the words were a cry in his heart, and now . . . And now, he thought, I will go on or I will die, but sometime I will join you.

"Mr. Malek . . ." David felt the rabbi's hand on his shoulder. "Is there anything I can do for you now?"

"No, thank you, Rabbi Witt. You've done more than I could have asked for. Thank you. I think I'll just go home, now."

"We'll come to visit you, for the prayers." David couldn't tell whether it was a statement or a question.

"Yes, that would be nice. You know where my cabin is, up on the mountain?"

"We'll find it. Tomorrow?"

"Yes. No, no, make it the day after. That would be better. Okay?"

"As you like. Your friends will take you home now?"

David looked down at the quickly filling grave and up at the trees bending bare branches in the wind. He was warm now, and felt no more loneliness, felt no longer alone. "Yes, my friends will take me home."

Malek walked through the cabin, feeling the different feel of the rooms. In Peg's studio, he looked at the covered easel, at the painting

continued on next page

which might or might not be finished. He went to it slowly, touching the cloth draped over it on a frame so that it would not come into contact with the canvas while the paint was wet. He lifted a corner, then dropped it slowly. No. Maybe tomorrow.

He heard his neighbors coming in, bringing food for him, companionship. He didn't want the emptiness now, though he didn't need the company. He welcomed them, showed the women where the plates were, the silverware. These were people used to wakes, he realized, people who drank and laughed and told stories about those who had died. It was a good tradition, and when finally everyone had left, and he fell into bed, he didn't expect to dream.

Dream Speaker was pulling Steps High Fawn, dragging her away, retreating with her. In front of Raven Eye, the horsemen were coming, riding right at him. His wife shouted, and he turned, saw the arrow piercing her right shoulder, the blood running down over her breast. Then the horses were on him.

The large, black bird fluttered its wings as it landed on the tree limb. A cold wind keened across the Plains, causing the People of Our Own Kind to curl in their sleep. They had won, and credit was given to the members of the Sweat Lodge society and to the bravery of the Dog-men and Lance Men. Raven Eye would be missed; and his woman, Steps High Fawn who had fought bravely beside him and was probably one of those captured.

She lay tied to some trees miles from the village. Dream Speaker would return for her, she knew that as she knew that Raven Eye was dead. She had heard his song and he had heard her screams. Now, she heard the shaman's approach, could smell the stink of him.

Spent, he slept. The bird in the tree cawed and flew down from its roost. On the ground, it cocked its head, looking at the woman covered in blood, her eyes closed, her breathing ragged. He hopped around the body of the man lying next to her and pecked at the rope holding her left arm to a branch. She felt the movement and opened her eyes, watched the bird climb and

continued on next page

soar against the circle of the full moon, then light on a branch, pecking at something.

Steps High Fawn pulled with her left arm, and felt the rope give. This was not her time to die. As she struggled, the bird returned, two strips of cloth in its beak. He cawed again.

She didn't realize that her hand was free; feeling was gone. It was when she felt it against her body that she knew. The bird hopped excitedly while the woman reached for the knife at Dream Speaker's hip. She cut her other hand free, then stood silently, staring at the man on the ground. With a scream that shook the mountains, she thrust the blade into his heart and then cut his head from his body, impaling it on a naked branch.

The black bird rose with a roar of wings and pecked at the head's lolling tongue. Steps High Fawn found her dress and put it on. She braided her hair, tying it with the pieces of ribbon the bird had brought. She looked back—this was her past now; she couldn't return to the People. She walked out of the copse, untied Dream Speaker's pony, and began her trek toward the morning sun, toward the beginning.

Eventually she reached a land of mountains and rushing waters. She found shelter and waited.

Malek woke to a perfect morning, the clouds threatening the snow of the day before blown clear. The sky blue and high; the sun brighter than it had any right to be in that place and that time. He knew he had dreamed in the night, but he couldn't remember what he had seen. It would come back, he knew. Just as he knew that it was time to look at Peg's painting.

He dressed and made coffee, delaying the moment until it demanded to be answered. Then he pulled the cloth away.

In the center, a large raven in silhouette against the moon. Surrounding it, scenes: The scenes from his dream. It made every bit of sense, really, once he stopped to think about it. And he did think about it, and remembered that there are no accidents.

continued on next page

All day, while he went about doing what had to be done, he thought about it, and nodded. And in the evening, he went down to Paulie Boy's, where they were surprised to see him, but he explained that life goes on, that all they had was that and time, and that Peg would have wanted this.

He drank at the counter for an hour, watching the room in the mirror. But no one came for him, no one came to lead him away. Had he been wrong? Was it all a ridiculous fantasy born out of his grief? Malek didn't know, and now he didn't want to think about it. He wanted only to sleep.

He started a fire in the bedroom fireplace, and crawled into bed. Tendrils of mist whispered up out of the ground and into the cabin as if seeking purchase; finding Malek, they wrapped themselves around him.

They pulled, and he knew he was right. The cave door slid open and the woman in white stepped into the room, her braided hair held by pink ribbons, the stain gone from her breast. She held out her hand and David rose.

"We have only time," the woman said.

"We have only time and more. Thank you for bringing me home, Steps High Fawn."

The cabin was a heap of ash by the time anyone from the town across the creek could get to it. They waited for the ruins to cool, joined by the rabbi and the members of the congregation who had come to pray with David Malek. The gray heap was relieved by one spot of color, a piece of pink ribbon caught by one of the rocks that had come sliding down the mountain, blocking the entrance to the cave.

The ribbon waved in the wind, and was torn loose, blowing down into the creek where it floated away, into the river and around Three Mile Curve. ◆

All the dreams have been added, the details checked. I had a South-ern Cheyenne dog soldier read it, went to the American Museum of Natural History and looked at the sashes and lances. The ghost is gone except in passing.

More changes, today, years after I wrote it? Sure.

But there comes a time when you have to let the story go. It's time had come, it had been seven or eight years in the writing. And it had gone through changes.

I had an opening line with nothing to use it for.

I had an idea about David and Bathsheba.

I had an urge to write a ghost story.

The three came together; the ghost story, which is what I set out to write, disappeared altogether.

The process of revision worked: After I chopped away at my quar-ried stone, the form that was there emerged; everything else was swept up and put in a box in the corner.

Waiting. . .

INDEX